Social Democracy

Global and National Perspectives

Edited by

Luke Martell

with

Christien van den Anker

Matthew Browne

Stephanie Hoopes

Phil Larkin

Charles Lees

Francis McGowan

Neil Stammers

First published 2001 by
PALGRAVE
Houndmills, Basingstoke, Hampshire RG21 6XS and
175 Fifth Avenue, New York, N. Y. 10010
Companies and representatives throughout the world

PALGRAVE is the new global academic imprint of
St. Martin's Press LLC Scholarly and Reference Division and
Palgrave Publishers Ltd (formerly Macmillan Press Ltd).

ISBN 0–333–80405–8 hardback
ISBN 0–333–80406–6 paperback

This book is printed on paper suitable for recycling and
made from fully managed and sustained forest sources.

A catalogue record for this book is available
from the British Library.

Library of Congress Cataloging-in-Publication Data
Social democracy : global and national perspectives / edited by
Luke Martell with Matthew Browne ... [et al.].
      p. cm.
    Includes bibliographical references and index.
    ISBN 0–333–80405–8
     1. Socialism—Europe. 2. Socialist parties—Europe.
    3. Globalization. I. Martell, Luke.

    HX238.5 .S6 2001
    335.5—dc21

                                        2001032131

10   9   8   7   6   5   4   3   2   1
10   09 08 07 06 05 04 03 02 01

Printed and bound in Great Britain by
Antony Rowe Ltd, Chippenham, Wiltshire

Contents

List of Tables and Figures

Notes on the Contributors

Yusaf Akbar is Assistant Professor of Economics and European Studies at IMC Graduate School of Budapest, Hungary

Christien van den Anker is a Lecturer in Global Ethics, Centre for Global Ethics, University of Birmingham

Matthew Browne is a Chargé de Mission at Notre Europe, Paris, France

Nick Cowell is a research student in the Social and Political Thought Programme at the University of Sussex

Stephanie Hoopes is a Visiting Fellow at the University of Sussex and lives in Mountain Lakes, New Jersey, USA

Phil Larkin is a Lecturer in Politics and Public Policy, Business School, University of Hertfordshire

Charles Lees is a Lecturer in International Relations and Politics, School of European Studies, University of Sussex

Luke Martell is a Senior Lecturer in Sociology, School of Social Sciences, University of Sussex

Francis McGowan is a Lecturer in Politics, School of European Studies, University of Sussex

Martin Shaw is Professor of International Relations and Politics, School of Social Sciences, University of Sussex

Neil Stammers is a Lecturer in Politics, School of Social Sciences, University of Sussex

Introduction

Luke Martell

In the British Labour Party in the 1980s a frequent discussion I participated in was about the possibilities for socialism if only social democratic parties were in power across Europe and even elsewhere. Capital would have nowhere to flee, as the only countries with workforces and consumer markets worth going to would be ones where other social democratic parties were in government. This would enable common regulations on capitalism, common social programmes and a shift away from the dominance of private capital and free markets. Businesses would be forced to make compromises with supranationally collaborating social democracy. At the start of the twenty-first century part of that dream (or nightmare, depending on your political views) seems to have come true. Across Europe the large majority of members of the European Union (EU) have social democratic governments. The Party of European Socialists in the European Parliament is coherent and well organized. There has even been a Democrat in the White House for much of the period of social democratic dominance, just to add the finishing touch to a perfect-looking picture.

Yet the fact of social democratic domination does not seem to be translating into the sort of progress for social democratic ambitions that were hoped for in those 1980s discussions. The EU is primarily a set of institutions with liberal economic goals. Of course, there are moderate social democratic EU policies and these are important, but they are subordinate to the primacy of open markets and the sort of macroeconomic policies determined by convergence criteria. In fact, some of the social democratic parties themselves seem more interested in pursuing the market goals of the EU than its social goals. They do not seem to need convergence criteria to persuade them to do so. Tony Blair fits into this category most obviously. But his prominent reluctance to support an EU committed to social regulation only conceals the record of many other European social democrats in pursuing liberal economic objectives. Blair is not only a reluctant regulator; he is also a reluctant integrator, blocking common policies such as tax harmonization in the name of governments retaining national autonomy to pursue their own competitive interest. So here is an instance of a social democratic party showing hesitance about some traditional social democratic-type goals, and also about common agreements and further solidarity and integration. Even in circumstances never really expected in the 1980s, of social democrats in power across the continent, there is little sign of the common socialist Europe dreamed of then.

But how fair is this picture? Is this where social democracy has got to, and if so what led it there? And where might it, or should it, go in the future? This book originates from a conference held at the University of Sussex in October 1998,[1] entitled 'Social Democracy: Current Ideological directions'. Over a year after Tony Blair and Lionel Jospin's electoral victories and soon after Gerhard Schröder's, all seizing power from the Right and apparently in the process of rethinking what social democracy meant, the aim of the conference was to look at the changing ideologies and policies of social democracy. We wanted to pin down the contemporary development and meanings of social democracy against the background of debates such as those about globalization and the future of Europe. Since then we have been charting ongoing events, ideological discussions and policy developments. The chapters in this book emerge from that conference and from subsequent analyses made by the authors.

There are three main themes in the book. The first is concerned with what the changing context has been for social democracy. Those aspects of the changing environment most discussed in the book are globalization and a lower level of supranationalism, European integration. For Martin Shaw, globalization is primarily a political process, already well developed in the form of a military-political 'western state'. Social democracy is involved in that state, but only as part of it and it needs to break free from its historical ties to the nation if it is to express another of its traditional links – with the movement for democratization – in new global regimes. Neil Stammers is more sceptical about what he sees as the capitalist and statist accommodations of globalist social democracy of the sort supported by Shaw and others. Yet he shares much of Shaw's analysis of the historical inability of social democracy to think beyond the confines of nation-state organization. Stammers outlines six characteristics of social democracy – commitments to liberal democracy, capitalism and mitigation of some of the worst effects of capitalism, and to elitism, statism and methodological nationalism – and argues that social democracy needs to go beyond the confines of these characteristics in order to become a true force for global democracy.

Matthew Browne and Yusaf Akbar take a different angle on globalization altogether. Their emphasis is on the discourse of globalization, not just as a tool used by politicians to justify policies that are really chosen for ideological reasons, but as a discourse that constitutes their knowledge of the world, their politics and agenda. Other authors also turn to the theme of globalization. Christien van den Anker suggests social democracy needs to find a way of reconstituting itself at global levels to provide a globally regulative antidote to free market capitalism. Such an international outlook is something the Dutch, the subject of her chapter, have long had a leaning towards. Francis McGowan is more sceptical about the possibilities for international forms of social democracy. He looks at a supranational form which exists concretely here and now with a strong social democratic element in its history – the European Union (EU). Like Stammers, McGowan draws on some valuable conceptual distinctions – between positive and negative integration in the EU, between traditional and modernizing social democracy, and between policies that are either compensatory in relation to liberal economic integration or countervailing to it. For McGowan, liberal integration has come to dominate the EU, and social democracy is too nationally divided and too domestically oriented at present to make inroads into reconfiguring the EU in a more social democratic direction, despite its numerical strength there.

A second key theme of the book is about how social democratic ideology has developed in response to changes such as globalization, or the perception of it, as well as in response to the influence of neoliberalism in some places, problems of Keynesianism and the welfare state and the changing social basis of social democracy. As already mentioned, McGowan distinguishes between traditional social democracy and the more economically liberal modernizing social democracy, exemplified by Blair, but evident elsewhere too. Stephanie Hoopes analyses the implications of changes in the media in the United States and United Kingdom for three forms of social democracy: traditional, modernizing and globalist. She argues that the new media increase the power of civil society in relation to the state, and also that of private enterprise, while having effects which go against equality and justice. These seem to threaten social democracy. Yet she also argues that the new media can strengthen democratization in civil society, which can in turn act as a force against private enterprise and in favour of equality and social justice. Furthermore, modernizing and globalist social democracy are in touch with the information revolution and global telecommunications. So there may well be ways in which social democracy can benefit from the new media as well as be negatively affected by it. Stammers makes a similar traditional/modernizing distinction to McGowan's adding, with Shaw and Hoopes, another recent type – globalist social democracy. What makes these types different is initially evident from the terms themselves, and I will leave the details to the authors in their chapters. Some of the authors also discuss national differences in social democratic development, McGowan for one seeing them as an obstacle to social democrats pursuing positive integration in pursuit of social democratic ends in the EU. Domestic constraints and national differences prevent social democratic governments from the sort of collaborative positive agreements they would need to forge to secure social democratic successes at a regional level.

Charles Lees provides a clear analysis of some of the differences between German and British institutions and political systems illustrating the impact that national contexts can have. There may well be similar policy agendas across nations like Germany and the UK – in this case between *Die Neue Mitte* and the Third Way – yet institutional differences are likely to lead to related debates and similar policy agendas ending up with differing outcomes. Such institutional and cultural factors, which may affect the development of social democratic policies, are also discussed by Nick Cowell and Phil Larkin. Their chapter seeks to pin down what New Labour is all about, arguing that interpretations of it need to stress Labour's relationship with its own history more than some analyses have done. They argue that policy agendas across European social democracy are more similar than rhetorical differences or commentators sometimes make them appear. Yet this is not at odds with Lees' conclusions because, like him, they see nationally-specific factors that will make similar policy agendas turn out differently across national boundaries. Christien van den Anker provides a complement to these views, her chapter analysing the recent and current state of the ideologies and policies of social democracy in the Netherlands. 'Similar but different' is also the story here. There are very similar features to modernizing social democracy between the Netherlands and elsewhere. In fact Dutch social democracy may be seen as an early modernizer. Yet politics in the Netherlands also has distinctive features which go against some of the economically liberal inclinations of modernizing social democracy – an emphasis on consensus, collaboration, consultation and continuity, for example, and a history of being involved in positive integration in international affairs. Van den Anker's own suggestions are for social democracy to take a more globalist and regulative role than some modernizers are currently apt to do.

This brings us to the third basic concern of the book – with critical and prescriptive arguments. How are we to assess modernizing social democracy's aims and goals? What alternatives are there to modernizing social democracy? And what sort of future might it or should it have? A number of the chapters touch on such issues. Browne and Akbar's argument, on the discourse of globalization, is clearly critical in the sense that they see its real function as not to give us a better handle on social reality, but more to constitute what political actors think and do. Van den Anker has her own prescriptions for a more global social democracy, which she sees as necessary if some more traditional social democratic goals are to be achieved. And she discusses criticisms of the direction modernizing social democracy has taken in the Netherlands. Stammers argues that social democracy needs to transcend its six defining characteristics if it has any hope of tackling the challenges of political globalization and establishing itself as a genuine force for global democracy.

My own conclusion to this book argues that this gives up too much strategically, and that capitalism and the state are necessary ingredients of any attempt to move towards global structures which can limit and regulate capital and extend democracy. Shaw identifies a similar historical deficiency on the part of social democracy in coming to terms with globalization as Stammers. But he pins his hopes on what he sees as an already existing force for democratic political globalization – the Western state. However, he argues that social democracy is only part of that state at present and, like Stammers, feels it needs to do some serious reconstituting of itself along global lines to become a participant with real influence on it. Shaw, though, does not see social democracy providing the values for the Western state, but rather the institutional levers through which they can be pursued. Such values can be brought in from elsewhere, from global social movements for example. This is where Shaw, Stammers and I stand on similar ground, agreeing on the importance of social movements in any future for social democracy at a global level. As I have outlined, McGowan's conclusions on all this are more hard-headed: global social democracy is a dream that is a long way in the future. Even at a regional supranational level, where social democracy has more of a foothold and history, it does not seem that capable of imposing itself coherently and effectively, at least in pursuit of its traditional goals. And he also shows how much social democracy, for good or ill, has lost of its traditional beliefs and how much it has failed to achieve them through the EU.

There are several distinctive features to the approach of this book. Like many other books in the area it has a European focus, although Stephanie Hoopes does provide a US angle on the discussions. This European focus is in part a result of the expertise of the authors involved. Yet social democracy and social democratic ideas are important elsewhere in the world, not just in more obvious places like Australia and New Zealand, but also in regions such as South America. Further analyses of social democracy will need to be more outward-looking to such regions, especially if they are to take globalization as a key theme as we have done in this book.

The book is not a country-by-country survey of different national social democracies. Hence we have not found it essential to include chapter-length studies of every relevant country with a social democratic history. But we have discussed themes that unite and differentiate national social democracies and which are relevant for and addressed in relation to countries far beyond those that get chapter-length attention here. Clearly, there are country-based chapters and a number of the contributions address comparative issues. But this is also a book which addresses common themes and concerns which go beyond individual nations or comparisons between them. It aims to provide an overall assessment of where social democracy is generally, of critical assessments of it, of supranational forms and global possibilities and at least some sense of possible alternatives to, or partners for, social democracy, in social movements and civil society, for example.

The book is also interdisciplinary. Charles Lees provides the sort of political science perspective often associated with books on this sort of topic, as does McGowan to some extent. But unlike many other books on social democracy the issue is also addressed from many other perspectives. The contributors to this book also represent approaches such as international relations, sociology, economics, European studies, social and political thought and discourse analysis. Cowell and Larkin, and Shaw, build in historical perspectives to their analyses. Many of the authors make good use of the concepts and perspectives of social and political theory, drawing important conceptual distinctions and definitions, and tackling some of the ideological and philosophical strands which are part of current social democracy. Shaw and others try to identify wider-scale social and political changes which are important to the rethinking of social democracy, while others, such as Browne and Akbar, try to deconstruct some of the discourses around those alleged changes. Perspectives come from both macro-and more micro-directions, and are both theoretical and practical. The book, like the conference on which it is based, creates the means for the interaction of these approaches. Together, they make for a more complete picture of the current state of social democracy and of the challenges and potentials for its future.

Finally, coming from all these perspectives, we go beyond merely describing what is going on in contemporary social democracy in this book. The aim is also to conceptualize it, explain it and provide critical and normative perspectives. We aim to give some conceptual meanings to different forms of social democracy, analyse why they are taking the directions they are, in response to what forces and changes, evaluating whether this is desirable and discussing prescriptions and recommendations.

Note

1 I am grateful to William Outhwaite for suggesting the idea of the conference. It was funded by the Centre for Critical Social Theory, of which he is Director, and supported by the Social and Political Thought Graduate Programme, both at Sussex University.

Many thanks to Christien van den Anker, Stephanie Hoopes, Phil Larkin, Charles Lees, Francis McGowan and Neil Stammers for their advice on this chapter.

1
Social Democracy in the Global Revolution: An Historical Perspective

Martin Shaw

Social democratic thinkers and politicians have rather mixed attitudes to 'global' processes.[1] Globalization is identified with the global free market, which is widely seen as the apotheosis of unbridled capitalism which John Gray condemns.[2] Some contemporary social democratic theorists, such as Paul Hirst and Grahame Thompson, even argue that globalization is largely mythical. They explain that nation-states retain the capacities to manage national economies which globalization is seen as eroding.[3] Only at the Blairite end of the social democratic spectrum does a more positive attitude to global change manifest itself, for example in the conception of the 'third way' advocated by Anthony Giddens.[4] As he himself notes, however, 'The critics see the Third Way . . . as warmed-over neoliberalism'; or as an unsympathetic Marxist puts it, 'not so much a powerful case for a refashioned social democracy as a rather depressing symptom of Giddens's own political and intellectual evolution to the right'.[5] Giddens can look after himself, of course, and his ideas about globalization are well established in influential texts, as well as supported by the empirical analyses of David Held and his collaborators.[6] Clearly, however, this principal 'globalist' vision of social democracy remains controversial.

The dismissal of the viability of social democracy in the global era, by post-New Right theorists like Gray as well as by Marxists, is undoubtedly, as Andrew Gamble argues, 'too final'.[7] Not only do governments have national discretion but the potential for international cooperation is also common ground between more traditional social democrats and advocates of the 'Third Way'.[8] As social democratic politicians dominated the turn of the millennium European Union, an internationalized, if not globalized, centre-left reformism was close to becoming the common sense of mainstream politics, with influence in North America too after the excesses of the Ronald Reagan and Newt Gingrich years. While statist socialism had become a forlorn doctrine and radical Marxism remained marginal, social democracy enjoyed a broad, if not necessarily very profound, worldwide renaissance in the reaction against the excesses of post-1989 neoliberal triumphalism.

This chapter seeks both to explore and further this expansion of social democratic politics on a world scale. It takes a position which is neither global-enthusiast nor global-sceptic, but which in Held's terms is 'global-transformationalist'[9] in a particular way. I argue, first, that the fullest meaning of 'globality' is more political than economic or technological; and second, that we are in the midst of a socio-political transformation on a world scale. This change, while apparently accommodating to western liberal democracy, is in fact profoundly challenging to all established forms of politics. Western social democracy, I will argue, needs to come to terms with revolutionary changes, in the non-western as well as western world, that are changing the face of world order. Not only most forms of mainstream social democratic thinking, including the 'Third Way', but established modes of critiquing social democracy – notably Marxism – are so thoroughly implicated in historic socio-political forms of western capitalism and state that they miss the central political questions of our time.

In order to pursue this argument, I first propose a revision of historical perspective on the theory and practice of social democracy. Not only does the unfinished global revolution present a fundamental challenge to our established ways of thought. The failure to grasp its significance also follows from a long history of failure on the part of theorists, practitioners *and critics* of social democracy. None of them has grasped the full significance of the world, and specifically international, contexts for the understanding of politics. In order to sharpen the presentation of current dilemmas, I need first to outline, however schematically, an historical theory. I shall try to show, from an historical-sociological point of view, how the changing implications of social democracy in world political change have been crucial to its evolution during the last century.

Historicizing social democracy in a world perspective

I emphasize two essential, closely interrelated points about the history of social democracy. On the one hand, we should never lose sight of the relations between social *democracy* and wider democratic movements and ideas. On the other, we need always to remember how closely developments in social democracy have been bound up with changes in the worldwide configurations of state power, especially the military relations of the major centres.

Although social democracy can trace its lineage to early nineteenth-, eighteenth-and even seventeenth-century democratic movements, there is no doubt that modern socialist parties emerged and became important political actors in the late nineteenth and early twentieth centuries. Social democracy became labour's dominant political expression in the period when, on the one hand, industrial capitalism spread across western Europe and North America, and on the other, the system of European empires achieved its greatest worldwide extent. As Michael Mann has shown, within this historical matrix, 'class' and 'nation' grew *together* as foci of collective social action.[10] Social democratic parties, and the broader social movements of the working class in which they were embedded, were from the start caught in the synthesis of these two powerful social forces.

From this period, labour as a social movement confronted not one but two powerful centres of social power. On the one hand, as Karl Marx and many other socialist thinkers emphasized, there was the growing social power of capital, as well as of older propertied classes. But on the other was the state, which was increasingly national and imperial in character, and in most places highly authoritarian and oligarchic. In the late nineteenth century, a major part of labour's task everywhere was to establish the conditions of democracy, based on freedom of expression, organization and action as well as on universal suffrage. Even Marx believed that the suffrage might be the key that, in some countries at least, unlocked the door to the social programme of the socialist parties.[11]

In adopting the name 'social democracy', socialists were simultaneously acknowledging their roots and role in the broader democratic movement *and* their specific goals of achieving social and economic democracy. In any socialist programme before 1914, the importance of democratic aims could hardly be minimized: hardly anywhere had universal male, let alone female suffrage been achieved; nowhere were political freedoms securely established. It was not until after 1945, indeed, that democracy became clearly established as the common political form of western capitalist states.

From the state's point of view, democratic rights were often conceded to the working class in return for military duty, which states increasingly expected all adult males to perform. (Mass armies became normal in Europe in the second half of the nineteenth century.) Similarly, recognition of social democratic parties as legitimate elements in the state depended on the parties' implicit acceptance of states' national and imperial claims. In establishing social democracy as a legal and constitutional party, its leaders also embraced these characters of the states within which they existed. Social democrats were of course organized 'internationally', but the potential for conflict between their aspirations for international cooperation and the realities of national power was always strong.

Social democrats' ideas left them ill-equipped to deal with the contradictions of the state system within which their movements were growing. Although most nineteenth-century socialist thinkers were critical of the centralized state, they had only limited understanding of the forces that were pushing in this direction. Even Marx mistakenly saw the main driving force as class conflict; his epigone, Lenin, was still repeating this argument decades later, even though it had become obvious that military mobilization was a far more powerful lever than class repression for building up state power.[12] Engels was a perceptive commentator on military power, but his misjudgement of its significance was shown in the comment that 'the warship is being developed to a pitch of perfection that is making it outrageously costly and unusable in war'.[13] Socialist thought was already characterized, as this remark showed, by the economism that remains a hallmark of all its main varieties to this day.

Mainstream social democratic leaders infamously bowed to national claims once the First World War broke out in 1914. While this is widely marked as a 'betrayal' of internationalist aspirations, it reflected the reality that social democracy had become deeply entrenched in discrete national-imperial centres of state power. Left-wing social democrats who broke away from their parties, eventually forming the basis of the new Communist International, argued that democracy was bound to suffer in conditions of inter-imperialist war. Certainly democratic institutions were precariously established in many European states; they eventually gave way to anti-democratic counter-revolution in Italy, Germany and elsewhere. However the new *soviet* democracy of workers' councils, led by the Communists, also gave way just as rapidly to Stalinist dictatorship. Only in the United States, Britain and its dominions, France and north-western Europe did some kind of parliamentary democracy survive. Only in these regions did social democracy (now clearly distinguished from the communist breakaway) continue to have a serious hold; but only in relatively marginal states like Sweden was it politically dominant.

Social democracy's dramatic revival in the 1940s and 1950s underlines how closely its fate was linked to configurations of power in the inter-state system and the role of democracy within these. It was because the United States and Britain were major victors of the Second World War that democracy was restored in north-western Continental Europe and imposed on Japan. It was because the war broke the backs of even the most victorious empires, that independent parliamentary democracies were instituted in the Indian subcontinent in 1947. It was because of the wartime participation effect that social democracy advanced strongly in Britain, leading to the first majority Labour government in 1945.[14] It was largely because war greatly strengthened the power of the state that everywhere statist ideas of economic and social planning (with which social democracy had become identified) became the new common sense. Everywhere in Europe urgent social needs were apparent in the aftermath of war: social democrats became parties of govern-ment in many European states, while even conservative and Christian-Democratic governments pursued broadly social democratic policies.

The linkage of social democracy to the western state was confirmed in the Cold War. On the one hand, even after the victory of the 'demo-cracies', only in North America, Western Europe, Japan and the British Commonwealth was democracy a widespread political form. Within these democratic zones, only in Western Europe and Australasia was social democracy strong. In much of Asia, Latin America and postcolo-nial as well as colonial Africa, democratic institutions were much more precarious and social democratic movements and ideas weaker. In the Soviet-dominated Eastern Europe, democratic institutions were extin-guished in the late 1940s and independent social democratic parties no longer allowed.

Given the subordination of Western Europe and the rest of the West to the United states, mainstream social democracy became, in conditions of Cold War, resolutely 'Atlanticist' – especially in Britain, Germany, Japan and Australasia. There were always pro-Soviet and neutralist minorities in Atlantic social democratic parties – and of course states with important social democratic influence, like Sweden, Finland and Austria, remained neutral throughout this period. In general, however, social democracy as a political movement sheltered within the Ameri-can-led western consensus throughout the Cold War period.

Cold War conditions had mixed effects on social democracy. On the one hand, social democratic governments and parties were implicated in US policies, including support for authoritarian, anti-Communist regimes. The disciplinary effect of anti-Communism was felt within social democratic movements, where autocratic right-wing groups often dominated party and union organizations. The social democratic Left's sympathies with Communist states in turn restricted its influence. Alliances with Communist parties, even where (as in Italy) the latter succeeded somewhat in emancipating themselves from Soviet tutelage, were always inhibited, and the division of the left helped to keep right-wing parties in power.

On the other hand, European social democracy was able to begin reconstructing its ideology and practice in more constructive ways. New conditions for international cooperation in Western Europe enabled Continental social democrats to play key parts in developing the European Economic Community. Although, with long periods of right-wing hegemony in principal member-states, the free market rationale remained dominant, the politics of integration always included a social democratic element. As the Community developed into the European Union of the 1990s, the role of social democrats, such as Commission President Jacques Delors, in defining its strategy became stronger. By the late 1990s, broadly social democratic governments held office in most member-states, including the four largest.

The conversion of European social democracy to integrationist politics was, of course, a long and conflict-ridden process. In Britain and Scandinavia, especially, social democracy as a whole was strongly wedded to national (in Britain, imperial) forms: in 1960 the Atlanticist Labour leader, Hugh Gaitskell, famously appealed to 'a thousand years of British history' to justify choosing the British Commonwealth over the European project. Left-wing social democrats were even more overwhelmingly opposed to European integration: for them, the project's connections to the Atlantic alliance, as well as its free market ideology, combined with nationalist ideology and even anti-colonialist solidarity, to overdetermine rejection.

At the beginning of the twenty-first century, it is easy to forget the extent of the divisions which Cold War politics caused in social democracy as recently as the 1980s, when the very term 'social democracy' became associated in some countries with Atlanticism. The social democratic name was chosen by several right-wing breakaways from the main labour or socialist parties, from the 1950s until as late as the 1981 foundation of the Social Democratic Party in Britain (although Labour was effectively social democratic, the name had never been widely used within the party). For right-wing 'social democrats', Atlanticism, nuclear deterrence and European integration were political totems. For left-wing 'socialists', as for Communists, all three were anathema.

It is remarkable that these divisions have been radically overcome in little more than a decade. Their transcendence is clearly connected with the end of the Cold War, which transformed the context of European social democracy. However it is also to do with *how* the Cold War ended, and the roles of social democrats in this process. Right-wing social democratic leaders like the German Chancellor Helmut Schmidt, and James Callaghan, the outgoing British prime minister, played key roles in the 1979 adoption by NATO of its 'dual-track' policy of deploying new intermediate nuclear systems in Europe while simultaneously seeking agreed reductions with the Soviet Union. The subsequent growth of peace movements, dedicated to preventing these deployments, played a large part in transforming the Cold War political situation in both parts of Europe, including in both left-and right-wing sections of social democracy.

The West European peace movements were unsuccessful in their manifest aims, and initially polarized politics – helping indeed to precipitate the right-wing 'social democratic' breakaway from the British Labour Party. However, their successful mobilization of wide swathes of public opinion across western Europe had a powerful impact. Opposition social democratic parties, especially in Britain and Germany, were largely converted to their aims. Left-wing social-democrats witnessed a vivid demonstration of the possibilities of pan-European cooperation: in Britain, particularly, the development of a Europeanist peace current, represented by European Nuclear Disarmament, was critical in shifting left opinion towards European integration. The international ascendancy of the Reagan–Thatcher New Right – Cold War nationalist as well as aggressively free-market – also pushed labour movements to see a more integrated social democratic Europe as an alternative.

These developments explain why, once the Cold War logjam broke, a major reconfiguration of western European social democracy was able to take place quite rapidly. We should not underestimate the extent of the changes. On the one hand, where barriers between old social democratic and Communist parties had become artificial these have been overcome, so that for the first time in almost a century European social democracy represents a single movement. On the other, old divisions within social democracy between pacifist Left and Atlanticist Right have equally been transcended. The ideological field of social democratic politics appears more fluid than for generations, and the relations between social democracy and other currents – liberal and Green as well as ex-Communist – appear more open than hitherto. Nowhere, perhaps, are these changes clearer than in Italy, where the main Cold War parties fell apart in the early 1990s and the post-Communist Party of the Democratic Left has formed the core of a New Left-reformist coalition. But the transformative trends are at work more widely, even where changes have been less dramatic.

If basic democratic concerns and changing international configurations have been central to the historical evolution of social democracy, as I have tried to suggest in this sketchy overview, then it would be naïve to believe that they have gone away. 'It's the economy, stupid', the watchword of Bill Clinton's first election campaign, has been widely understood as the bottom line of left electoral politics in Western societies. Certainly, fixing economic conditions to produce a satisfied majority is a *sine qua non* of electoral success. But in a broader historical perspective, other forces shape changes in political forces and ideologies. It is the argument of this chapter that the larger historical questions of world order, which have overshadowed social democracy's evolution to date, remain central to its development. Neither the narrow economism of electoral politics nor the broader economism of socialist thought, to which I referred earlier, helps social democracy to be aware of either the constraints or the possibilities that this situation creates. But it is vital that those concerned with the future of this movement, whether as politicians, citizens or indeed academics, grasp the meaning of the global challenge.

Social democracy and the globalized Western state

What I call the global revolution has two principal dimensions, centred on transformations in the relations of state and society. On the one hand, there is a fundamental change in the state system, on the other, a worldwide political upheaval (centred on democracy and human rights) that is bringing about a crisis in power relations. Both these closely linked changes have their origins in the Cold War period, but they are coming to fruition in new ways in the era that opened in 1989.

The transformations in the state system, upon which I have already touched, are in their superficial expressions widely acknowledged. The demise of the Soviet Union and the supremacy of the West are obviously fundamental changes. However, their causes and implications are more far-reaching than is generally recognized. The structural basis of the nation-state has been radically altered within the West. The anarchic system of nation-state empires within which social democracy developed until 1945 has been replaced within half a century by an increasingly integrated Western state. The interdependence of the expanded West, which many saw as a contingent result of American supremacy after 1945, and of the Cold War itself, has been confirmed in the new post-1989 conditions. Both the pressures of the global revolution and the logic of institutional development have been powerful factors in this development.

Economic rivalry between Europe, America and Japan takes place now on the basis of military and political unity, and of common structural arrangements in the Western-defined world economy. Western political elites collaborate within myriad international organizations as well as through bilateral relations. Although there is a veritable mess of overlapping national and international jurisdictions, in effect the Western state has become a single, if complex and internally differentiated, conglomerate of state power.[15] The Western state mobilizes, moreover, the resources of the world's largest and richest economies. Its combined expenditures dwarf those of all other states. Its military forces are the strongest, the most sophisticated, with capabilities of projection which greatly exceed those of the great non-Western powers (Russia, China, India, etc.). The war over Kosovo (1999) exposed the central paradox of this form of state: a (more or less) single, integrated military machine, run by political institutions comprising 19 national governments each 'spinning' the war differently to its national constituency. The West's political influence in legitimate world institutions (such as the United Nations Security Council) is indisputably dominant, if (as Kosovo again showed) certainly not undisputed. The West's economic model, the free market, and its political model, liberal democracy, are widely attractive to populations and to increasing extents accepted (or at least paid lip-service to) by political elites everywhere.

In essentials, this power of the Western state was already mobilized during the Cold War, when there was a transition in the principal form of the state from the rivalry of national empires to that of international blocs. The West and the Soviet blocs appeared symmetrically opposed, the twin pillars of the bipolar world. However while the rivalry of the Soviet bloc – with its alternative social and political model – partially limited the West's dominance, its greater importance was to mask the fact of dominance.

The Soviet bloc-state appeared as the twin of the West, but it lacked most characteristics of the latter's success. Its economic resources were always decidedly weaker. Its economic model had some attractions for anti-imperialist elites seeking an alternative to the world market, but it

became manifestly inefficient. Its political model lacked extensive legitimacy, especially in the outer reaches of the quasi-imperial bloc. Its military rivalry with the West was achieved at the cost of economic burdens
that only exacerbated both national and social contradictions. Despite
the Communist ideology of international cooperation, the Soviet bloc
never succeeded in developing cohesive integration. On the contrary,
unequal power relations between Soviet and non-Soviet elites meant that
many of the latter sought increasing economic integration with the West;
while conflicts between Russia and China and their Vietnamese and
Cambodian clients degenerated in the 1970s into open war.

The collapse of the Soviet bloc, and then the Soviet Union itself, in
1989–91, allowed the real supremacy of the West to become manifest. At
the same time, however, it greatly extended the scope of Western political and ideological, as well as economic, power. The former Communist economies – and those Third World economies that had attempted
development outside – were already increasingly, if unevenly, integrated
into the Western-dominated world economy. Now the biggest barriers to
world market flows were removed, western capital became dominant on
a fully world scale. Likewise, however, Western political and military
power became manifestly supreme. Post-Soviet Russia, although (like
China) still nuclear-armed and with a seat in the Security Council, is a
shadow of the former superpower. The West became the clear centre of
world economic, military and political power and all the problems of
world order landed at its door. These problems, especially those caused
by political upheaval and violence, are far more demanding than anyone foresaw in 1989, and well beyond the capacities of Western institutions and the political will of Western leaders.

These transformations of the relations between Western and non-
Western centres of state power have also transformed relations within
the West, both between different national centres and between nation-
states and international organizations. Long before 1989, of course, a
shift in economic relations was apparent, in which American dominance was challenged by revived European and Japanese economies.
This became reflected in a more genuinely multilateral character for
western political and (to a lesser extent) military institutions. The
other two corners of the Western triangle became increasingly influential. The paradox of the 1990s has been that while the relative dominance
of the American economy has been restored, while Japan and Europe
have faltered, internationalizing processes in the Western state have
strengthened. Indeed America has encouraged other sectors of the larger
West to shoulder the military and political burdens of world order.

Three complementary features of the transition from Western to global state have accentuated the role of Western Europe.

First, the problem of European order was central to the Cold War, and the creation of a stable order in Europe has been manifestly central to the 'new' world order. (Indeed some of the most acute military-political crises resulting from the collapse of the Soviet bloc have arisen in southern and east-central Europe.)

Second, maturating Western unity and its extended global reach have been accompanied by extensive international institutionalization. Since America has largely relied on projecting its vastly superior national power, it has often shown a limited, even opportunistic commitment to international organization. For European states, in contrast, the development of the European international institutions has been a central concern; in addition, a number of states have made particularly strong contributions to the United Nations and other wider international organizations.

Third, in contrast to the United States where even levels of electoral participation are exceptionally low, in Europe democratization has been an ongoing process. Both the geographical spread of democracy and the reform of institutions in existing democracies has been more intense, a process which has been reinforced by the development of European institutions – both in the unique development of a directly elected international parliament, and in the democratic criteria for admitting new member-states.

To the extent, therefore, that global state development is about settling the European order, developing mature international institutions and consolidating democracy, there is a distinct European contribution. None of these aspects arises in any simple way from the greater importance of social democracy in European than in American – or Japanese – politics. Rather, the social democratic influence is probably best seen as a parallel aspect of Europe's distinctive contribution to the Western state. The importance of this is growing, however, because in the aftermath of the economic crises in Asia, Russia and Latin America in the late 1990s, the excesses of the unrestrained free market are increasingly recognized.

The unprecedented social democratic hegemony in the European Union at the end of the 1990s partly reflected the recognition of the need for international as well as national regulation of markets, as well as of social protection, in the process of market liberalization. The renewal of social democracy in Western Europe is matched by a modest movement in east-central parts of the continent, too, towards social democratic politics, whether of newly formed parties or of reformed Communist parties (although it is true that the social democratic label is also used by largely unreconstructed ruling parties).

The potential social democratic contribution to the development of global institutions depends, however, on social democratic politicians recognizing the radical scope of the demands for change in the contemporary world. As Giddens, a sympathetic critic, remarks, 'In spite of their electoral successes, social democrats have not yet succeeded in creating a new and integrated political outlook.'[16] The problems we face are not restricted to reconciling social welfare and cohesion with developments in Europe-wide markets and globalization; or even to the 'enlargement' of Europe to include the much poorer 'transitional' economies. As is obvious in the European Union's relations with Turkey as well as former Yugoslavia, economic and social problems are entirely bound up with national, democratic and human rights questions, and with military order. The agenda for social democracy in the twenty-first century remains, as it has been throughout the twentieth, profoundly connected with basic democratic issues on the one hand, and the nature of world order on the other.

Social democracy in the global-democratic revolution

The difference today is that these two questions are intertwined as never before. The old idea that democracy is a question of the political relations *within* states and world order one of the relations *between* states is outmoded. There is nothing less than a worldwide upheaval that is simultaneously bringing into question national and international political arrangements. The demand for democracy within national borders is interlinked with the demand for global standards and institutions. It presents profound challenges to the Western state, within which social democracy is established, and to existing world institutions. It also raises the more radical challenge to social democracy to reconstitute itself, not merely with a national or a European programme, but as a genuinely worldwide and global politics.

The literature speaks of 'democratization' as a process, which is spreading worldwide in a rapid way.[17] Before 1989, only a minority of the world's states were formally democratic, and a minority of the world's people lived in them: the majority were still controlled by Communist, military or other authoritarian regimes. A decade later, the positions are reversed, although substantial proportion of the world's population still lives in states that are manifestly not democracies (especially China).[18] It is obviously true that in a large number in states where democracy is newly instituted, it remains insecure or shallow in terms of the accountability of state for society. By any standards, however, this is a very significant transformation.

Some accounts stress the role of changes in Western, especially American, policy in producing democratization.[19] It is clearly true that during the 1980s, American policy began shifting from the support of authoritarian, anti-Communist regimes in the Third World, towards support of democratic reform movements. In Europe, the tentative moves towards democracy promotion in the Helsinki negotiations with the Soviet bloc gave way to more wholehearted support of democratic reform. However the West, especially America, always lagged behind movements for change, which were deeply rooted in society.[20] Official Western institutions maintained strong links with state elites and institutions, in the crumbling Soviet bloc as well as the Third World, and were often caught out by the pace of change from below.

In this respect, the 1989–91 transition in the Soviet bloc was not the exception to the general world pattern, but the standard experience. Neither Soviet nor Western elites anticipated the extent and speed with which Gorbachev's reform process would cause state institutions and the whole bloc to dissolve. The driving forces for change – notably in Poland, East Germany, Czechoslovakia and Romania – were spontaneous popular movements, led by loose new political coalitions in which (Romania apart) members of old 'dissident' groups played key roles. Certainly, once the revolution had been achieved in Central Europe, sections of the old elites re-formed into new parties and would-be ruling groups. In much of the Soviet Union, once the Stalinist counter-revolution was defeated, the democratic revolution was largely bypassed. It was quickly overtaken by self-interested elites using nationalist language and limited democratic reforms to consolidate new forms of corrupt, authoritarian rule based on the market.

The democratic revolution has spread to most parts of the world in the 1990s but everywhere it has met with resistance and/or manipulation by local elites, combined with a confused mixture of policies towards the consequent conflicts by Western and global state institutions. Where democratic change has occurred within relatively homogeneous existing nation-states, with only moderate economic dislocation and good links with the western state, reform has been relatively successful. The principal Central European states, Asian 'tigers' and possibly some of the more advanced Latin American states provide examples. Where democratic change has occurred within more diverse quasi-imperial states, raising deep national issues with greater economic dislocation and weaker western links, it has had more dangerous consequences. Overt counter-revolutionary violence has been the response of state elites from China to Yugoslavia, Burma to Indonesia.

In the 'new wars'[21] which have resulted from these conflicts, democratic movements – in both the zones of conflict and the West – have emphasized the universal principles of human rights which were proclaimed globally after 1945 but given little more than lip-service during the Cold War. In this sense, the democratic revolution today is 'global-democratic', demanding common standards of freedom and democracy on a world scale, enforced by legitimate global institutions and the dominant global power. These demands, together with the plight of the victims of violence, have forced the Western state to back increasingly widespread international interventions – in political, military, legal and socio-economic forms – in non-western regions from Yugoslavia to East Timor and many parts of Africa.

In this global-democratic revolution, the West is deeply compromised, of course, by its association with anti-democratic forces during the Cold War. Moreover, Western governments see continuing political interests in maintaining close relationships with those in power in all but the most recalcitrant states, and parallel economic interests in arms sales and general market access. The Iraqi regime of Saddam Hussein had earlier received tacit Western backing in its 1980s war with Iran. During the Yugoslav wars, the West attempted to use the Milosevic regime as a guarantor of the Bosnian settlement – turning against it only when it became responsible for a third major conflict, in Kosovo. The West continued to arm the Indonesian military even as it destroyed East Timor in 1999, necessitating a western-led UN intervention. And of course, in the really big states, like Russia and China, the West always seeks close relations with those in power, even while it criticizes their human rights records.

Many, especially smaller, Western states have better records of support for global-democratic change than that of the United States. Predominantly social democratic countries, notably in Scandinavia, provided more consistent support for human rights at times when the US was backing ultra-repressive regimes – in Chile and El Salvador, for example. In the new global era, they have pushed for the development of international institutions, often in the teeth of US resistance – for example, over global environmental standards and the new International Criminal Court.

Nevertheless the smaller Western states, including those with social democratic governments, have failed to develop a clear alternative to the national *realpolitik* of successive US administrations. On the one hand, social-democrats and left-liberals in the West have often seemed to set the agenda of 'development' above that of human rights, justice and democracy in the Third World. Thus left-leaning politics has its own history of compromises with less than democratic regimes outside the West.[22] On the other hand, new attempts to define human rights-oriented world policies are often compromised by historic commitments of Western states to economic cooperation with (and arms sales to) repressive regimes. Thus the Blair government's commitment to an 'ethical dimension' in foreign policy has often been tarnished by the realities of Britain's role as one of the world's major arms-producing states.

The global-democratic revolution poses a fourfold challenge to social democracy. First, global change is centred, not in its traditional homelands of the advanced West, but in the crises of the non-Western world. Second, global demands are first and foremost to consolidate the democratic agenda, to protect human rights and create local institutional accountability, as a precondition of economic and social advance. Third, global reform demands a high priority for creating viable international institutions, in which global norms are embedded, and which protect and strengthen local democracy in the democratizing regions. And fourth, the spread of democracy does not mean that traditional social democratic concerns with economic and social welfare are irrelevant: on the contrary, it raises the prospect that these issues will be raised on an unprecedented worldwide scale and with a huge expansion of militancy. Quite clearly, once the impoverished peoples of democratizing regions have gained basic political freedoms, they are going to demand improved economic and social conditions. Globalizing social democracy will mean something more than a modest increase in the aid budget, even to the best levels achieved by the best social democratic Western government.

Some of this agenda has become increasingly visible to liberal as well as social democratic politicians and analysts since the end of the Cold War. Two of the characteristics of 'Third Way' social democracy – that it takes globalization seriously and its emphasis on individual as well as collective development – fit well with the enhanced global politics of human rights. Giddens' attempt to elaborate a 'renewed' social democratic politics includes a final chapter, 'Into the global age', with a brief outline of a project for global governance. In line with David Held's programme for 'cosmopolitan democracy',[23] Giddens would create global bodies on the lines of the European Union: a parliament, an executive and developed legal institutions.[24] He champions, too, the idea of the 'cosmopolitan nation': the national project reinvented in global terms.

However, even in his version, the new social democratic project – like most of the liberal discourse of global governance of which it is a distinct variant – very seriously underestimates the violent consequences of the clashes between global revolution and counter-revolution. There is something of a paradox here: Giddens was one of the first major sociologists of recent times to re-emphasize the importance of war in modern society.[25] Writing of Bosnia and Rwanda, he rightly argues that, 'appalling as these last episodes of violence were, they indicate a change in the pattern of war, away from the earlier geopolitical wars of nation-states.'[26] But such genocidal wars are constantly reproduced in the current era and represent a central challenge to any kind of world order. Giddens' account probably also underestimates the dangers of major war between states: as clashes between nuclear-armed India and Pakistan have reminded us, old-fashioned inter-state conflict is hardly dead yet.

The contemporary social democratic project has barely got to grips, either, with the vast scale of the poverty and social inequality that exist world-wide, and the extent to which more global markets, society and governance are likely to thrust these problems on to the world agenda. Although social democracy has contributed to Western liberal thinking, so that addressing these issues is now an obligatory part of any progressive politics, the extent of the political and economic change which is necessary to make an impact on them has hardly been understood. The long-term shift in world society, which is seeing the most dynamic growth in population outside the old West, implies a much more radical shift in politics over the medium term than European social democrats are recognizing.

We can see these limitations both in the discourse and in the practice of contemporary social democracy. The structure of *The Third Way*, in which the penultimate 'global' chapter is an add-on to thematic discussions cast essentially within the framework of national politics, indicates the kind of political audience that Giddens is addressing. Social democracy is still largely a political doctrine within national parameters; it has been internationalized on a European level, but it has hardly yet made the leap to serious global politics. Other evidence comes from the experience of the Blair government. Elected on an overwhelmingly domestic programme, it has been preoccupied far more than its leaders predicted with international issues. The 1999 Kosovo war, for example, represented a major diversion of energies and resources. Blair appeared, however, much better prepared ideologically than his counterparts in other social democratic European governments, many of whom could manage no more than an uneasy mismatch between the rhetoric necessary to assuage party and popular constituencies, and their commitment to the NATO campaign.

At the beginning of the twenty-first century, therefore, social democracy does indeed face a challenge of 'global' renewal, but this is far more profound than its most enlightened thinkers have yet imagined. It is true, in a sense, as was previously said of neoliberalism, that 'there is no alternative'. A global society, based on increasing awareness of commonality as well as the realities of global markets and communications, is rapidly developing. Unbridled markets pose so many dangers of instability that even former neoliberals now recognize the inevitability of global forms of regulation. After the disastrous experience of the Russian transition, the needs for both regulation and social protection are increasingly understood. At the same time, Marxism is still discredited, and the Marxist critics of new social democracy, trapped in the ideology of Cold War anti-imperialism, have little to offer. The spirit of the times is favourable to a renewal of social democracy: and yet there are only small beginnings for the kind of radical reconstruction which would make it truly a global politics for the century now beginning.

In these circumstances, it may be that we should look for sources of global social democracy beyond the conscious social democratic tradition, in the broad renewal of democratic thought including international institutionalism, radical liberalism, ecological and feminist politics. Certainly, what formally constituted social democratic politics has to learn from social and political movements, especially in the non-western world, is as important as what it has to contribute. In this context, social democracy itself will not necessarily be a specific political movement, but may often be a current within broad social movements. It will be distinctive not so much for distinctive policies or institutional goals, which may be shared ground with these other sets of ideas, as in the ways that it pulls them together. The distinctiveness of social democratic contribution will be its emphases on the importance of developing formal world institutions, the relationships between national and international frameworks in this process, and the need to make all of these serve the broad socio-economic as well as political needs of the majority.

Notes

1   In this chapter I treat social democracy as a broad political current, centred in concrete political movements around which quite varied intellectual trends crystallize. Since the meaning of social democracy and the extent to which it can be defined by a distinctive intellectual position are themselves variable – and contested – features of the social democratic tradition, I shall not attempt a tighter *a priori* definition. Instead, I shall try to show how the meaning and intellectual parameters of social democracy have been historically transformed.

2   J. Gray, *False Dawn: The Delusions of Global Capitalism* (London: Granta, 1998).

3   P. Hirst and G. Thompson, *Globalization in Question* (Cambridge: Polity, 1996).

4   A. Giddens, *The Third Way: The Renewal of Social Democracy* (Cambridge: Polity, 1998).

5   Giddens, *The Third Way*, 25; A. Callinicos, 'Social Theory Put to the Test of Politics: Pierre Bourdieu and Anthony Giddens', *New Left Review*, I: 236 (1999), 82.

6   A. Giddens, *The Consequences of Modernity* and *Modernity and Self-Identity* (Cambridge: Polity, 1990, 1991); D. Held, A. McGrew, D. Goldblatt and J. Perraton, *Global Transformations* (Cambridge: Polity, 1999).

7   A. Gamble, 'The Last Utopia', *New Left Review*, 236 (1999), 126.

8   Compare Hirst and Thompson, *Globalization in Question*, with Giddens, *The Third Way*.

9   Held *et al.*, *Global Transformations*, 2–14.

10   M. Mann, *The Sources of Social Power*, Vol. 2 (Cambridge: Cambridge University Press, 1993).

11   K. Marx, cited by S. Hook, *Understanding Karl Marx* (New York: n.p., 1933).

12   V. I. Lenin, *The State and Revolution* (London: Lawrence and Wishart, 1933); see M. Shaw, 'War, Imperialism and the state System: A Critique of Orthodox Marxism for the 1980s', in M. Shaw, (ed.), *War, State and Society* (London: Macmillan, 1984). The point here is that military mobilization for interstate war tended to determine 'internal' repression of subordinate classes, rather than the other way round as Marxists tended to assume.

13   F. Engels, 'The Force Theory', quoted in B. Semmel (ed.), *Marxism and the Science of War* (Oxford: Oxford University Press, 1981), 57.

14   Paul Addison, *The Road to 1945* (London: Quartet, 1975).

15   I have developed this argument further in 'The State of Globalisation', *Review of International Political Economy*, 5: 2 (1997), 497–512. The theoretical justification, which rests on the idea that distinct 'states' can only be identified in discrete military-political centres, is most fully expressed in *Theory of the Global State: Globality as Unfinished Revolution* (Cambridge: Cambridge University Press, 2000). The fact that the Western state includes Japan emphasizes that 'Western' here is a political rather than a geographical or cultural term.

16   Giddens, *The Third Way*, 24.

17   David Potter, David Goldblatt and Margaret Kiloh, *Democratization* (Cambridge: Polity, 1996); Robin Luckham and Gordon White (eds.),

Democratization and the South: The Jagged Wave (Manchester: Manchester University Press, 1996).

18   Potter, Goldblatt and Kiloh, *Democratization*, 9.

19   William I. Robinson, *Promoting Polyarchy* (Cambridge: Cambridge University Press, 1996).

20   There is much scope for reflection on left-wing reluctance to recognize the independent social sources of democratization, seeing it as a consequence rather than a cause of US policy shifts. See my inaugural lecture, 'The Unfinished Global Revolution: Intellectuals and the New Politics of International Relations', http://www.sussex.ac.uk/Users/hafa3/unfinished.pdf, 1999.

21   M. Kaldor, *New and Old Wars: Organized Violence in a Global Era* (Cambridge: Polity, 1999).

22   Thus social democrats have often been sympathetic to Communist and other 'left' dictatorships.

23   D. Held, *Democracy and Global Order* (Cambridge: Polity, 1995).

24   Giddens, *The Third Way*, 144–6.

25   A. Giddens, *The Nation-State and Violence* (Cambridge: Polity, 1985).

26   Giddens, *The Third Way*, 139.

2
Social Democracy and Global Governance

Neil Stammers

Introduction: transformation and global governance

The present intensity of processes of globalization indicates that we may be entering a period of fundamental social transformation, one at least as significant as the industrial revolution, if not the transition to modernity itself.[1] If so, none of our existing forms of social organization nor any of our intellectual and political categories can be taken for granted. In particular, we need to acknowledge the severe difficulties involved in predicting the future beyond the very short term and to recognize that most of our familiar macro-level explanatory models of societal change have proved woefully inadequate: often tending towards simplistic monocausal forms of explanation,[2] economic reductionism being prevalent among these. Having said that, current trajectories of change strongly suggest that the next 50 years or so may witness the construction of increasingly extensive and dense networks of global governance. Such forms of global governance will become highly significant for everyone on this planet: perhaps crucial to our (and its) very survival. If all this sounds overly apocalyptic, the views of the Co-Chairs of the Commission on Global Governance writing in 1995 made the same points, albeit in somewhat more measured tones:

> This report deals with how the world has been transformed since 1945, making changes necessary in our governance arrangements.... Time is not on the side of indecision. Important choices must be made now, because we are at the threshold of a new era.[3]

Now governance does not imply or necessitate government as it has been traditionally understood. Governance is, rather, a wider and looser term for the variety of possible ways in which humans might administer and manage their affairs.[4] This is an important distinction, for governance without government, governance without the state, is not only a possibility, it has *in fact* been a ubiquitous social reality throughout human history.[5] The importance of this distinction for thinking about global governance arises both negatively and positively. On the negative side, there is the danger of conflating ideas about global governance with the existing assumptions about governments and states. Such conflation raises the spectre of 'world government' or a 'global state' with all the authoritarian potentials that such notions carry.[6] On the positive side, the pressing need to think about global governance provides us with an opportunity to consider afresh the relationship between governance and government and, consequently, issues relating to participation, representation, accountability and democracy. In short, how do we make 'one world' a genuinely 'democratic world'? Any proposals for global governance clearly demand serious and deep interrogation. How such networks are constructed is critical to their democratic and participatory or, alternatively, their authoritarian and oligarchic potentials.

So we need to ask what lessons or ideas can usefully be drawn from our existing traditions of political thought and practices? It is in this context that the objective of this chapter is to consider what the social democratic tradition offers us in terms of thinking about global governance. In the next section I set out my understanding of social democracy within a historical framework. I then look at contemporary variants described as 'traditional', 'modernizing' and 'globalizing' forms. My overall analysis will be critical, but it should not be assumed that analyses of other political traditions would be any less so. As indicated above, it seems to me that the rapidity of change in contemporary conditions requires a degree of conceptual reconstruction such that no assumptions, outlooks, or categories should be regarded as sacrosanct.

What is social democracy?

As an intellectual and political tradition social democracy has always been a moving target, so defining it is a difficult, contingent and contentious task. I will use a framework which is broad in some respects but quite precise in others. Conceptually, my usage will include the 'social' or 'developmental' strand of liberalism associated with the work of John Stuart Mill in the nineteenth century and of L.T. Hobhouse, J.M. Keynes and William Beveridge in the twentieth. While such usage is open to criticism, it does mean that recent particular identifications of social democracy – such as Tony Blair's argument that 'modernized social democracy' is a synthesis of themes from 'democratic socialism and liberalism'[7] – are not excluded.

The extent of any fundamental philosophical differences between social democracy and 'social' or 'developmental' liberalism has always been doubtful. Indeed, a case can be made that, under closer scrutiny, social democratic concepts ultimately collapse back into the categories of mainstream liberal thought.[8] But, that said, in the case of social democracy, there is even less merit than usual in trying to consider or judge ideas abstractly, purely in terms of their intellectual coherence or lack of it. This is because social democracy has always attempted to be strategically pragmatic – and therefore it needs to be assessed in terms of the historical development of its praxis,[9] rather than by its ideas alone.

Another defining feature of what I mean by social democracy is its party form and the manner in which such parties have functioned inside liberal democratic polities. From the time of the First World War onwards, organized, party-based social democracy has been understood on the left as the exclusive political expression of one pole of a binary opposition between reformism and revolution. Much ink (and, unfortunately, blood) has been spilt defending one of these poles whilst denouncing and berating the other. While both analytically and empirically this idea of an exclusive opposition between reform and revolution should have always been deeply suspect, it nevertheless framed and set limits to the terms of debate about socialism throughout the twentieth century. Furthermore, since the main revolutionary traditions also adopted organized, party-based forms, until recent decades little thought had been given (apart from within the anarchist tradition) to the oligarchic implications and consequences of the organized, party-based form itself, despite persistent debates about problems of intra-party democracy.[10]

It seems to me that the strategic pragmatism referred to above has been a potentially major strength of social democracy in contrast to the teleological, and often theological or messianic, impulses of the dominant revolutionary traditions. However, I want to divorce this strategic pragmatism from the assumption that political expressions should necessarily take organized, party-based forms. There are many other forms of political (as well as economic and cultural) activity which are strategically pragmatic but which are not social democratic in their organizational form and orientation towards the political system.

Many non-governmental organizations and social movements fall into this category, and I have argued elsewhere that social movements in particular may have the capacity to contribute to transformative social change: a possibility which remains inadequately understood and largely untheorized – especially by those still committed to 'the party' and an exclusive binary opposition between reform and revolution.[11]

Six characteristics of social democracy

So let me now be more specific about what I mean by the social democratic tradition by setting out six points which, in my view, have historically constituted its central tenets and framed its practices. The first three comprise the ideological terrain upon which the vast bulk of arguments for and against social democracy were contested during the twentieth century. They are that:

1. Social democracy assumes that liberal democracy works: that is, societies with a liberal democratic polity are already democratic in a fundamental sense – even if further democratization is advocated.
2. Social democracy perceives capitalism as both inevitable and also inherently dynamic – the source of growth and wealth creation. Thus, it also necessarily accepts the logical and structural imperatives of a capitalist market economy.
3. Social democracy recognizes that inequalities and deprivation are generated by a capitalist market economy but believes these can be effectively mitigated by some (greater or lesser) form of economic and/or social intervention and regulation.

These points should be relatively uncontentious. For proponents, it was the possibilities for change inferred by universal suffrage from the end of the nineteenth century which led them to advocate electoral politics and a parliamentary road to change. This quickly sedimented into 1) above which has become a central – largely unquestioned – assumption. In contrast, it has been considerations of 2) and 3) and the nature of the relationship between them which has framed most of the key debates within social democracy during the twentieth century. In particular, 2) was not initially a characteristic of social democracy and some might still contest its inclusion here. It has nevertheless been an operational axiom of social democratic leaders for many decades. More recently, since the apparent crisis of Keynesianism, much more debate has centred on what 3) should consist of – for example, whether demand-side interventions are still viable in a global economy.

The essential core of the traditional critique from the left rejects the positive aspects of all three of these characteristics. Proposition 1) is rejected on the grounds that substantive asymmetries of power in social relations, particularly in economic relations, operate so as to deform liberal democracy – which in any case is typically a limited structure of formal or legal political democracy. In respect of 2) and 3), while the dynamism of capitalism is not disputed, it is the negative consequences of such dynamism which are seen as *the* defining characteristics of capitalism; not only in terms of the gross inequalities necessarily generated in a market economy, but also in terms of the destruction of all forms of social relations which stand in the way of profit seeking and commodification.[12] Furthermore, social democracy's necessary acceptance of the logical and structural imperatives of a capitalist market economy in 2) means that any attempts at mitigation as per 3) are necessarily limited and subordinated to those imperatives.

Many key elements of the debate between proponents of social democracy and left critics raise issues which remain unresolved even at a basic empirical level. I will come back to this well trodden – if still very thorny – path later. However, now I want to shift focus because, when thinking about global governance, we need to grasp three further characteristics of social democracy which have rarely been given the attention they deserve either by proponents or critics. These are:

4. Social democracy is largely wedded to an elitist understanding of the potential relationship between people and political leadership and tends to assume a top-down, hierarchical model of governance.
5. The social democratic tradition has been almost entirely 'statist' both internally, in terms of its orientation towards the intervention and regulation referred to in 3) above, and externally, in respect of its approach to foreign policy and international relations.
6. Social democracy has been both united and split by a commitment to methodological nationalism: a privileging of 'national' levels of debate, analysis and policy over other possible levels, whether local, regional or global.

Historically, the importance of 4) has been uncritically accepted for the most part and can be linked to the adoption of the party-based form of organization discussed above. There are many factors at work here, for example, underlying assumptions about the need for elite rule and the inevitability of a link between organizational hierarchy and efficiency. In short, pyramidal structures of power and organization are seen in practical terms as the only way to get things done. The Fabian Society in Britain has always embraced such assumptions, but they have also been positively endorsed academically, for example in Joseph Schumpeter's celebrated arguments for elite rule in *Capitalism, Socialism and Democracy.*[13] This characteristic in social democracy can also be conceptually linked to, and is bolstered by, a strong commitment to technocratic rationality: a belief that knowledge and control should be achieved through the calculated application of scientific, managerial and organizational expertise.[14] An extreme example of this link in policy practice can be seen in the 'ethnic hygiene' sterilization programme of successive social democratic governments in Sweden until 1976.[15]

These oligarchic and hierarchical tendencies of social democratic parties have rarely been examined critically from within social democracy but there are exceptions dating back to Michels' classic, if flawed, study of the German SPD.[16] More recently, in the context of debates about the need to 'modernize' social democracy, Escudero has attacked what he calls the age-old problem of organizational oligarchy and hierarchy and Giddens has criticized what he calls 'classical social democracy' for seeking to create an 'elitist state'.[17]

With respect to the statism of 5), the historical *raison d'être* of social democracy was to improve the condition of the working class by using state power to harness the dynamism of the market for social ends and to mitigate the worst inequalities generated by capitalism. Although social democracy has largely abandoned class analysis in recent decades, the aim of using state power to aid 'the least well-off' remains broadly similar (but see further discussion below). It is important to stress, though, that social democratic statism goes further and deeper than this. This is simply illustrated by the fact that social democratic governments have rarely considered anything other than state ownership on the few occasions when the question of the socialization of the means of production has been considered at all. Again, a strong commitment to technocratic rationality is involved here in so far as it assumed that it is the state which is best suited to mobilizing expertise and resources in order to regulate and intervene. While there is currently much talk about the limits to state action, a reflex towards statist solutions remains strong within social democracy as we shall see below.

The importance of characteristic 6) – the commitment to methodological nationalism – is found in the way in which social democracy has configured its understanding of community, identity and the national/ international. It was typically assumed that the boundaries and the most fundamental meanings of identity and (political) community ought to be coterminous with the understanding and boundaries of the nation. While class analysis was traditionally also a central feature of social democratic understandings of identity and community, Martin Shaw (in this volume) notes how 'nation' and 'class' emerged together and were irretrievably intertwined within European social democracy. Furthermore, and importantly, Shaw argues that social democratic understandings of 'nation' and 'state' are bound up with the historical formation of the inter-state system and the extant relations and structures of power within that system.[18]

Once the methodological nationalism of characteristic 6) is tied up with the statism of 5) we can grasp a key social democratic outlook, one that privileges the search for a near-perfect match between 'community, nation and state'. While national social democracies share this goal they must nevertheless aspire to it separately. Foreign policy (international relations) and internationalism are thus usually configured and understood as the *inter*national: that is, as a realm of activity that is – and should be – dominated by relations between nation-state actors. While social democratic approaches may not be unswervingly 'realist' in international relations terms, (in that the importance of international organizations and non-state actors is not denied) the 'internationalism' of the leadership of social democratic parties has not stretched much beyond 'looking to create solidarity between like-minded political parties', as Giddens puts it.[19]

Although perhaps obvious, it is important to stress that none of these six characteristics is unique to social democracy. Indeed, despite a few exceptions, they have – from the time of Hobbes onwards – framed much enlightenment and modernist thinking. In particular, characteristics 4), 5) and 6), commitments to elitism, statism and methodological nationalism have been pervasive assumptions throughout virtually all domains of social praxis in the West. But this should not blind us to the historical importance of these latter three characteristics as core dimensions of social democracy. Indeed, I would argue that social democracy cannot be understood without grasping their relevance. It is around an apparent loosening of points 5) and 6) that we can see the emergence of what we might call a 'globalizing' form of social democracy. Before discussing that, however, let me turn first to what I will call 'traditional' and 'modernizing' forms and their relation to global governance.

'Traditional' social democracy and global governance[20]

Given that the six characteristics identified above have constituted the central core of social democratic thinking for much of the last 100 years, it is hardly surprising that sections of social democracy should seek to defend 'traditional' configurations of that core despite the breadth and depth of current social transformations. Yet 'traditional' social democracy clearly has serious difficulties in coming to terms with the nature and impact of globalization. It has even more difficulty in thinking about global governance.

Let us begin with the point that an important social democratic tenet seeks to match 'community, nation and state' in the combination of points 5) and 6) referred to above. 'Traditional' social democracy has so far been largely sceptical of accounts of globalization which suggest that there is anything much more going on than an increasing degree of economic interdependence and capital mobility. Analyses which suggest that nation-states are losing their capacity to govern, or that historical constructions of community and national identity are being undermined, tend to be discounted. So 'traditional' social democracy fails to identify any threat to liberal democracy or, indeed, any significant change 'inside' the nation-state arising from processes of globalization. Similarly, since traditional social democracy continues to privilege the nation-state as the appropriate 'container' for democratic community, it tends to be suspicious of any threats to state sovereignty from 'outside' the nation-state. This leaves 'traditional' social democracy, at best, trying to forge *inter*national agreements through which intervention/regulation might take place.[21] At worst, there might be a collapse towards, as John Gray put it in the context of responding to economic globalization, 'sovereign states...waging a war of competitive deregulation'.[22] So the core characteristics of 'traditional' social democracy provide little basis beyond *inter*national cooperation for thinking about community, identity or political democracy at the global level. In short, there is little conceptual space for thinking about global governance as a political project at all.

When we shift focus fully onto the questions of economic intervention and regulation, the limitations of traditional social democracy become stark indeed. Although there is a good deal of debate about the extent to which economic globalization limits the capacity of nation-states to manage their economies, even globalization sceptics such as Paul Hirst recognize that there have been fundamental changes in recent years.[23] Arguably, these changes leave traditional social

democracy in a dangerous double-bind. While a capitalist market economy is still seen as the dynamic force in the creation of economic
growth, the use of a national economic strategy to mitigate the worst
effects of that market is constrained by the need to avoid weakening the
national position in the global market. Linking the impact of economic
globalization to the constraining effects of statism and methodological
nationalism in terms of thinking about global governance, David Miliband has noted:

> while the power of social democracy as a national project is comprom-
> ised by economic interdependence, international political institu-
> tions are too weak for an effective supranational strategy.[24]

It is primarily the fact that these arguments have been accepted by the
leaderships of most social democratic parties – perhaps most strongly in
Britain – which have led to the emergence of 'modernizing' social
democracy to which I now turn.

'Modernizing' social democracy and global governance

There can be no doubt that European social democracy has been transformed over the last two decades,[25] yet of the three analytic categories
used here, 'modernizing' social democracy is probably the least unified and most unstable. So what then are the boundaries and what
features does 'modernizing' social democracy possess which justifies
the epithet?

The boundary between 'traditional' and 'modernizing' social democracy is marked most evidently by different understandings of the nature
and impact of economic globalization and, consequently, by a changed
assessment of the relationship between characteristics 2) and 3) above –
the nature of capitalism and the possibilities for mitigating its negative
effects. But there are also some differences in respect of 5) and 6), statism
and methodological nationalism, in so far as 'modernizing' social
democracy appears much more willing to look beyond the nation-state
towards either a pooling of state sovereignty or else an attempted
reconfiguration of community, identity and democracy in regional
confederal structures.

The boundary between 'modernizing' and 'globalizing' social democracy is again marked by differences in respect of characteristics 5) and 6)
yet, in this case, 'modernizing' social democracy holds to more statist
and methodological nationalist positions (including here a perceived

need for them to be re-instantiated at a regional level) while 'globalizing' social democracy apparently seeks to transcend them.

Another way of thinking about the boundary between these categories is in terms of focus. 'Modernizing' social democracy tends to focus on economic globalization and its effects 'inside' the nation-state (and/or region) whilst 'globalizing' social democracy tends to focus on broader political restructuring which might be necessary to cope with globalization 'outside' the nation-state (and/or region).

It is also important to note that underlying this difference is an ambivalence within 'modernizing' social democracy towards the impact of cultural globalization 'inside' the nation-state. At one end of this spectrum, some elements of 'modernizing' social democracy share the 'traditional' view that historical constructions of community and identity are not being significantly transformed by processes of globalization. From this perspective, any arrangements to pool sovereignty are purely a response to economic change. Others – best exemplified perhaps in Anthony Giddens' rendition of 'the Third Way' – argue for the necessity of reconfiguring understandings of the nation and the state as necessary responses to the impacts of cultural globalization 'inside' the nation-state.[26]

The most controversial aspect of 'modernizing' social democracy within social democratic parties is undoubtedly the analyses of economic globalization and the policy prescriptions which flow from them. Sassoon has made the point that 'the last 20 years have witnessed the effective termination of the main European model of capitalist regulation: national Keynesianism' and that globalization is the force behind what he calls the 'unprecedented, Europe-wide convergence of the parties of the left'.[27]

While it is impossible to explore the detail of these sorts of debates here, we can consider what changes are implied in characteristics 2) and 3) above. The first thing to note is that the belief in the capitalist market to deliver wealth and growth has, if anything, been strengthened in 'modernized' social democracy. Giddens has recently stated that 'there are no alternatives to capitalism' and that, instead, it is the dynamism of the market which needs harnessing and regulating for the social good.[28] Taking that argument further, Blair has claimed that 'with the right policies market mechanisms are critical to meeting social objectives, entrepreneurial zeal can promote social justice'.[29]

It is with respect to characteristic 3) that significant change is most clearly evident. The possibilities for mitigating deprivation and inequalities are now seen in quite different terms from the 'traditional' emphasis on Keynesian demand management and a universalist welfare state. These are now seen as hampering the capacities of national economies to compete successfully in the global economy. In contrast, supply-side interventions in terms of, for example, developing education and training are seen as the best approach to mitigation since they enhance economic dynamism and competitiveness. Many critics argue that this shift represents a straightforward capitulation to a neoliberal agenda of creating an unfettered global market. But it is important to recognize that 3) has not been abandoned as such and, in that sense, 'modernizing' social democracy remains within the mainstream. Indeed, critics who argue that 'modernizing' social democracy has sold out to global capitalism[30] are conveniently forgetting that the leaderships of 'traditional' social democracy – particularly when in government – have believed in the dynamism and inevitability of capitalism for many decades.

Furthermore, a case could be made that the limitations of 'modernizing' state intervention at the national level could be compensated for by transformed approaches and objectives at the regional, international or global levels. Certainly, social democratic enthusiasm for European integration could be understood in this light and undoubtedly this project is historically unprecedented. Proposals for a new international architecture for global finance and trade – involving reform of the IMF, World Bank and World Trade Organization – could also be seen as a potentially innovative response. Yet, significantly, these proposed reforms are limited and remain firmly based on a traditional model of *inter*national agreements. For example, the Paris Declaration of the 21st Congress of the Socialist International in the Autumn of 1999 was dedicated to addressing 'the challenges of globalization'. However, their concrete proposals for restructuring of international institutions were restricted to increasing the number of permanent members on the UN Security Council, 'some changes' to the IMF, the World Bank and World Trade Organization and the establishment of a UN Economic Security Council.[31] The declaration emphasized instead regional cooperation as 'the most appropriate way of meeting the challenges which cannot be met efficiently by Nation-States acting on their own'.[32] So while some 'modernizers' like Giddens recognize the need to move towards some form of cosmopolitan democracy,[33] generally 'modernizing' social democracy offers few proposals for the substantive reform of international institutions or the inter-state system. There is certainly not even a hint of thinking about any process of political democratization at the global level.

So 'modernizing' social democracy too looks to be in a potential double-bind. On the one hand, there is a recognition that economic globalization is creating a powerful global economy which is limiting the ability of nation-states to regulate national economies. Yet, on the other, they are unwilling or unable to consider establishing global structures which might be essential for the establishment of adequate regulatory frameworks, nor entertain the possibility of developing a political project of global democratization. European social democracy's assumption that an expanded and more fully integrated Europe will be able to 'mop up' what cannot be dealt with by nation-states may be over-optimistic given the current pace of change and the considerable ambivalence of national public opinions towards the European project.[34] For some hints of what transformed institutional structures might look like we need to turn to what I have called 'globalizing' social democracy.

'Globalizing' social democracy

'Globalizing' social democracy appears to make a significant break from the statism and methodological nationalism of characteristics 5) and 6) above. In so doing, it also appears to make a shift in respect of characteristic 1) – the belief that liberal democracy works – in that issues of democracy and the accountability of institutional structures are recognized as problems 'beyond' the liberal democratic nation-state. In other words, the political issue of global democratization is taken up in detail, as is the cultural question of the possible transformation of constructions of community and identity 'outside' the nation-state. Note, however, that the proposals below have very little to say regarding the impact of globalization 'inside' nation-states. The examples considered here are the work of Commission for Global Governance and David Held's proposals for cosmopolitan democracy.

Some shift away from statism and methodological nationalism by the Commission on Global Governance is most clearly indicated by its call for the establishment of a global civic ethic, major reforms of the United Nations – including the establishment of an economic security council, a people's assembly and a civil society forum – and the limitation of state sovereignty through an increasing embedding of a global rule of law.[35] Furthermore, in an apparent parallel break away from the strong thread of elitism running through social democratic thinking, the Commission strongly emphasize the potential role of global civil society organizations in offering a non-bureaucratic approach to global governance, seeing them as having the capacity to broaden effective representation in an emerging global society.[36] Similarly, in talking of the need for enlightened leadership in the global neighbourhood, it stresses that this leadership must be 'dispersed and democratic'.[37] Global governance, it is stipulated, must be underpinned by democracy at all levels and it must 'subject the rule of arbitrary power – economic, political or military – to the rule of law within global society'.[38]

In contrast to 'modernizing' social democracy, these proposals represent a distinctly radical agenda. Yet closer examination shows that there are still significant limits here. First, statist and national frames of *international* politics are not in fact transcended. Rather, they are partially reconfigured. So, for example, the proposed membership of the economic security council comprises state representatives and, likewise, membership of the peoples' assembly is drawn from those delegated from state assemblies.[39] In contrast, the civil society forum which is intended to give a voice to non-state actors is restricted to a 'discussion-only' body. Allowing that these proposals may be only a first step, a beginning, not an end-state of global democracy, core elements of social democratic thinking around statism, methodological nationalism and elitism still seem to be at work here. Indeed, emphasizing its elitist credentials, Richard Falk has characterized the Commission's report as 'social democracy globalized through the agency of an enlightened, empathetic sector of the leadership cadre in the established order'.[40]

If we turn to the economic trajectory of the Commission's report, an unreconstructed social democratic pedigree is clear. The report evinces a strong commitment to a capitalist market economy yet notes that '[b]oth the dynamism and the instability of the process of global economic integration are linked to the fact that it largely originates in the private sector'.[41] What is required, they say, is a global framework of economic regulation which can harness that dynamism and seek to limit that instability. Yet, at the same time, they also praise the virtues of free trade and economic liberalization in a manner more reminiscent of 'modernizing' than 'traditional' social democracy.

Turning to Held's model of cosmopolitan democracy, the first thing to note is that his case for democratic reconstruction rests partly on the argument that globalization processes are undermining liberal democracy as it is currently constituted 'inside' nation-states. His short-term proposals are similar to those of the Commission, but his longer-term vision appears rather more radical. He makes the case for the establishment of a global parliament and the entrenchment of what he calls 'cosmopolitan democratic public law' with a new charter of rights and obligations locked into and constraining different domains of political, social and economic power. This democratic public law is ultimately backed up by military force, the jurisdiction for which is gradually shifted from the hands of nation-states to global institutions. Held also stresses the importance of civic associations, NGOs and social movements in establishing enhanced degrees of participation and lines of accountability within cosmopolitan democracy.

Yet in a further parallel with the work of the Commission, a closer look at Held's proposals reveals similar limitations. Elements of statism and elitism can still be discerned in his work although he is apparently less constrained by methodological nationalism given his notion of cosmopolitan citizenship. For Held, states remain primary actors within the framework of cosmopolitan democracy and direct political representation does not appear to extend much beyond the sphere of the nation-state. So, for example, it is existing *inter*national institutions and organizations which are expected to construct and entrench cosmopolitan democracy. Held's concern with procedural mechanisms and the emphasis given to democratic public law seems to suggest a reliance on institutional structures which are more likely to favour elite control over democratic accountability. In this connection it is notable that, like the Commission, Held too is concerned to set limits to participation. He does so on the basis of needing to defend the principle of autonomy from the dark side of popular participation, the potentially 'undemocratic' action of citizens and their social movements.[42] While Held is right to point to this as an important issue, at the same time he assumes that fully legitimated political structures have somehow already been brought into existence. Yet, given existing asymmetries of global power, 'unruly' political action including civil disobedience might well be necessary as part of popular struggles to achieve and establish such institutional structures in the first place.

The importance of this last point is reinforced if we look at how Held approaches the relationship between cosmopolitan democracy and the capitalist market economy. He is much less sanguine about the impact of capitalist relations than the Commission and 'modernizing' social democracy. Indeed, as well as recognizing that capitalism creates economic inequalities and deprivation, he points to the impact of the logic and structural imperatives of capitalism on the political process:

> A government's policies must...follow a political agenda that is at least favourable to, that is biased towards, the development of the system of private enterprise and corporate power.[43]

In other words, Held questions characteristic 1), that liberal democracy is necessarily democratic, by recognizing that capitalism significantly constrains this possibility. That said, Held feels capitalism has strengths as well as weaknesses. So he argues for 'reframing the market' – regulating and constraining it to compensate for the structural biases he identifies. Cosmopolitan democratic public law should thus be entrenched and enforced across economic life, nationally, regionally and globally. It is important to stress that Held does not argue for simply accepting the logical and structural imperatives of the capitalist economy: his proposals are not framed in terms of mitigation but in terms of achieving economic democratization. But then how are such changes to be achieved? We are back to the question of how a transition to cosmopolitan democracy might occur and it is not at all clear that Held – having kept social movements and social struggles at arm's length – has any sort of answer to this question. As McGrew puts it:

> . . . it might be argued that without stronger mechanisms for taming the power of global capital the idea of cosmopolitan democracy remains seriously deficient.[44]

Notwithstanding my criticisms, I would stress that Held's work and that of the Commission on Global Governance are challenging and interesting. At points they push at the boundaries of the core characteristics of social democratic thinking. They do at least attempt to tackle some of the most complex questions which will probably have to be faced in the next few decades. That they do so in ways that I have criticized is no doubt partly due to differing understandings of appropriate forms of strategic pragmatism under contemporary conditions. But in my view it is also partly due to a continuing commitment by both the Commission and Held to elements of the core characteristics of social democratic thinking. So where do we go from here in terms of thinking about the relationship of social democracy to global governance?

Conclusion: global governance beyond social democracy

My contention is that continued uncritical adherence to any of the six core characteristics identified above constitutes a serious impediment to constructive and imaginative thinking about the possibilities for democratic global governance. But reflection on these characteristics and their historical instantiation may also help us to think about how we might go beyond the limits of social democracy in approaching the issue. A lot could be done in this direction but here I must confine myself to a few brief remarks.

First, as noted earlier, characteristics 4), 5) and 6) (elitism, statism and methodological nationalism) are so deeply embedded within the thought and practices of western modernity that they have been natur- alized and reified and have set the limits to what is often perceived as politically possible. Such assumptions have never, of course, been inno- cent in respect of relations and structures of power. In the broadest terms, they have served to legitimate capitalism and sustain various forms of political power organized around elite rule, nation-states and the inter-state system. So, it seems to me that we have to question these assumptions *as assumptions* in order to make a full exploration of the possibilities for establishing any form of democratic global governance. While any trajectory towards global governance has to start from where we are – a set-up of nation-states and an inter-state system suffused with asymmetries of power and forms of elite rule – that should not entail wearing the same blinkers that got us to where we are in the first place!

Second, while the above characteristics may not have been confined to social democracy, characteristics 2) and 3) (a commitment to a capit- alist market economy whilst seeking to mitigate its worst effects) have been the keystone, the hallmark of social democracy. Yet, at the same time, social democracy has always struggled to find ways of reconciling the inherent tensions within these two positions. In terms of the response of social democracy to economic globalization and issues around global governance, two things seem particularly curious. If the apparent failure of the national Keynesian model was an early indicator of the vastly increased intensity of economic globalization, what is the basis for believing that effective mitigation is any longer possible? Pro- posals to re-embed particular forms of intervention and regulation across local, regional and global domains could work, but we need to recognize that this is a distinctly new version of characteristic 3) and one without – as yet – much evidence to support claims for its utility. Quite simply, social democracy is making an unsupported claim here instead of considering whether characteristics 2) and 3) should be more sub- stantively questioned under contemporary conditions.

Furthermore, it seems strange indeed that elements of 'modernizing' social democracy have responded to economic globalization by appar- ently reconfiguring the relationship between characteristics 2) and 3) in favour of the former. The emphasis turns towards the capacity of capitalism to pull the world's poor out of poverty through its assumed capacity to deliver wealth through growth. Interestingly, there is a significant difference on this point between elements of 'modernizing' and 'globalizing' social democracy – with the latter retaining much more of an emphasis on 'traditional' approaches to intervention and mitigation.

What I find most telling about these responses is the extent to which the belief in the positive aspects of the dynamism of capitalism does not appear to have been subjected to interrogation at all. Yet many would argue that the rapid processes of economic globalization over the last 20 years or so are, once again, demonstrating that the dynamism of capitalism is predicated on the generation of vast inequalities and gross deprivation. While it may be true that 'the definition of, and attitude towards, capitalism has been a fault line in the left for generations',[45] unless all evidence and analysis is seen as nothing more than ideology or rhetoric (in a hideous sort of Marxist/postmodernist mélange!) the veracity of social democratic assumptions around this point ought to be amenable to coherent assessment and analysis.[46] Yet, currently, in so far as such evidence is taken into account at all, social democrats tend to explain it as a consequence of the political hegemony of neoliberalism in major western states and the international financial institutions over the last 20 years. In other words, such evidence is explained in terms of a *contingent political problem* rather than being understood as inherent to capitalist dynamics.[47]

My final points also concern social democratic assumptions about capitalism – assumptions that appear to be the least questioned of all. Third, then, is the belief that capitalism is inherently dynamic, the driving force behind wealth-creation and growth, actually true? Or is it an unquestioned assumption, which is also embedded in classical liberal thought and, as I noted earlier, Marxist critiques of capitalism? The fact that it is such a shared and pervasive view points to the possibility that it is, in fact, an unjustifiable form of economic reductionism inherited from nineteenth-century political economy.[48] So perhaps a case could be made, for example, to show that it is technological innovation and development which impels economic dynamism rather than the other way round.[49] No doubt these two (and many other) dynamics cannot be easily disaggregated, but that does not detract from the point that some – perhaps much – of the dynamism attributed to capitalism could be explained in other ways. Since we appear to be on the verge of another quantum leap in technological innovation and development, perhaps we need to look at such relationships again rather than relying on reductive and monocausal explanations at a time of such complexity?

My fourth and final point is disarmingly simple, but perhaps the most fundamental of all. Is capitalism inevitable? The leadership of mainstream social democracy has assumed so for many years, but what is it that is supposed to be inevitable about capitalism? Two arguments stand out here. The first is the belief that only capitalism is dynamic enough to create the wealth and growth necessary to promote and facilitate human well being. This has already been questioned above. The second argument for capitalism's inevitability is, as Held argued:

> . . . [it] has distinct advantages . . . over all known alternative economic systems as an effective mechanism to co-ordinate the knowledgeable decisions of producers and consumers over extended territories.[50]

Well, maybe, but Held is dealing here only with the 'allocative' aspect of capitalism. Does this necessarily entail an acceptance of the other central aspect of capitalism – the huge concentrations of economic power under corporate ownership and control? It should also be noted that Held talks of the advantages of the allocative aspect of capitalism over 'all known economic systems'. However, while there may not presently seem to be a viable macro-level economic blueprint as an alternative to capitalism, much innovative work is being done – most notably by green economists – which could significantly alter and constrain the current trajectory of capitalist development.[51] Furthermore, the evident failures of statist command economies does not mean the search for alternatives should be abandoned. Capitalism is neither natural nor a stage in historical development with unfolding immanent contradictions. It is a social construction resulting from human praxis. Human praxis can transform it.

At the beginning of this chapter I stressed that strategic pragmatism has been a potential strength of social democracy. That strength, however, has been seriously and increasingly diluted by adherence to the six core characteristics described above. What I have tried to show is that, to date, most social democratic responses to the challenges posed by current transformations remain largely wedded to those characteristics. Yet, while these have been the intellectual tradition of social democracy and frame its political heritage, strategic pragmatism today entails recognizing and discarding unquestioned assumptions and unnecessary baggage from the past. To make positive contributions to the debates on, and the construction of, democratic global governance, social democrats need to move decisively beyond social democracy as it has been historically understood.

Notes

1 By globalization I mean multidimensional and dialectical processes of political, cultural, economic and technological change which are increasing the degree of interconnectedness and 'stretching and deepening' of all forms of social relations around the globe. This contrasts with very common but much narrower accounts of globalization as an economically driven phenomenon. For further discussion of the orientation to globalization used here, see D. Held *et al.*, *Global Transformations* (Cambridge: Polity Press, 1999), Introduction; A. Giddens, *The Consequences of Modernity* (Cambridge: Polity Press, 1991); D. Held, *Democracy and the Global Order* (Cambridge: Polity Press, 1995); A. McGrew (ed.), *The Transformation of Democracy* (Cambridge: Polity Press, 1997).

2 Actor-centred and structuralist models of social explanation dominated much thinking in the social sciences throughout the twentieth century. Both have, in my view, seriously impaired our capacity to understand the world, let alone change it. For an introductory discussions of these matters see C. Hay, 'Structure and Agency', in D. Marsh and G. Stoker, *Theory and Methods in Political Science* (Basingstoke: Macmillan, 1995), 189–206; and A. McGrew, 'A Global Society', in S. Hall, D. Held and A. McGrew, *Modernity and its Futures* (Cambridge: Polity Press, for the Open University, 1992).

3 Commission on Global Governance, *Our Global Neighbourhood* (Oxford: Oxford University Press, 1999), xvii and xix.

4 For alternative definitions of governance, see P. Hirst, *From Statism to Pluralism: Democracy, Civil Society and Global Politics* (London: UCL Press, 1997), 3; and The Commission on Global Governance, *Our Global Neighbourhood*, 2.

5 From Hobbes on, the hegemonic traditions of western political thought are saturated with assumptions about states being the only form of governance able to mediate the competition and conflict which is the 'natural' human condition. The cooperative side of human behaviour visible through the ages has been largely ignored in terms of its theoretical significance. Yet as soon as one moves away – even slightly – from the universalised and timeless Hobbesian view of human nature, the possibilities of non-coerced cooperation take on great significance in terms of conceptualizing governance.

6 This threat is widely recognized. For example, The Co-Chairs of the Commission on Global Governance state: 'We are not proposing movement toward world government, for were we to travel in that direction we could find ourselves in an even less democratic world than we have [at present]' (Commission on Global Governance, *Our Global Neighbourhood*, xvi).

7 T. Blair, *The Third Way: New Politics for a New Century*, Fabian Society Pamphlet No. 588 (London: Fabian Society, 1998), 1.

8 I have taken up this question previously in N. Stammers, 'A Critique of Social Approaches to Human Rights', *Human Rights Quarterly*, 17:3 (August 1995), 488–508.

9 By praxis here I mean the dynamic fusion of ideas and practices in the social construction of reality. The concept does however also have a more complex relationship to my approach to understanding social reality and social change which lies close to 'structurationist' and 'critical realist' positions. For an overview of some of these issues and a discussion of praxis, see I. J. Cohen,

Structuration Theory: Anthony Giddens and the Constitution of Social Life (New York: St. Martin's Press, 1989), Chs 1 and 2.

10   It is symptomatic that when the so-called 'new social movements' came to question oligarchic and hierarchical models of social and political organization from the 1960s onwards, their intellectual point of reference was Michels' famous work on the 'iron law of oligarchy' first published in 1911. For an introductory discussion of the orientation of 'new social movements', see A. Scott, *Ideology and the New Social Movements* (London: Unwin Hyman, 1990). See also R. Michels, *Political Parties* (New York: Free Press, 1962).

11   See N. Stammers, 'Social Movements and the Challenge to Power', in M. Shaw (ed.), *Politics and Globalization: Knowledge, Ethics and Agency* (London: Routledge, 1999).

12   This was poetically encapsulated by Marx and Engels in terms of the transition to capitalism. 'All that is solid melts into air, all that is holy is profaned.' *The Communist Manifesto*, (Harmondsworth: Penguin Books, 1967), 83. For a contemporary rendering of the same point in respect of economic globalization, see V. Shiva, 'Diversity and Democracy: Resisting the Global Economy', *Global Dialogue*, 1:1 (Summer 1999), 19.

13   J. A. Schumpeter, *Capitalism, Socialism, Democracy*, sixth edition (London: Allen & Unwin, 1987).

14   This also resonates with aspects of a broader, Weberian understanding of processes of rationalization in modernity. For a brief account, see W. Outhwaite and T. Bottomore, *The Blackwell Dictionary of Twentieth Century Social Thought* (Oxford: Blackwell Publishers, 1993), 546–7, entry on 'rationalization' points 3–5.

15   'Sweden Pays for Grim Past', *The Guardian* (6 March 1999), 15. The article adds: 'As in Britain, where some of eugenics' most enthusiastic supporters were on the political left, liberals and Social Democrats backed the Swedish programme and sustained it for decades.'

16   Michels, *Political Parties*.

17   M. Escudero, 'Re-inventing Politics', in D. Miliband (ed.), *Re-inventing the Left* (Cambridge: Polity Press, 1995); and A. Giddens, *The Third Way: The Renewal of Social Democracy* (Cambridge: Polity Press, 1998), 16.

18   For a useful discussion of the history of the inter-state system, see Held, *Democracy and the Global Order*, Ch. 4

19   Giddens, *The Third Way*, p. 11.

20   I want to make it clear that the use of the categories 'traditional', 'modernizing' and 'globalizing' primarily serve as analytical aids here. They should not be taken as firm, factual descriptions of discrete positions within social democracy. Indeed, the various strands of social democratic praxis overlap and contradict each other and – currently – could just as easily be seen as part of a complex, and rapidly changing continuum.

21   Within the context of the European Union, where one might expect a considerable degree of convergence and the growth of shared perspectives, analysts of social democracy appear to continue to prioritize 'national' outlooks. See, for example, J. Woldendorp, 'The Review', *ECPR News: The Circular of the European Consortium for Political Research*, 10:(3) (1999), 30–1.

22   J. Gray, *False Dawn: The Delusions of Global Capitalism* (London: Granta, 1998), 78.

23 Hirst, *From Statism to Pluralism*, Introduction.

24 Miliband, *Reinventing the Left*, 13.

25 H. Kitschelt, *The Transformation of European Social Democracy* (Cambridge: Cambridge University Press, 1994); and J. Hopkin, 'Social Democracy: Globalization, European Integration and the European Social Model', *ECPR News: the circular of the European Consortium for Political Research*, II(1) (Autumn 1999), 21.

26 Giddens, *The Third Way*. See also J. Krieger, *British Politics in the Global Age: Can Social Democracy Survive?* (Cambridge: Polity Press, 1999).

27 D. Sassoon, *Looking Left: European Socialism after the Cold War* (London: I. B. Tauris, 1997), 2, 5 and 11.

28 Giddens, *The Third Way*, 100.

29 Blair, *The Third Way*, 4.

30 See, for an example, H. Radice, 'Taking Globalization Seriously', in Panitch and Leys, *Socialist Register 1999*, 22–3.

31 *Declaration of Paris: The Challenges of Globalization*, XXI Congress of the Socialist International, Paris, 8–10 November 1999, pp. 8 and 9. www.socialistinternational.org/5Congress/XXISICONGRESS/DeclParis-e.html, accessed 3 December 1999.

32 Ibid., 9.

33 Interestingly, given Giddens' previous work, his endorsement of 'cosmopolitan democracy' in *The Third Way* appears somewhat 'tacked on' at the end. Furthermore, given his references to the inevitability and dynamism of capitalism (*The Third Way*, p. 100) it is not at all clear that Giddens could endorse the specific proposals for economic democratization in David Held's proposals for cosmopolitan democracy (see discussion of Held's proposals in 'globalizing social democracy').

34 There was a certain irony that, at the very same time the Socialist International was proclaiming the virtues of regional cooperation, the social democratic governments of Britain and France were completely at loggerheads over the safety of beef from Britain.

35 Commission on Global Governance, *Our Global Neighbourhood*.

36 Ibid., 33.

37 Ibid., 37.

38 Ibid., 5 and 48.

39 Ibid., 158–60.

40 R. Falk, 'Liberalism at the Global Level: The Last of the Independent Commissions', *Millennium*, 24:3 (1995), 575.

41 Commission on Global Governance, *Our Global Neighbourhood*, 137.

42 Held, *Democracy and the Global Order*, 157–8 and 285.

43 Ibid., p. 247.

44 McGrew, *The Transformation of Democracy*, 253.

45 A. Finlayson, 'Third Way Theory', *The Political Quarterly*, 70:3 (1999), 271–9.

46 I was struck by two claims which I read within a day or two of each other whilst preparing this chapter. The first was a positive expression of characteristic 2) from a Fabian Society briefing paper:

> The globalising world economy, and the growth in world trade that has accompanied it, has brought benefits to millions of people. More people

have escaped from poverty in the last fifty years than during the previous five centuries. (J. Crowe, *Globalization: Meeting the Challenge*; Fabian Society, 1999, 1)

In contrast, in a contemporaneous expression of the traditional left critique (albeit from an ostensibly postmodern legal theorist):

In the twentieth century, more people died of hunger than in any of the preceding centuries, and even in the developed countries the percentage of the socially excluded, those living below the poverty line (the "interior Third World"), continues to rise. (B. De Sousa Santos, *Towards a New Common Sense: Law, Science and Politics in the Paradigmatic Transition*, New York: Routledge, 1995, 8)

The point is not whether these two claims are compatible. They probably are. What is relevant is the extent to which the underlying assumptions of each framework ensures that 'facts' are selected so as to support those assumptions. Supporters and critics of social democracy have had it far too easy dismissing each others' arguments and talking past each other for the last 100 years.

47   For example, and following on from the last footnote, the very same statistics on the rapidly increasing gap between the world's rich and poor (UNDP Development Report, 1997) which have been used in radical/left critiques of the effects of global capitalism, are accounted for in the Fabian briefing paper in terms of the hegemony of neoliberalism rather than being used to question the benefits of the globalizing world economy.

48   Colin Hay raises the same issue in a different context in C. Hay, 'Globalization, Social Democracy and the Persistence of Partisan Politics: A Commentary on Garrett', *Review of International Political Economy*, 7:1 (Spring 2000) 139–52.

49   A similar point is made by Finlayson, 'Third Way Theory', 278.

50   Held, *Democracy and the Global Order*, p. 250.

51   See for example the work of the New Economics Foundation; M. H. Clayton and N. J. Radcliffe, *Sustainability: A Systems Approach* (London: Earthscan, 1996).

3
Globalization and the Renewal of Social Democracy: A Critical Reconsideration

Matthew Browne and Yusaf Akbar

Talk of globalization has been prevalent for some years. The current 'Third Way' renewal of social democracy is, however, a more recent phenomenon. Since April 1999, when the conference 'Progressive Governance for the 21st Century' was hosted in Washington DC,[1] the Third Way movement has gained increasing notoriety and importance in both the Anglo-Saxon and the Continental European political economies.[2] The self-prescribed or proclaimed aim of this movement is to identify a progressive, social democratic politics for the twenty-first century, a politics that can successfully negotiate both the caprices and opportunities of a globalized information economy. The movement has, however, been criticized by a number of commentators who appear sceptical about its attempts to unite globalized capitalism and business interest with social justice. For many, the movement has failed to maintain any left-wing outlook due to what appears to be its acceptance of, or capitulation to, neoliberalism.[3]

In light of these concerns, the purpose of this chapter is to offer a critical reconsideration of the relationship between globalization and the Third Way renewal of social democracy. First, an analysis of the way in which the relation between globalization and the renewal of social democracy has been theorized both in the academic literature, and within the Third Way movement itself, will be presented. Here, it will be shown that there are two broad categories of theories or perspectives that emerge. On the one hand, there are those who believe that economic globalization has ushered in an era of epochal change in which the traditional – what might be termed Keynesian welfare state – social democratic policies and practices are neither effective nor viable (practicable). On the other hand, there are those who are sceptical of the globalization narrative, arguing that the degree of 'economic globalization' achieved, as well as the consequences of the global interdependence this implies, are either overstated, or at the least are nothing new. Here, then, globalization is often understood as an obfuscating narrative or ideology, an ideology that hides the interests of those who benefit from these developments.

Having presented the central tenets of each of these perspectives, the chapter will argue that both these understandings of the relationship between globalization and the renewal of social democracy are inadequate. Both approaches presuppose that economic globalization can be understood in terms of quantifiable economic indicators (for example, the level of trade flows or capital movements), between supposedly interdependent, yet discrete units. If it can be shown, as the first approach argues, that the degree of capital mobility or global trade is notably higher than during previous periods, then it is assumed that globalization has ushered in epochal change. If such a difference cannot be identified, as the second approach contends, then the globalization narrative must be understood as a myth or ideology. In both of these accounts, globalization discourses or narratives stand in a secondary position to their supposed material determinants. Accordingly, a second task of this chapter is to outline an alternative approach within which one might offer an alternative evaluation of the role and function of discourse within this relation: namely critical discourse analysis.

Having outlined the theoretical and philosophical basis of this approach, the chapter will then seek to offer an alternative evaluation of the relationship between the renewal of social democracy and globalization. Here, it will be argued that the predominance of the orthodox construction of globalization is an essential element in the foreclosure of debate about the nature and direction of potential policy responses to current developments within contemporary capitalism. It will be argued that this foreclosure is achieved through the naturalization of the neoliberal order, and in particular through its presentation (or rather construction) as a 'given' or achieved state. This is not to argue that the policies proposed and pursued by some, if not all, social democratic parties can simply be reduced to neoliberalism. Nor is it to claim that the naturalization of the neoliberal order is reducible to ideology. Rather, what we would argue is that the social democrats' self-understanding of their responses as technical, pragmatic, yet superior methods of managing national economic affairs in the era of globalization has had two notable consequences. First, the central aspects of the neoliberal critique, which stressed the virtues of the market and the private sector over all others are essentially solidified and accepted as given, objective – almost scientific – truths. Second, politics is essentially degraded to local-level management, the technical application of best practice. With these aims in mind let us now consider the orthodox construction of the relation between globalization and the renewal of social democracy.

Globalization and the renewal of social democracy

The rationalization for and explanation of the renewal of social democracy in terms of strategic or necessary responses to the advent of economic globalization is a relatively new approach to thinking about this transformation. Previous explanations, having assumed a stable and unchanging international context, forwarded accounts based on internal politics. These included accounts based on the contradictions embedded in the welfare state itself, the normalizing effects of industrialization, the retreat of the working class and/or the rise of the middle class, as well as shifting priorities in the preferences of policy-makers.[4] These, accounts, however, often encountered difficulties in explaining why broadly similar transformations were taking place simultaneously across Europe. Here, it should be noted that explanations presenting globalization as the major causal factor are not solely focused on the international context, but more specifically on the relation *between* the international context *and* the national political economy.[5] Underlying this focus is a more general consensus that social democracy – in its traditional form – was viable only within a relatively autonomous national economy.[6] Hence, it is not so much that 'traditional' social democracy has difficulties coming to terms with globalization, but rather that it is impracticable in an economically interdependent world. Indeed, it is this line of argument that has led some commentators to assert that it is globalization that is the force behind a general and unprecedented convergence of social democratic parties across Europe.[7]

The historical coincidence of the primacy of the Fordist regime of accumulation, the predominance of Keynesian economics and the international order of 'embedded liberalism' are of particular importance here.[8] This was an era of limited international capital mobility and a mass organized working class. The state also had, at least in principle, the *de facto* capacity to manage local and national economic activity. The relative strength of organized labour and the relative weakness of financial capital – when combined with the *de facto* capacity of the state to manage national economic activity – permitted the mediation of class antagonisms and the provision of a stable environment for economic growth and full employment. Here, then, the advent of social democracy becomes intimately tied to the establishment of a corporatist, Keynesian welfare state. Thus while Shaw (this volume) is correct to note that the historical emergence of class and nation developed in a symbiotic relation with European social democracy, it is in large part the international regime of this period which facilitates or permits its institutionalization.

Within this context social democracy, at least until the 1970s, is neither necessarily dependent upon, nor directly linked to, the political hegemony of a social democratic or centre-left party. Under the conditions identified above, it is politically expedient and economically rational for all governments, whether 'Right' or 'Left', to seek to maintain full employment and relatively low inflation. Moreover, through Keynesian demand management policies and collective bargaining agreements, these goals should be attainable.[9] From this perspective, the crisis of 'old-style' or 'traditional' social democracy is generally regarded to stem from a two-fold transformation in the nature of the economy: the rise of interdependence through the growth of transnational and later global capital markets, and the intensification of international and regional trade; and the movement from a Fordist to a post-Fordist regime, and from secondary to tertiary production. This dual movement then results in and internationalization or globalization of the national political economy, which destabilizes the central tenets of 'old-style' social democracy.

First, given its increased mobility and the relative immobility of labour, capital is empowered to the detriment of labour. Moreover, in an environment in which social costs of labour in a particular member state can no longer be passed directly on to the consumer, who is free to choose from products produced under alternative regimes which may have lower labour costs, high-skill, high wage labour becomes difficult to protect.[10] Second, capital is also empowered *vis-à-vis* the state. On the one hand, 'punitive' tax regimes are likely to precipitate capital flight.[11] On the other hand, the rate of return on financial investment is now set by global capital markets rather than by domestic interest rates. Thus the traditional macroeconomic mechanisms used for shifting financial investment towards job-creating investment are no longer viable, while the taxation base upon which redistributive transfers are based is increasingly under threat. This has led a number of scholars to hail the hegemony of global capital, and to observe an increased convergence towards neoliberal labour market norms due to the policing effect of speculative capital flows.[12]

In addition, this new economic environment transforms the opportunity structures facing different sectors of society, as well as the organizational practices of the workplace. Here, then, when one considers that the 'internal' or 'domestic' accounts of the renewal of social democracy identified above – the normalizing effects of industrialization, the retreat of the working class and/or the rise of the middle class, as well as shifting priorities in the preferences of policy-makers – one might argue that such developments should be viewed as consequences of economic integration, and thus part of what needs explaining rather than constitutive of an explanation in and of themselves.

Here, the shifting priorities and preferences of policy-makers should be considered of particular importance. Within this dual economic transformation Keynesian welfare state public policy becomes viewed as both enviable and impracticable. On the one hand, national economic activity can no longer be controlled by macroeconomic policy. That is to say, the level of national economic activity is now determined by a particular state's competitive standing in the international division of labour, and not by publicly agreed domestic economic indicators. On the other hand, traditional industrial policy is not suited to the requirements of a flexible information and service economy. Here, it is not simply that attempts to maintain or even extend traditional social democracy are damaging to the economic well-being of a particular state, although – as the French socialist parties' experience in 1983 demonstrates – this certainly appears to be the case. Rather, policies intended to bring about a particular effect are more than likely to have opposite or contrary results. The situation is well summarized by Scharpf:[13]

> It was not fully realized at the time ... how much the success of market correcting policies did in fact depend on the capacity of the territorial state to control its economic boundaries. Once this capacity was lost ... the 'golden years' of the capitalist welfare state came to an end ... [If] a government should now try to reduce interest rates below the international level, the result would no longer be an increase in job-creating real investment in the national economy, but an outflow of capital, devaluation and a rising rate of inflation.

In terms of policy preference and choice, the apparent incapacity of the state can be seen as part of a process through and within which

increased economic interdependence mediates and motivates a transformation away from the welfare state towards the competition state, or
Schumpetarian workfare state.[14]

Here the advent of the competition or Schumpetarian workfare state
refers to a general a shift away from concentration on macroeconomic
demand management to meso-and microeconomic supply-side measures. Here, the role of the state is itself transformed. Full employment
and redistributive transfers are rejected as guiding principles in favour of
the provision of an environment conducive to private investment, particularly foreign direct investment, and the entrepreneur. This rationale
is clearly reflected within the Third Way literature, along with the belief
that renewed social democracy actually provides a more viable means of
producing such a 'competition state'. Consider, for example, the Department of Trade and Industry's (DTI) description of the necessities
demanded by globalization:[15]

> In the increasing global economy of today, we cannot compete in the
> old ways. Capital is mobile, technology can migrate and goods can
> be made in low cost countries and shipped to developed markets...
> business must compete by exploiting capabilities which its com-
> petitors cannot easily match or imitate...knowledge skills and cre-
> ativity.

Or the following statement, by Giddens:

> Old-style social democracy concentrated on industrial policy and
> Keynesian demand measures, while the neoliberals focused on de-
> regulation and market liberalization. The Third Way needs to
> concern itself with different priorities – with education, incentives,
> entrepreneurial culture, flexibility, devolution and the cultivation of
> social capital.[16]

It is, however, this very shift away from Keynesian macroeconomic
policy, collective bargaining and full employment and redistributive
transfers as guiding principles that has led many to question whether
the advent of globalization has not led to a reversal of Polanyi's 'Great
Transformation'.[17]

In opposition to this view, both the DTI and Giddens imply that while
globalization and the emergence of an information and service economy have rendered old-style or traditional social democracy outdated,
social democratic values can be maintained within this context. Here,

then, what needs to be understood is that within this renewal of social democracy there has been a movement away from a 'protecting' role for the state towards an 'enabling' one. Here, the role of the state is not, cannot and indeed should not be to protect from 'cradle to grave'. Such a policy would, we are told, be likely to limit individuality, entrepreneurial zeal and creativity. This movement is evident in the importance the Third Way – at least rhetorically – places on education, life-long learning and retraining. Providing citizens with the skills they need to survive and thrive in a global information order, through equal access to life-long learning and education conveniently unites the demands of the new global economy with the social democratic values of social justice and equality.[18] The focus on education, life-long learning and retraining, it is argued, is merely the presentation of old-values in a new context.

Thus, as Blair contends 'market mechanisms are critical to meeting the social objectives, entrepreneurial zeal can promote social justice'.[19] Similar arguments are also forwarded with regards to 'welfare-to-work' policies and supply-side job creation. On the one hand, this marks a movement from a passive, purely market-based employment policy to one aimed at combating structural unemployment. On the other, the reduction of working hours, the advent of job sharing and the improved status of part-time and contract work is an attempt to combine the supposedly – according to neoliberal logic – incommensurable goals of increased security and quality of life with the need for flexibility.[20] For advocates of the Third Way, these are policies and values that, if responsibly taken up by citizens, imply an increased standing in the international division of labour for any given country that initiates them. Rights and responsibilities, social justice and competition, at least rhetorically, are united and regarded as mutually reaffirming and beneficial.

Clearly, both this view of globalization, and the Third Way's own self-understanding of the renewal of social democracy along the above noted lines have been the subject of much critique. Hirst and Thompson, for example, have argued that the economic interdependence that exist today is nothing new. While they do not contest that this interdependence has increased during the last three decades, they claim that it is not quantitatively different from that which existed in the nineteenth century of laissez-faire capitalism.[21] However, as Giddens has noted, this 'later point is fairly easily challenged. Even if the current period were only a replay of a century ago, it would still be quite different from the postwar era of the Keynesian welfare state. National economies were much more closed then than they are now'.[22] Hay, Watson and Wincott – among others – have also noted that arguments about the degree of interdependence and capital mobility have been overstated.[23] However, their analysis is tempered by the observation that, while the consequences of globalization are often exaggerated, 'it is clear that *ideas* about globalization, if not the extent of globalization itself, continue to inform public policy decisions in contemporary Europe'.[24]

Other analyses have sought to critique the way in which the globalization thesis tends to reside on a form of economic determinism, reducing national politics and the state in particular, to little more than a transmission belt from the global economy to the national level.[25] Such critiques underpin more general concerns regarding the way in which globalization is often presented, particularly in public discourse, as an 'agent-less' process, or as an achieved state. Pierre Bourdieu, for example, has noted that for those who aspire to the formation of an even more interdependent or globalized economy the routine representation of its prior existence is a powerful symbolic resource.[26] Another explicit and detailed analysis of linguistic constructions and the use of language more generally is offered by Norman Fairclough. In his analysis of ' "New Labour's" new language', Fairclough argues that multinationals are often present within the Third Way discourse merely as 'ghosts in the machine'. That is to say, rarely, if ever, do they gain explicit recognition as one of the primary and most active agents in the globalization process. Consider here Fairclough's analysis of the above cited extract from the DTI White Paper. In the second sentence, as Fairclough notes, the manufacturing of goods in low-cost countries and their shipping to the developed markets are represented as actions, but actions 'without any responsible agents'. Moreover, the statement that capital is mobile is not even presented as a action 'but as a relation of attribution, though the attribute (*mobile*) does imply action', but 'again without a specified agent'. The most striking rhetorical use of language is found in the analysis of technology. Here it is technology itself that is represented as an agent in a process. This is achieved through the use of a metaphor from the natural sciences. Technology ' "migrates", like birds in the winter'.[27]

Such rhetorical devices, when combined with a number of key nominalization's[28] such as the representation of the economy as entity in and of itself, rather than a set of social relations and processes, are – for Fairclough – ideological, little more that the 'powerful using discourse to enhance their power'. Fairclough's understanding of the relation between observable material transformations associated with increased economic interdependence and the globalization narrative is similar to the account forwarded by Robert Cox. For Cox, states – having become willy-nilly more accountable to forces in the global economy than their citizens – have been 'constrained to mystify this accountability in the eyes and ears of their own publics through the new vocabulary of globalization, interdependence, and competitiveness'.[29] Here, then, the construction of globalization as an inevitable process must be linked to a managerial class who are active agents in this change, agents who apparently consciously – and in an implied sense maliciously – seek to obfuscate their role in this process. While the arguments forwarded in this chapter have much in common, as well as a certain degree of sympathy with those forwarded by Fairclough and Cox, the construction of the discourse of globalization in terms of ideology is, we would argue, inadequate. It presupposes, in the final analysis, that the aforementioned agents are not themselves subject to the rationality of this discourse. It is with regard to this inadequacy that this chapter will now consider the theoretical and philosophical underpinning of discourse analysis.

Critical discourse analysis

The aim of critical discourse analysis is to evaluate the relationship between language and power. This is well summarized by Norman Fairclough, when he argues that language and discourse have a dual relation to power. 'On the one hand they incorporate differences of power, on the other hand they arise out of – and give rise to – particular relations of power.'[30] The notions that texts and discourse can be both barometers of current orders of power, and themselves central to the constitution and maintenance of particular power relations, is itself anathema to more orthodox conceptions of power. Behavioural or what Lukes has termed 'first dimensional power' tends to view power in a very narrow manner.[31] The study of political power forwarded by this approach is, in Dahl's terms, concerned with determining 'for each decision which participants had initiated the alternatives that were finally adopted, had vetoed alternatives initiated by others, or had postponed alternatives that were turned down'.[32] In short, it is concerned with determining 'who actually prevails in community decision-making'.[33] Here, language and discourse have a two-fold status. On the one hand, rhetorical devices or debating skills could be considered as political resources through which particular actors make a *de facto* influence of the decision-making process. On the other hand, a discursive analysis can be used as a heuristic aid for tracing the dominance of a particular group's interests. In both cases, it should be noted that discourse itself is not considered as central to the constitution of interests and power *per se*.

However, as a number of scholars have noted, this notion of power is deficient as it presupposes that 'power is totally embodied and fully reflected in concrete decisions'.[34] As such it 'inevitably takes over the bias of the political system under observation and is [therefore] blind to the way in which its political agenda is controlled'.[35] One can, therefore, note a further dimension of power, what Lukes has termed the second dimension, a dimension concerned with the way in which a particular group of actors organize the mobilization of bias within a given system. This is a bias that discourages the development of overt conflict in the political realm through the creation of barriers to the public airing of particular views. This second dimension of power thus refers to the way in which public agendas reflect existing relations of power within society thereby foreclosing alternative perspectives from arising in public debate. To this extent, policy agendas embedded in White Papers, Green Papers and the like already narrow the agenda, and thus the space in which formal decision-making coheres. Here, then, texts become hermeneutic aids for identifying the inter-subjective parameters within which public conflict of interests cohere, but are not themselves directly implicated in the development and maintenance of particular power relations and interests.

This second, pluralist notion of power offers only a limited critique of the behaviourist notion, as it is itself too closely commitment to the behaviourist study of overt or 'actual conflict'. It assumes that if individuals or social groups have no grievances, then they necessarily 'have no interests that are harmed by the use of power'.[36] However, this is not necessarily the case, as Lukes argues:

> Is it not the supreme and most insidious exercise of power to prevent people, to what ever degree, from having grievances by shaping their preferences, cognitions and preferences in such a way that they accept their role in the existing order of things, either because they see it as natural and unchangeable, or because they value it as divinely ordained and beneficial?[37]

For Lukes, this is the third dimension of power: a dimension within which latent conflict may be specified, conflict that may never be actualized or appreciated. It is this dimension of power that underpins Fairclough's analysis of the language and discourse of New Labour. Fairclough's concern is that the particular discursive construction of globalization underpinning the Third Way, if it is taken at face value, may co-opt – for want of a better term – those whose interest it works against. While this dimension of power has been marginalized within mainstream or orthodox social science, it is quite possible to see consensual relations as relations of power none the less.[38] Indeed, this was a dimension of power that was central to the poststructuralism movement. Foucault, for example, argued that 'the notion of repression is quite inadequate for capturing what is precisely the productive aspect of power'.[39] Here, the juridical or repressive view of power theorized power in terms of a force of prohibition, as is implied in the first and second dimension identified above. However, this is to marginalize the productive aspect of power, the aspect which traverses and produces discourse and knowledge. It is here that a problem emerges with Fairclough's analysis of the Third Way.

In a sense, Fairclough's critical discourse analysis of the relation between power and language is rather limited. Viewing discourse as ideology, the rhetorical and discursive constructions embedded in the globalization narrative are simply understood as resources or political tools of the dominant class.[40] In a similar manner to the way in which Marcuse assesses techno-rationality, the ruling classes are regarded to stand in a privileged position to this discourse, thus not being subject to its productive powers.[41] In opposition to this view, Foucault refused to associate the productive or formative aspect of power with ideology. For Foucault, the concept of ideology was difficult to make use of because it always stood in virtual opposition to something that was to count as truth. This opposition, argued Foucault, was misplaced. The central problem here should not 'consist in drawing the line between that which comes under some other category, but in seeing historically how effects of truth are produced within discourses which in themselves are neither true [n]or false'.[42] To paraphrase, the central problematic here is the following: how can history have a truth if truth has a history.

Here, then, Fairclough's construction of the globalization narrative as an ideology rather than a truth regime, is based on the claim that the current Third Way renewal of social democracy subordinates the interests of labour and the socially excluded, for example, to those of transnational capital. This may well be the case, but under these conditions Fairclough's critique is one that is directly aimed at both capitalism in general *and* social democracy *per se*, and not uniquely at the Third Way or New Labour.[43] Let us consider, here, one of the key nominalizations noted by Fairclough, namely the representation of the economy as an entity in and of itself, rather than a set of social relations and processes. The emergence of the notion of the economy as an existentially 'separate' field of social activity was a long historical process. It was both concrete and abstract, and as scholars as diverse as Weber and Marx both noted, it was intimately linked to the dissolution of classical political economy and the emergence and establishment of capitalism.[44]

To this extent, one might consider this – at least – partially conceptual construction as part of what Bourdieu terms the *habitus*.[45] Here, the term *habitus* refers to the schemes of perception, and of thought and action, that are embedded within social understandings of how the world is organized. These schemes are the product of history, and thus must be understood as a 'present past' that tends to perpetuate itself into the future by reactivation into similarly structured practices. Continuity and regularity are thus not reducible to immediate concerns and intentions, but are actually part of the process through which these concerns and intentions themselves emerge. Here, then, a reconsideration of the politics – economics relation within social democracy might prove instructive. As Stammers notes in this volume, the belief that a capitalist market economy is both inevitable *and* a positive source of growth and wealth creation has been central to social democratic thinking. Social democracy has also presupposed that liberal democracy worked. To this extent, Stammers is quite correct to assert that social democracy collapses back into the categories of mainstream liberal thought. Within the social democratic heritage, politics and economics have always been construed as existentially separated, if interdependent spheres of social activity.

Here, while one might assert that within the current renewal of social democracy, this construction, and faith in the market have become even more marked, it is questionable to what extent this constitutes a qualitative distinction from previous social democratic renewals. In the introduction to this chapter it was argued that the discourse of globalization and the renewal of social democracy had two particular consequences. First, that the central aspects of the neoliberal critique, which stressed the virtues of the market and the private sector over all others are essentially solidified and accepted as given, objective – almost scientific – truths. Second, that politics had been degraded to local-level management, the technical application of best practice. In order to substantiate these claims, and in order to clarify what we regard to be the qualitative difference between the current and previous forms of social democracy, it is perhaps worthwhile considering the nature and function of a number of key motifs embedded in contemporary schemes of perspective, thought and action.

Neoliberalism and the reinvention of social democracy

As Andrew Sayer[46] has noted, embedded within contemporary understandings of how the world is organized are a number of key dualism, what Derrida[47] referred to as *logo*centric dichotomies. *Logo*centric dichotomies are linguistic constructions, or dualisms within which two terms are opposed to one another; for example 'fact' to 'value', 'individual' to 'collective', 'pragmatism' to 'ideology', 'objective' to 'subjective', 'quantitative' to 'qualitative', 'economic' to 'political', 'private' to 'public', 'science' to 'tradition', 'is' to 'ought', and so on. These oppositions are ordered in such a manner that each element within the dualism is held to be existentially separable from the other, that is, self-contained. However, within each dualism one of the two terms is prioritized. That is to say that one particular term is considered the pure form, or the *logos*. Within the dualism, the other term is defined, or understood in terms of what it lacks *vis-à-vis* the other, the *logos*.

The above, despite its apparent abstract nature, has important consequences for how we might analyse the renewal of social democracy, and its relationship to discourses, theories and practices of globalization. It implies that the way in which we understand social phenomena and processes, in this case globalization and the renewal of social democracy, or rather the way in which such phenomena are made comprehensible to us, is at least partially determined by these habitually received schemes of perception and understanding. That is to say discourse, understood here not simply as texts and narratives, but also in terms of the 'ordering scripts' embedded in perception, thought and action, could be considered to have determining or causal properties.

Here, it is important to note that the above dualism emerged contemporaneously with the dissolution of classical political economy. This was a supposedly positive movement, as it was believed it would allow for a more scientific investigation of society. Scientific investigation was understood, here, to reside in the value-free analysis of society. While this movement essentially presupposed, spuriously, that the social practices being observed where themselves not necessarily value-laden, the emergence and gradual predominance of positivism and empiricism within the social sciences provided fertile ground upon which economics could establish itself as the pre-eminent social science. The 'science' of economics was more readily amenable to the analysis of quantitative 'variables', and the development of quantifiable theories and laws, and could thus be more easily adjudged to be value-free (at least in the non-numerical sense). Here the language of economic cycles, inflation, supply and demand present themselves in a similar fashion to the changing of the seasons or other natural phenomena. To the economist they were phenomena, albeit social, that could be analysed, comprehended and, finally, controlled.

This rationale of control also has a long structural history within the history of the Left. From as early as Saint-Simon, there have been those that have argued that competency, rather than private property was key political and economic resource. Here, the future of society resided in the capacity to plan and deliver that highest utility to the highest number of people. Saint-Simon and Comte where aware that there was a danger in the technocratic ideal. Namely, that the depoliticization entailed by the rationality of competence, expertise and the drive for disinterested knowledge ran the risk of prioritizing material values over all others. However, the technocratic ideas that crossed the Atlantic in the twentieth century – namely Taylorism – expressed no such concerns. Taylorism was quite explicitly aimed at both the practical reorganization of the workplace to increase productivity, and the dissolution of industrial antagonisms in an era of mass mobilization. As Taylor himself asserted, under the principles of scientific management, 'what constitutes a fair day's work will be a question for scientific investigation, instead of a subject to be bargained or haggled over'.[48] Here, then, the extension of this rationality through what Maier has termed a politics of productivity embedded in Fordism can be seen as instrumental in providing stability for the postwar era.[49] Moreover, as Burnham had noted, the role of Keynesian demand management, under its welfare state formulation, had allowed managers to assume even greater power leading to what he argued to be a structural convergence towards, the managerial society.[50] Burnham's view was also complemented by Daniel Bell's argument that technical decision-making was itself now undermining ideology.[51] To this extent, as Foucault noted, a key strand in the western art of government should be understood as 'government in the name of "truth"'.[52]

Here, however, it is worth noting that the 1960s was a period in which the 'truths' of economics were also subjected to what might be termed a Kuhnian revolution.[53] During this period, neoclassical academic economists – of which Milton Friedman was in the vanguard – argued that unless a radical reformulation of economic policy were to take place, the industrialized countries were sure to be victims of an 'over-burdening state'. According to this group of economists, it should have come as no surprise that by the 1970s the macroeconomic performance of virtually all of the industrialized economies had stagnated as a consequence of falling growth rates, increased unemployment and price inflation.

In practical terms, Friedman and others proposed a number of policy reforms, ranging from cuts in individual and corporate taxation, to more general programmes of privatization and liberalization. In many quarters, this was viewed as a process of depoliticizing the economy and, thereby, removing both the state and the economy from the shackles of embedded interest representations. It was a process that would champion the private over the public sector in order to promote the 'objective' – that is, supposedly non-value-laden – and therefore universally, that is to say in principle non-partial, economic processes carried through by the market mechanism. These arguments easily meshed with the neoliberal consensus developing in international organizations such as the Trilateral Commission. During the 1970s, the Trilateral Commission began to argue that democracies were becoming ungovernable.[54] Asserting that under capitalism there was essentially a trade-off between democracy (or democratic input in the political process) and efficiency. According to these commentators, this balance had been tipped heavily in favour of input, leading to inefficient decision-making, ineffective policy and an 'overloaded state'.

Here, then, the neoliberal challenge and response to the crisis of the welfare state effectively reinstated the liberal dualism of the separation of politics and economics which had, to a certain degree, been challenged through the institutionalization of social democracy in the guise of the welfare state. As Foucault noted, this was a challenge that the 'Left' was singularly ill-equipped to respond to, particularly as it had never possessed its own distinctive art of governing.[55] As traditional social democratic policies began to flounder, social democratic parties essentially collapsed into neoliberalism. The early implementation of programmes of deregulation and privatization by the French Socialist Party (PSF) from 1983 onwards highlights the extent to which the economic and social dimensions of neoliberalism quite quickly transcended ideological differences. The perceived and substantive failures of the Keynesian experiment between 1981 and 1983 [56] precipitated a split within the PSF. Led by the moderates, Jacques Delors and Laurent

Fabius, the party was steered towards a more neoclassical policy. The French regulatory apparatus was relaxed, as were price and credit controls, and the virtues of a flexible labour market found a public voice. From 1983 onwards, the PSF also began to permit the sale of non-voting shares of publicly owned companies.[57] Here, it is important to note that this policy reversal was seen as a technical, pragmatic response to the crisis of the national economy in the face of economic interdependence.

It is in this sense that one might argue that the re-presentation of the separation of politics and economics within neoliberalism takes on a qualitatively new form. To the extent that neoliberal programmes are regarded as essentially technical, pragmatic response to problems caused through economic interdependence. Thus, the separation of the political and the economic is itself re-presented as a technical necessity. Here, then, it is not so much that the nominalization of the economy and the presentation of capital and productive mobility as agent-less that is of central importance.[58] Rather, understanding the 'art of government' as essentially the 'rationality of government'[59] the emergence and predominance of a particular art of government entails knowing what the activity consists in, and how it might be carried on.

> A rationality of government will thus mean a way or system of thinking about the nature and practice of government (who can govern; what governing is; what or who is governed), capable of making some form of activity thinkable and practicable both to its practitioners and to those upon whom it is practised.[60]

Accordingly, central importance must be attached to the reactivation of neoliberal motifs within the Third Way. The argument here is that in taking global economic interdependence, and the consequences of such interdependence as a given and unchangeable starting point, the theoretical 'ought' of neoliberalism, namely that the state or public institutions should not proactively seek to manage or control the economy, is transformed into a practical, or objective 'is'. That is to say that within such a discourse neoliberal motifs are engrained in the 'is', the truth about how the world is organized, and thus what can be governed. Accordingly, the 'ought' forwarded by modernizing or Third Way social democrats is contained within the neoliberal orthodoxy. In a peculiar sense social democracy has been inverted. From a political movement that once sought to control and manage the economy to the benefit of society, it has been transformed into a doctrine which seeks to manage and facilitate the adaptation of that society to the requirements of the economy. In this sense, the Third Way renewal of social democracy should be considered as the acceptable face of neoliberalism. Through its attempt to unite social justice and competitiveness the Third Way provides a means through which economic globalization becomes both thinkable and practicable – and potentially acceptable – to those who practise it, and those upon whom it is practised. While, the Third Way seeks to unite competition and social justice – in asserting that either is necessary for the other to be achieved – it simultaneously presents itself as a technically superior method of managing national economic affairs. It is in this sense, then, that we would argue that politics has been degraded to localized management, localized management which is increasingly dependent upon advisory boards, think tanks and un-elected ministers that possess the expert knowledge social democrats require to find practical and pragmatic resolutions to the globalization conundrum. This definition of who is to wield power, or 'who is to govern', might well be characterized as an expert based rationalization of the *res publica*.

Here, however, it is also important to note who is to be governed within this framework. As Stammers has noted, within modernizing social democracy, the traditional social democratic motif of methodo-logical nationalism is heavily engrained. Nowhere is this more evident that in New Labour's association of its own renewal with national renewal *per se*. Nevertheless, this still begs the question as to why mod-ernizing social democracy has prevailed over globalizing social democ-racy or, put differently, why has there been no social democratization of globalization? In response to this dilemma, Stammers, citing Miliband, argues that 'while the power of social democracy as a national project is compromised by economic interdependence, international political institutions are too weak for an effective supranational strategy'.[61] As most commentators note, even in the European Union, which has the most developed post-national political and democratic institutions, sufficient progress has not been made to establish democracy – let alone social democracy – that transcends the nation-state.[62] In short, these institutions lack the legitimacy of a pan-European civil society with a common identity within which they might be embedded.[63]

However, here we would wish to suggest that the explanation for the failure of such a movement to emerge resides no so much in the institu-tional weakness of these institutions, but rather in the very design of these institutions, and the set up of inter-institutional relations themselves. One might argue, for example, that while the European

Parliament is a very good at the technical scrutiny of legislation, it is very poor at politics in the traditional sense. Indeed, Joseph Weiler has recently argued that the dual processes of European integration and Europeanization have been instrumental in the degradation of politics *per se*.[64] This view is echoed in the work of Majone, although with a rather more positive interpretation. For Majone, the 'first and probably the most important lesson' to be drawn from European integration 'is the rediscovery of the old liberal principle of the separation of politics and economics'. He adds that 'despite the ambiguities of the founding treaty, the disjunction of state and market turned out to be the most striking characteristic of the process of European integration'.[65] Here, then, Majone identifies two developments that are of central importance to the dilemmas facing social democracy. First, the restriction of the freedom to intervene in national economies when such interventions interfered with the smooth functioning of the single European market. Second, the extensive delegation of rule-making and adjudication to supranational institutions – such as the European Commission and the European Court of Justice – enjoying a considerable degree of independence from national governments and the European Parliament. Here, what becomes clear is that the *de facto* incapacity of the state associated with the advent of economic globalization is translated, in the context of the EU, into a *de jure* removal of sovereignty. These, combined with the fiscal and budgetary constraints placed on member states who are members of Economic and Monetary Union represent practically impossible obstacles for traditional social democracy to overcome, even if the consequences of economic globalization are overstated. This is particularly so when one considers that to alter this order of play requires a treaty amendment that has to be agreed by all 15 member states, and thus can be blocked by one recalcitrant partner.

Conclusion

In this chapter we have attempted to offer the outline of an alternative analysis of the relationship between globalization and the renewal of social democracy. Adopting a critical discourse analysis we have argued that globalization should be understood neither in terms of simple economic indicators, nor in terms of a legitimating or obfuscating ideology, but rather as a 'global truth regime'. Here, the construction of a neoliberalized global economy as an achieved state, and the acceptance of this by social democrats, has re-presented the traditional liberal separation of politics and economics. However, in the current European political economy, this re-presentation of the separation of politics and economics is qualitatively different from previous representations. On the one hand, this separation is constitutionalized in a legal order that is both embedded in, and superior to, the national political system. It thus cannot be directly changed within the national polity. On the other hand, and in our opinion more importantly, this separation is embued with a technical quality. Here, both the theories and practices associated with a globalized economy appear to render necessary the reduction of national politics to local-level management. Due to spatial limitations and the nature of the analysis offered, this outline has been largely abstract and general. A more complete analysis would require not only a more in depth review and presentation of previously forwarded analyses of this relationship, but also a more detailed concrete evaluation of the particular resolutions of this relation across the European continent. Such an evaluation, we would argue, should concern itself, although not necessarily exclusively, with analysis of the extension of management practices such as targeting and the cost-benefit analyses into the public sector. The presentation of such tasks, we would argue, further solidifies the re-presentation of these policies and programmes as technical matters.

However, we would like to stress once more that while we have set out to argue that the Third Way renewal of social democracy has resulted in both a naturalization of neoliberalism, and the degrading of national politics, we do not contend that this renewal can be reduced to neoliberalism. Indeed, the current revival of social democracy on the European continent is in part due to its apparent ability to provide a more current and successful management strategy. While Third Way social democracy may collapse into neoliberalism, as traditional social democracy collapsed into liberalism, both offer adaptations which differ in important respects to liberalism or neoliberalism *per se*. It is true that many commentators have criticized the Third Way for its failure to maintain any left-wing outlook. We shall not pass judgement on this issue, at least for the time being. Nevertheless, it is perhaps worth noting– or restating – that the critiques forwarded by many of these commentators are ones that could quite easily be aimed at social democracy *per se*. To this extent, they are perhaps misplaced. While the self-proclaimed aim of this movement is the development of a radical and progressive politics for the twenty-first century, this is perhaps too much to expect. Social democracy has been, and is likely to remain, a reactionary political project. Whether this current renewal of social democracy will be able to successfully combine competition and social justice, only time will tell.

Notes

1 The Democrat Leadership Council, and in particular their Progressive Policy Institute (Washington, DC), have played an influential role in the development of the Third Way. In 1996, they published the *New Progressive Declaration* while, more recently (25 April 1999), the institute held the Third Way conference on 'Progressive Governance for the 21st Century'. The conference was hosted by the DLC President, Al From, and Bill Clinton, and attended by a number of notable European leaders: Tony Blair, Gerhard Schröder, Massimo D'Alema and Wim Kok. They were joined by other leading DLC members from the United States: DLC Vice-Chair Roy Romer (Former Colorado Governor); Kathleen Kennedy Townsend (Maryland Lt.-Governor), Mike Thrumond (Georgia Labor Commissioner) and Denver Mayor Wellington Webb.

2 It should be noted that the supposed Anglo-Saxon roots of the Third Way have led commentators such as Tuomioja to assert that the movement has little if any relevance to the political economies of Continental Europe. E. Tuomioja, 'Blairism May Not Work Elsewhere in Europe', *Newsletter of Finish Institute* (July 1998). Torfing and Etherington have forwarded a flip-side to this view. They claim that the Third Way is essentially what the Danish have been doing. J. Torfing, 'Workfare with Welfare: Recent Reforms of the Danish Welfare State', *Journal of European Social Policy*, 9:1 (1999), 5–28; D. Etherington, 'From Welfare to Work in Denmark: An Alternative to Free Market Policies?', *Politics & Policy*, 26:2 (1998), 147–61. This view has also been echoed by Clinton, who stated at the Washington *Progressive Governance* Conference, that 'Wim Kok, from the Netherlands, actually was doing all this before we were; he just didn't know that – he didn't have anyone like Al From who could put a good label on it'. Democratic Leadership Council, *The Third Way: Progressive Governance for the 21st Century* (Washington, DC: National Press Club, 25 April 1999), 2.

3 See, for example, P. Collins. 'A Game of Give and Take', in *The Third Way* (London: Social Market Foundation, 1999); R. Dahrendorf, 'Whatever Happened to Liberty?', *New Statesman* (6 September 1999); S. Hall, 'The Great Moving Nowhere Show', *Marxism Today* (November/December 1998); D. Halpern and D. Mikosz, *The Third Way* (London: Nexus, 1998); D. Kunset and R. Teixeria, 'The Third Way and the Future of Social Democracy', *Dissent*, 46:3 (June 1999); C. Mouffe, 'The Radical Centre: Politics without an Adversary', *Soundings*, 9 (1998); A. Ryan, 'Britain; Recycling the Third Way', *Dissent*, 46:2 (1999).

4 See here, for example, C. Offe, in J. Keane (ed.), *The Contradictions of the Welfare State* (Cambridge, Mass: MIT Press, 1984); C. Kerr, J. T. Dunlop and C. A. Myers, *Industrialism and Industrial Man* (London: Penguin Books, 1964); G. Esping-Andersen, *Politics against Markets* (Princeton, NJ: Princeton University Press, 1985); P. Abrahamson, 'Social Class and Political Change in Western Europe', *Comparative Political Studies*, 4 (1971), 131–55; T. Notermans, 'The Abdication from National Policy Autonomy', *Politics and Society*, 21 (1993), 133–68.

5 Indeed, here, some might argue that the globalization has rendered the very distinction between international and domestic invalid. See, for example, R. B. J. Walker, *Inside/Outside: International Relations as Political Theory* (Cambridge: Cambridge University Press, 1993).

6 See, for example, J. W. Moses, 'The Social Democratic Predicament and Global Economic Integration: a Capital Dilemma', in W. D. Coleman and G. R. D. Underhill (eds), *Regionalism and Global Economic Integration: Europe, Asia and the Americas* (London: Routledge, 1998); F. W. Scharpf, *Crisis and Change in Social Democracy* (Ithaca, NY: Cornell University Press, 1991); H. Kitschelt, *The Transformation of European Social Democracy* (Cambridge: Cambridge University Press, 1994); D. Sassoon (ed.), *Looking Left: European socialism after the Cold War* (London: I. B. Tauris, 1997).

7 Sassoon, *Looking Left*.

8 For a presentation of the central elements of 'Embedded Liberalism', see J. G. Ruggie, 'International Regimes, Transactions, and Change: Embedded Liberalism in the Post-war Economic Order', *International Organization*, 36 (1982), 379–415. On the importance of Fordism for providing stability, see C. Maier (ed.), *In Search of Stability* (Cambridge: Cambridge University Press, 1979), and *Changing Boundaries of the Political: Essays on the Evolving Balance between the state and Society, Public and Private in Europe* (Cambridge: Cambridge University Press, 1987); or M. Rupert, *Producing Hegemony: The Politics of Mass Production and American Global Power* (Cambridge: Cambridge University Press, 1995).

9 C. Crouch, 'The Conditions for Trade-Union Wage Restraint', in L. N. Lindberg and C. S. Maier (eds.), *The Politics of Inflation and Economic Stagnation* (Washington, DC: Brookings Institute, 1985); G. Garret and P. Lange, 'Government Partisanship and Economic Performance: When and How Does "Who Governs" Matter?', *Journal of Politics*, 51 (1989), 676–93; P. Hedström, 'The Evolution of the Bargaining Society: Politico-economic Dependencies in Sweden', *European Sociological Review*, 2 (1986), 20–9; D. Hibbs, 'Political Parties and Macroeconomic Policy', *American Political Science Review*, 71 (1977), 1467–87; P. Lange, 'Unions, Workers and Wage Regulation: The Rational Basis of Consent', in J. H. Goldthorpe (ed.), *Order and Conflict in Contemporary Capitalism* (Oxford: Clarendon Press, 1984).

10 S. Strange, *Retreat of the State: The Diffusion of Power* (Cambridge: Cambridge University Press, 1996).

11 H. Kitschelt, *The Transformation of European Social Democracy* (Cambridge: Cambridge University Press, 1994); H. Kitschelt et al., *Continuity and Change in Contemporary Capitalism* (Cambridge: Cambridge University Press, 1999); P. Kurzer, *Business and Banking* (Ithaca, NY: Cornell University Press, 1993).

12 T. Iverson, 'Power, Flexibility and the Breakdown of Centralised Wage Bargaining', *Comparative Politics*, 28 (1996), 399–436; R. G. Ehrenberg, *Labour Markets and Integrating National Economies* (Washington, DC: Brookings Institute, 1994).

13 F. Scharpf, 'Negative and Positive Integration in the Political Economy of European Welfare States', in G. Marks *et al.*, *Governance in the European Union* (London: Sage, 1995), 16.

14 On the advent of the Schumpeterian workfare state, see B. Jessop, 'Transition to Post-Fordism and the Schumpeterian Workfare State', in R. Burrow and

B. Loader (eds), *Towards a Post-Fordist Welfare State?* (London: Routledge, 1994). On the emergence of the competition state, see P. Cerny, *The Changing Architecture of Politics* (London: Sage, 1990).

15   Department of Trade and Industry, *Building the Knowledge-Driven Economy*, White Paper (London: Stationery Office, 1998).

16   A. Giddens, *The Third Way and Its Critics* (London: Polity Press, 2000), 73.

17   For a discussion of whether, and how, globalization has resulted in the reversal of Polanyi's 'Great Transformation', see, for example, S. Gill, 'Theorizing the Interregnum: The Double Movement and Global Politics in the 1990s', in B. Hettne (ed.), *International Political Economy: Understanding Global Disorder* (London: Zed, Books, 1995).

18   M. Latham, *Civilizing Global Capital: New Thinking for Australian Labor* (St. Leonards, NSW: Allen and Unwin, 1998), and 'Economic Policy and the Third Way', *Australian Econmic Review*, 31:4 (1998), 384–98; J. E. Roemer, 'Egalitarian Strategies', *Dissent*, 46:3 (1999), 64–74.

19   T. Blair, *The Third Way: New Politics for the New Century* (London: The Fabian Society, Pamphlet 588, 1998), p. 4.

20   Consider here, for example, David Lawday's analysis of the French 35-hour working week introduced by Martine Aubry. In assessing the view that the reduction of average working hours from 39 to 35 hours was an attempt to increase employment, he argues that this was 'never more than wishful thinking'. According to Lawday, what is happening is that 'rigidly run France is becoming flexible despite itself'. This is so because employers and unions have tended to multiply working hours up over and entire year. Some weeks, when demand is higher, can thus be longer. Other weeks, when demand is low, can be shorter. A side-result of this, then, is that the 'French are getting even longer holidays that they did before – seven to eight weeks a year instead of five or six'. D. Lawday, 'The NS Profile: Martine Aubry', *New Statesman* 18:9 (14 February 2000), 19.

21   P. Hirst and G. Thompson, *Globalization in Question: The International Economy and the Possibilities of Governance* (Cambridge: Polity Press, 1996).

22   A. Giddens, *The Third Way: The Renewal of Social Democracy* (Oxford: Polity Press, 1998), 29.

23   C. Hay and M. Watson, *Rendering the Contingent Necessary: New Labour's Neoliberal Conversion and the Discourse of Globalisation*, Centre for European Studies, Programme for the Study of Germany and Europe Working Paper 8.4, (Harvard University, 1998).

24   C. Hay et al., *Globalization, European Integration and the Persistence of European Social Models*, ESRC One Europe or Several? Working Paper 3 (1999).

25   L. Panitch, 'Globalization and the State', *The Socialist Register (Special Edition on Globalization)* (London: Merlin Press, 1994).

26   P. Bourdieu, 'A Reasoned Utopia and Economic Fatalism', *New Left Review*, 227 (1998), 25–30.

27   N. Fairclough, *New Labour, New language?* (London: Routledge, 2000), 23–4.

28   Simply understood, nominalization is the representation of a process as a noun.

29   R. Cox, 'Political Economy and World Order: Problems of Power and Knowledge at the Turn of the Millennium', in R. Stubbs and G. Underhill (eds),

Political Economy and the Changing Global Order (Oxford: Oxford University Press, 2000), 26.

30 N. Fairclough, *Language and Power* (London: Longmans, 1989), 1–2.

31 S. Lukes, *Power: A Radical View* (London: Macmillan Press, 1974).

32 R. A. Dahl, *Who Governs? Democracy and Power in an American City* (London: Yale University Press, 1971), 336.

33 N. W. Polsby, *Community Power and Political Theory* (London: Yale University Press, 1963), 113.

34 P. Bacharach and M. S. Baratz, *Power and Poverty: Theory and Practice* (Oxford: Oxford University Press, 1970), 16.

35 Lukes, *Power*, 57.

36 Lukes, *Power*, 24.

37 Ibid.

38 R. Simon, *Gramsci's Political Thought: An Introduction* (London: Lawrence and Wishart, 1982).

39 M. Foucault, *Selected Writings*, (London: Verso, 1984), 71.

40 Here, it should be noted that Lukes' view of the third dimensions is similar to the ideology argument forwarded by Fairclough. Lukes, for example, argued that in theorizing conflict in the third dimension of power one must understand that latent conflict exists in the contradictions between the 'interests of those exercising power and the real interests of those they exclude'.

41 H. Marcuse, *One-Dimensional Man: Studies in the Ideology of Advanced Industrial Society* (London: Routledge and Kegan Paul, 1964); or *Negations: Essays in Critical Theory* (London: Beacon Press, 1968).

42 Foucault, *Selected Writings*, 60.

43 Here, for example, some commentators have argued that the consensual relations that developed between labour and capital under traditional social democracy were beneficial for both parties. See, for example, F. Castles, *The Social Democratic Image of Society* (Cambridge: Cambridge University Press, 1978); A. Przeworski and M. Wallerstein, 'The Structure of Class Conflict in Democratic Capitalist Societies', *American Political Science Review*, 76 (1982), 215–38. Others commentators have viewed either labour or capital as the victor under these scenarios. For examples of those who consider capital as the loser, see D. Hibbs, 'Political Parties and Macroeconomic Policy', *American Political Science Review*, 71 (1977), 1467–87; W. Korpi and M. Shalev, 'Strikes, Power and Politics in Western Nations, 1900–1976', *Political Power and Social Theory*, 1 (1980), 301–34; J. D. Stephens, *The Transformation from Capitalism to Socialism* (Atlantic Highlands, NJ: Humanities Press, 1980). For those who view labour as the loser, see C. Offe 'The Attribution of Public Status to Interest Groups: Observations on the West German Case', in S. Berger (ed.), *Organizing Interests in Western Europe* (Cambridge: Cambridge University Press,1981); L. Panitch, 'The Development of Corporatism in Liberal Democracies', *Comparative Political Studies*, 10 (1977), 61–90; or 'Recent Theorizations of Corporatism in Liberal Democracies', *British Journal of Sociology*, 31 (1980), 159–87.

44 P. Fougeyrollas, *Sciences sociales et marxisme* (Paris: Payot Press, 1979).

45 P. Bourdieu, *Outline of a Theory of Practice*, translated by R. Nice (Cambridge: Cambridge University Press, 1989).

46 A. Sayer, *Method in Social Science: A Realist Approach*, second edition (London: Routledge, 1992).

47 For a discussion of these points, see C. Johnson, *Derrida: The Scene of Writing* (London: Phoenix Press, 1997).

48 F. W. Taylor, *The Principles of Scientific Management* (New York: Harper Brothers, 1925), 142.

49 Maier, *In Search of Stability*.

50 For a discussion of this argument, see C. Radaelli, *Technocracy in the European Union* (New York: Longman, 1999), 21. J. Burnham, *The Managerial Revolution: Or, What is happening to the World Now?* (London: Putnam, 1941).

51 D. Bell, *The End of Ideology: On the Exhaustion of Political Ideas in the Fifties* (New York: Free Press, 1962).

52 For a more detailed discussion of this argument, see G. Barcell et al., *The Foucault Effect: Studies in Governmentality, With Two Lectures by and an Interview with Michel Foucault* (London: Harvester-Wheatsheaf, 1991), 8.

53 Here, for example, Friedman's famous 1967 Presidential address to the American Economics Association, *The Role of Monetary Policy*, in which he outlined the monetarist policy prescriptions, is widely regarded as one of the most important moments in the development and acceptance of monetarism. Here, he rejected the then conventional wisdom, that of demand management and full employment. Moreover, he suggested severe constraints on the general effectiveness of government intervention and fiscal policy in particular.

54 M. Crozier et al., *Report on the Ungovernability of Democracies* (London: The Trilateral Commission, 1975).

55 An additional factor could be the incapacity of the Left to offer any new programme following the establishment of welfare state social democracy.

56 It should be noted that this failure actually had very little to do with the ownership of the nationalized industries and banks, as most had be returned to profitability under public management.

57 For a more detailed discussion of the implementation of these policies, see M. Feigenbraum *et al.*, *Shrinking the State: The Political Underpinnings of Privatization* (Cambridge: Cambridge University Press, 1998).

58 However, the rearticulation of such narratives along the lines suggested by Fairclough might themselves be important with regard to the mobilization of opposition to the Third Way.

59 As Barcell notes, these terms were used interchangeably by Foucault. Barcell *et al.*, *The Foucault Effect*, p. 3.

60 Ibid.

61 D. Miliband (ed.), *Re-inventing the Left* (Cambridge: Polity Press, 1995), 13.

62 See here, for example, V. Bognador, 'The European Union, the Political Class and the People', in J. Hayward (ed.), *Elitism, Populism and European Politics* (Oxford: Clarendon Press, 1996); F. Scharpf, *Governing in Europe: Effective and Democratic?* (Oxford: Oxford University Press, 1999); and W. Wallace and J. Smith, 'Democracy or Technocracy: European Integration and the Problem of Popular Consent', *West European Politics*, 18:3 (1995), 137–57.

63 For a discussion of these shortcomings, see D. Beetham and C. Lord, *Legitimacy and the European Union* (London: Longman, 1998); B. Laffan, 'The Politics of Identity and Political Order in Europe', *Journal of Common Market Studies*,

34:1 (1996), 81–103; E. Meehan, *Citizenship and the European Community* (London: Sage, 1993); A. D. Smith, 'National Identity and the Idea of European Unity', *International Affairs*, 68:1 (1992), 55–76; J. H. H. Weiler, 'After Maastricht: Community Legitimacy in post-1992 Europe', in W. J. Adams (ed.), *Singular Europe: Economy and Polity of the European Community after 1992* (Ann Arbor: University of Michigan Press, 1992); and J. M. Welsh, 'A people's Europe? European Citizenship and European Identity', *Politics*, 13:2 (1993), 15–31.

64 J. H. H. Weiler, 'Democracy, Constitutionalism and Legitimacy', Keynote speech delivered at the Sussex European Institute Conference 'Constitutionalism and Legitimacy in the EU and the WTO', University of Sussex, 20 June 2000.

65 G. Majone, 'State, Market, and Regulatory Competition in the European Union: Lessons for the Integrating Economy' in A. Moravcsik (ed.), *Centralization or Fragmentation? Europe Facing the Challenges of Deepening, Diversity and Democracy* (Washington, DC: Council of Foreign Relations, 1998), pp. 94–5.

4
Social Democracy and the European Union: Who's Changing Whom?

Francis McGowan

Introduction

In the summer of 1997, following the victories of Tony Blair and Lionel Jospin, there was much speculation that the trajectory of European integration would take a leftward turn. Speculation had turned to expectation a year later with the election of Gerhard Schröder's SPD, bringing to 13 the number of governments either led by or including centre-left parties in the European Union (EU). For some, this shift in the centre of political gravity raised the prospect of a turn away from the neoliberal policies which had prevailed at the EU level since the mid-1980s towards a more social democratic agenda. However, the following months were to demonstrate the difficulties in reorientating the EU, and by the time of the 1999 European Parliament elections (which reversed the small majority already enjoyed by the centre left in that institution), it appeared less and less likely that the coincidence of so many centre-left governments would change the character of EU policies. On the contrary it appeared that the economic orientation of European integration and its embodiment in the rules, institutions and policies of the EU was not only a constraint upon European social democracy but was also contributing to its redefinition.

In this chapter we put these developments into the context of how social democracy and European integration have evolved, or 'co-evolved', in the postwar – and post-Cold War – era. Coevolved because, on the one hand, social democrat parties and politicians have been important protagonists in the EU and have helped to shape it (though not as much as their domestic strength might have merited) while, on the other, the values of the EU have increasingly set the limits of social democratic (and other partisan) policies within member states. The starting point of the chapter is the idea that, notwithstanding the political aspects of the European project, the process of integration has been conceived and developed on the basis of economic principles which can be described as 'liberal', save for some limited exemptions and compensatory mechanisms. These principles were 'constitutionalized' within the Treaties and institutions of the EU, even if they were not apparent for the first few decades. Instead, this liberalism was for a long time 'embedded' (borrowing Ruggie's[1] term) by the postwar settlements reached within member states and submerged by the deadweight of the EU policy-making process.

Over the last two decades, however, the underlying liberal bias has emerged as the primary catalyst for economic integration and has, as a result, increasingly constrained national policies (particularly – though not only – those of a social democratic bent). This constraint has, moreover, proved hard to overcome, reverse or dilute because of the institutional character of the EU.[2] There have, it is true, been different emphases in EU policy-making over time and these have occasionally brought in policies which are more in tune with social democratic concerns. There is, moreover the potential for reinforcing such elements given the scope for governments and/or parliamentarians to propose policies or Treaty changes which might 're-embed' the EU's liberalism. Yet the record over time, and particularly the recent past, has been poor due to a combination of the machinery of integration (which 'locks in' member states to an *acquis communautaire* and which moves at a pace slower than that of national decision-making processes) and the disparate positions of the governments themselves which work against the development of a concerted position which could be translated into policy changes.

This chapter locates social democratic responses to European integration in the context of the wider challenges it has faced and, drawing on the development of a range of European policy initiatives, considers whether it has been – or is – possible to refocus integration along more social democratic lines. The chapter is in four sections. We start by discussing the nature and evolution of the European integration process, highlighting the liberal orientation and the implications of this for social democracy. We then chart the evolution of policies towards the EU by social democratic parties noting how attitudes have changed over time and have varied across member states. These two elements are brought together in a review of recent developments in the coevolution of integration and social democracy which looks at debates within the movement as a whole and the conduct of the main protagonists inside and outside the EU policy-making context. We then look more closely at aspects of the EU policy regime, considering how it acts as a constraint upon social democracy and at how far it is possible to counter that influence by bringing in new policies and changing the content of existing ones.

European integration as embedded liberalism

The EU is unique as a model of 'deep integration', combining an intense economic 'integratedness', a dense pattern of interaction amongst politicians and officials, and a set of institutions and rules which involve a substantial sharing of sovereignty.[3] No other attempt at regional integration has been able to advance so effectively on all of these fronts: earlier attempts at cooperation in other parts of the world foundered on the gap between grandiose ambitions and minimal commitments,[4] while the so-called 'new regionalisms' have been characterized by rather lean structures and a narrower focus on economic liberalization.[5] The EU's own history demonstrates, moreover, that the path to integration has been marked by many obstacles and the occasional reverse. The future, too, is uncertain as the prospect of further enlargement puts considerable pressure on the structures and practices of the EU which have already been under increased pressure as a result of shortcomings in performance and concerns about legitimacy.[6] Yet, 50 years on from the Treaty of Paris which established the European Coal and Steel Community (ECSC), the scale of what has been achieved in the EU is remarkable. That success is normally attributable to a mix of factors including the political commitments of member state governments, the interactions between national and European officials and pressure groups and, not least, the history of the European continent itself. However, it could be argued that an essential element in the successful pursuit of economic integration has been the essentially 'liberal' economic project upon which European integration has been based.

While it might be thought today that European integration, or even regional integration *per se*, is intrinsically liberal, the idea and practice of integration has embraced a much wider range of options for development.[7] The postwar debate on regional cooperation focused as much on the planning and pooling of resources as it did on removing barriers to trade. Indeed, in the 1960s and 1970s many regional integration schemes were associated with policies of economic nationalism and protectionism. Yet in practice such ventures were unsuccessful: protectionism eroded the credibility of many regional agreements and attempts at joint planning also failed.[8] Instead, integration seems to have been most effective where it has been concerned primarily with the removal of tariff and other barriers to trade, so-called 'negative integration', and where governments have been prepared to commit to such a regime by limiting their scope to intervene in the economy.[9] As Hayek recognized in a (pre-EEC) discussion of the prospects for European integration, any successful federation would have to 'possess the negative power of preventing individual states from interfering with economic activity'.[10]

Yet in the context of the early postwar era, it was not at all obvious why such a model should emerge. The economic orthodoxy of continental Europe was traditionally very far from being liberal and, if anything, the political and social settlements which were made in European states after the Second World War were as much about equity as they were about efficiency.[11] And yet reconstruction and then integration were premised upon a broadly liberal economic project. Why was the basis for such a regime established in such unpropitious conditions? It could be argued that European integration in the postwar period was an extension of the principle of 'embedded liberalism', Ruggie's characterization of the postwar compromise between a liberalized and open economy on the one hand and broader economic and social objectives on the other.[12] He uses the term to describe the bargain between the US and other powers (primarily European) to establish a liberal multilateral trade and payments regime which also provided governments with enough autonomy to develop their own economic models and welfare systems. Arguably, the term can also be used to refer to the experience of European integration, as governments agreed to a regime which embraced 'common markets' but also left them with the space to pursue social and regional policies and to mitigate the effects of market liberalization. Indeed, there was a relationship between the process of multilateral liberalization and European integration: the United States was keen to encourage integration on these terms within Europe as demonstrated by its sponsorship of the OEEC and support for the ECSC.[13] Nor was it only the United States which sought such a regime. Monnet and others in France were keen to see economic cooperation premised upon market integration as a means of modernizing their societies as well as a stepping stone to a federal Europe.[14]

The market integration that was at the core of the 1951 Paris Treaty and the 1957 Rome Treaties, therefore, was basically 'liberal' but it was also 'embedded'. The original institutions and debates were concerned as much with planning mechanisms as they were with free markets.[15] Moreover, the integration project was qualified by other considerations, both principled and pragmatic, such as the political ideal of integration, the political reality of member states protecting their sovereignty, the attempts to develop 'positive integration' policies which mitigated the effects of liberalization and a certain reluctance to pursue and/or implement the logic of liberalization.[16] These factors effectively limited the pace and timing of economic liberalism in the EU, leaving member states with considerable autonomy in the domestic realm. This in turn left enough space for governments to pursue social democratic policies.

The full implications of the Treaty commitments (particularly in terms of their impact on economic policy) were not recognized by many at the time. Instead the politics of integration revolved around either grander or more mundane concerns. For the postwar generation of political leaders, economic integration was a means to a political end.[17] For officials and lobbyists, economic integration itself was a source of 'low politics', whether technical issues which were addressed as problems to be solved by experts or bones of contention to be negotiated upon by various national or sectoral interests.[18] As we will see, however, the ideological implications of integration were not lost on everyone – there were those on the Left who viewed the European Communities as a 'capitalist club'[19] – but the concern that integration would undermine the postwar social democratic settlements was not widely held.

In any case, the initial steps in the integration process, such as removing barriers to free trade within the Community, did not of themselves undermine the social compromises and state interventions upon which the postwar settlement in Europe was based. Many would argue that social democracy and the general growth of the government role in western economies were quite compatible – even complementary – with increased trade liberalization and European integration.[20] Moreover, while the supranational institutions and practices of the European Community originated in the treaties, the full implications of such a major shift in sovereignty were not to manifest themselves for some time. Indeed, for much of the early part of the EU's history, national authorities were to assert their predominance in the integration process.[21]

This tendency for national sovereignty to prevail was reinforced in the 1970s by the combined processes of enlargement and economic recession. This period is often referred to as one of 'Eurosclerosis', a term which originally referred to the rigidities within the European labour market but often used more generally to refer to the combination of structural economic problems and institutional logjams which bedevilled the EU at the time.[22] While important steps towards economic union were taken in this period – most notably the agreement on the European Monetary System – the period is often characterized as one when attempts to reform the European economy became bogged down. Ironically, the period also marked the highwater mark of European social democracy as exemplified by centre-left governments in many member states including Britain and Germany, corporatist-type arrangements in many states and serious (if largely unsuccessful) challenges to the mixed economy from the Left.[23]

Yet if the 1970s saw the tension between social democracy and European integration resolved – at least temporarily – in favour of the former, by the middle of the 1980s the tables were beginning to be turned. The changing economic and political climate – manifest in the emerging neoliberalism of the Thatcher government in Britain, the reversal of socialist policies in Mitterrand's France and the symbolic reformism of Kohl's *die Wende* in Germany – provided both the catalyst for and the content of the relaunch of the EU.[24] The Single Market, the acceptance of market liberalization for other economic activities beyond trade in manufactures and the use of competition policy as a lever to reform old industrial structures and tackle the conduct of both firms and governments were the instruments of a reinvigorated EU.[25]

This revival built very much on the original blueprint for integration. Ideologically, the emphasis on the market and competition as the drivers of integration drew upon the Treaty provisions. In contrast to the past, however, the Commission and at least some member states were more prepared to follow through the logic of these ideas and were less prepared to accept the prevailing structures and practices as a block on reform: liberalism became less embedded as the resonance of postwar social settlements diminished. Institutionally, the legal status of those original commitments was highlighted by Court judgments and Commission actions, constituting the mechanisms for reform. Thus, although the overall powers of the Commission and the Court were agreed in the 1950s and the principles governing European law were articulated in the following decades, they were not utilized effectively until the Delors Commission. Moreover they were to be supplemented by the additional powers granted in the 1986 Single European

Act, particularly the reinforcement of majority voting in the Council of Ministers.[26]

Economic growth and positive public opinion – 'Europhoria' – helped to maintain the momentum of integration in the late 1980s. The case for further reform, particularly for Economic and Monetary Union (EMU), became more compelling; to be truly effective, it was argued, a Single Market required a single currency.[27] The Intergovernmental Conference which culminated in the Maastricht Treaty took integration to a new stage, in the process establishing a monetarist model of macro-economic policy. While Maastricht extended the EU's competence in a range of other policy areas (as did the Single Act), the powers in areas such as environmental and social policy were for the most part less robust than the very real powers designed to bring about the Single Market and EMU.[28] The recession of the early 1990s and disenchant-ment with the EU in some member states saw a reaction against integra-tion in some member states but left the core of these liberal economic policies untouched. If anything the condition of the European economy raised a broader set of questions about whether more rather than less liberalization was needed. From the Delors White Paper of 1993 to the Lisbon summit declaration of 2000, EU economic policy leant more in the direction of market liberalization (whether of public services or labour markets) and of reining in the state's economic role.[29]

Thus, whether as a conscious strategy of elites (some officials had recognized the underlying thrust of the Community from the very beginning) or as unintended consequence, economic liberalism has come to prevail as the driving force of European integration. Although political objectives underlay the project initially, the chosen path for integration was economic and 'negative' in its orientation, backed up by a strong legal base which was supranational in character. The full implications of this model were not apparent for some time, but prevailed in the 1980s as the overall intellectual and policy climate swung in favour of the market. The highly institutionalized nature of European integration meant that member states were locked in to a more or less irreversible set of commitments (though, given their ideo-logical orientations in the key period of the late 1980s and 1990s, most governments were untroubled by the economic direction of policies). By contrast attempts to build 'positive' integration on the back of common policies were relatively unsuccessful, not least because of the absence of either effective countervailing institutional/legal constraints or a shared commitment on the part of member states. Over time, in other words, the embedded liberalism of the original treaties was eroded while attempts to 're-embed' were of only limited success.

The evolution of social democratic attitudes to the European Union

How have social democrats viewed European integration? There is a long tradition of international solidarity on the Left which should have rendered socialists in Europe well disposed towards integration: one of the earliest proposals for European integration – the Briand Plan – was drawn up by social democratic politicians.[30] Yet, historically, social democratic attitudes to the EU have been ambivalent and divergent, for a mixture of ideological and domestic political reasons. Ideologically, there have been some social democratic parties, along with many to the left of social democracy, which regarded the EU as a capitalist club: the German social democrats of the 1950s, the French socialists of the 1970s and the British Labour Party in the 1970s and 1980s. Others were at ease with the idea of a common market and saw the potential of the EU as a force for modernization: the French socialists in the 1950s, the Spanish and Portuguese from the 1970s on and the British and Swedish socialists in the 1990s. However, economics was not the only (and at times not the most important) factor in shaping the approach of the centre-left attitudes towards the EU. Politics were often in command, as variously manifest in federalist idealism which regarded the economic project as a means to a federal end, concerns for sovereignty which sought to defend national autonomy and diplomatic statecraft (UK isolationism, Franco-German rapprochement, the Cold War). These factors, as much as any questions of economic policy choice or ideology, shaped social democrat attitudes to the EU. Thus the British Labour Party's original hesitation over membership of the ECSC and ambivalence during the negotiations for the EEC reflected postcolonial great power pretentions, while the French socialist leadership was concerned to move away from interwar mentalities and, in the wake of Suez, share sovereignty to retain international influence.[31]

The economic character of European integration was to emerge in debates on the Left, particularly in the 1970s and early 1980s. The split in the British Labour Party over Europe owed much to questions of sovereignty, but there was also an underlying concern with the economic character of the Common Market and how far socialist policies could be pursued in that framework.[32] Those splits were to persist into the 1980s with a 'left Euroscepticism' in the ascendant (coinciding with

– though probably not causing[33] – the party's fall in public popularity). Elsewhere there was a similar radicalism to economic policies (French nationalizations, Swedish wage earner funds) which was accompanied by a real ambivalence towards the EU.[34] One exception to the trend was in Spain where the prospect of membership of the EU was seen as important for anchoring the country's new democracy. The *Partido Socialista Obrero Español* (PSOE) abandoned their Marxist rhetoric as they grew in popularity in the late 1970s and saw membership of the Community as an important means of modernizing Spain (rather than of accelerating socialism). Arguably, the Spanish were to be in the vanguard of macro and microeconomic rigour followed by other parties of the left by the end of the decade.[35]

While undoubtedly a special case – given the late transition to democracy – the Spanish socialists' view of Europe as a means of modernization was also to be embraced by other parties (even if the paralell is rarely recognized). The coming to terms with capitalism enshrined in the Kinnock leadership of the British Labour Party and in a similar modernization in Sweden attached considerable importance to the EU (effectively repudiating earlier ambivalences and oppositions to integration).[36] The same shift can be seen in the embrace of 'Europe' by Mitterrand followed the 1983 U-turn in economic policy, itself prompted by the decision of the socialists not to leave the European Monetary System, a measure which would have been required had they maintained their original reflationary policies.[37] Since that time one could argue that Social Democracy as originally conceived has been on the defensive against economic liberalism, and that increasingly Social Democratic movements which are 'modernizing' have embraced economic liberalism (and, with it, the EU).

There now appears to be a consensus amongst social democrats regarding the desirability of European integration, with only pockets of 'left Euroscepticism' in some Scandinavian parties.[38] This consensus extends to a good deal of coordinated action amongst European socialists, most notably in the European Parliament where the Party of European Socialists is one of the most cohesive groups.[39] However, it would be wrong to suggest that there is a uniform vision of how fin de siècle social democracy should inform the content of EU policies. On the contrary there remain serious divisions between parties and in some cases within them as well (the differences on labour market policy between the UK on the one side and the French on the other; the divisions between Schröder and Lafontaine over monetary policy). These differences seem to reflect more general differences in national debates and orientations,[40] and reinforce the impression of the importance of the national context in shaping social democratic policies towards the EU. Whatever their roots, however, these divergent attitudes have effectively acted as a constraint upon the ability of European social democrats to reorientate the thrust of European integration.

Fin-de-siècle social democracy and the European Union: an opportunity missed?

The coevolution of European integration and European social democracy reached a critical stage in 1997. After many years of being on the defensive and in opposition, the centre-left found itself in power across much of the EU. However, it was not clear how far (and for whom) the ideological tide had turned; in some countries power was regained only after much debate and reform within the movement, generally away from traditional social democratic values. Of course, coming to terms with capitalism is nothing new for social democrats, but in embracing economic liberalism – a 'triple distilled' ideological variant – a more radical reorientation was taking place. For some, arguably in Sweden and certainly in the UK, the scale of adjustment was dramatic.[41] The embrace of the market and macroeconomic rigour had been paralleled by a more positive approach to European integration.[42]

However, while the victories of the British Labour Party and the French socialists in 1997 were symbolically important and opened up the possibility of a reorientation of the EU, it was also clear that there were serious differences between these two movements in their expectations of what the EU was for and in their approaches to economic management. These differences manifest themselves at a meeting of the leaderships of the centre-left at Malmo in June 1997.[43] The British prime minister lectured his colleagues from the rest of Europe on the need for more flexible labour markets and liberalization, a message which not all of them appreciated. There seemed to be very divergent attitudes amongst the centre-left on core issues of economic management. When they reconvened with the other heads of state at the Amsterdam Intergovernmental Conference, these differences meant that the changes to the EU treaties were rather modest and bore only small signs of a social democratic imprint, with the key provision – on employment – a weak compromise between traditional and modernizing attitudes.[44]

The apparent gap between modernizers and traditionalists widened over the following year. A conference of the 'Third Way' held in New

York and attended by Blair and President Clinton (as well as the then prime minister of Italy Prodi) again emphasized the need to move away from traditional social democratic positions.[45] The electoral victory of the German SPD highlighted the tension, by embodying both aspects: on the one hand, *Die Neue Mitte* of Chancellor Gerhard Schröder, apparently keen to embrace a modernizing agenda; on the other the robust traditionalism of Oskar Lafontaine, Minister of Finance. Lafontaine's outspokenness, particularly on EMU, raised the prospect of a neo-Keynesian macroeconomic policy, an option welcomed by many in the French government. Towards the end of the year, a meeting of European socialist leaders, seemed to endorse an model of economic government for EMU which was closer to these ideas than those of Blair and other modernizers.[46] Meanwhile the British were back in their traditional position within the EU. If it was in the vanguard of the debate on reforming the centre left, the Blair government was still in its more traditional position as laggard in EU policy-making. Quite apart from its absence from the Eurozone, the British found themselves at odds with almost all its partners over tax harmonization, and demonstrated little enthusiasm for deepening EU social policy.[47]

Hopes (or fears) of a social democratic turn in EU policy came to very little, however. Lafontaine left the German government within a matter of months and Schröder asserted a much more modernizing line in public debates. In a series of venues – the Milan Congress of the PES to agree the manifesto for the European elections, the joint Anglo German declaration of June 1999, the Florence 'Third Way' meeting – modernizing ideas appeared to be in the ascendant, albeit at the expense of the alienation of the French socialists. Jospin's rejection of the Anglo-German initiative[48] and the French exclusion of any mention of the Third Way from the communiqué of the Socialist International Congress held in Paris that November[49] seemed to suggest a widening gap between the two models of social democracy.

More recently, there seems to have been a truce in the battle of rhetoric between the British and the French, as the two have recognized how much they have in common in policy – if not symbolic – terms.[50] Meanwhile in Germany the unpopularity of *Die Neue Mitte* prompted the arch-pragmatist Schröder to soft pedal the issue and invoke a more left populist stance (on matters such as the takeover of Mannesmann by Vodafone and the rescue of a major construction firm) while securing a major reform of corporate taxation which is likely to unravel many aspects of the 'Rhineland' model of corporate governance and industrial relations.[51] On balance it appears that the various parties have moved closer to the model advocated by Blair as borne out by the endorsement of liberalization in public utilities and flexibility in labour markets at the Lisbon Summit.[52] If the last few years have made a difference in the relationship between European integration and social democracy, it has been in the attempts by modernizing social democrats to replicate national strategies at the European level rather than the refocusing of EU policies to fit traditional social democratic agendas. This process has required more of an alignment of social democracy with the economic liberalism of European integration than the other way round.

The European Union and Social Democracy: asymmetric transformation?

In a number of national and European settings, therefore, there has been a vigorous debate on how the centre-left should orient itself and how it should shape the European policy agenda. While there has been an apparent clash of ideologies, the extent of the differences between the main protagonists is not clear, obscured in large part by a fog of rhetoric primarily designed for domestic consumption. It is clear, however, that where these debates have taken place in a policy environment, the decisions have tended to favour one argument more than most: at the risk of oversimplification, where economic liberalism and social democracy have been in tension with one another, economic liberalism has generally prevailed. This suggests an asymmetric dynamic between the two, with EU policies constraining (and contributing to a reorientation of) national social democratic options more than vice versa.

To understand why this is so we have to return to our earlier account of the nature of the EU as an economic (rather than a political) project and the distinction between negative and positive integration. European economic integration has been largely achieved by a combination of removing barriers to trade and competition and ensuring compliance with these obligations through the rule of law. In essence the process is one of 'negative integration', backed up by legal commitments, restraining member states from protecting local producers or otherwise reneging on their commitments to a more open economy. That is not to say that member states and firms have been at all times prepared to go along with this model but it has been broadly the case since the mid-1980s. Member states have been prepared to remove barriers on the grounds that they gain both reciprocal advantages from a bigger market and incentives to enhance their productivity and competitiveness. By limiting their room for manoeuvre, moreover, such commitments protect them from local lobbies which might otherwise seek protection or special treatment; in committing to negative integration, governments impose a self-denying ordinance upon themselves, enhancing their own credibility in the international economy.[53]

The attempt to pursue positive integration – agreeing common policies which would coordinate the activities of governments and firms and which might mitigate the adverse effects of market liberalization and/or redistribute resources around the EU – has been much less successful. Member states have been much less willing to surrender sovereignty for the uncertain benefits of a European policy and have been particularly reluctant to transfer financial resources to the European level. Since social democracy can be seen as a form of positive integration, relying upon the intervention of public authorities to pursue policies of welfare and economic development, and to maintain social harmony, the difficulty of not only recasting EU policies but also of maintaining national policies becomes apparent. Thus the overall thrust of European integration places limits on the scope of what is possible in national policy-making while attempts to reconfigure these tasks at a regional level face considerable problems.

In what follows we note how negative integration constrains national social democracies. We look at three related areas of policy – competition policy, the Single Market and Economic and Monetary Union – which are geared towards removing barriers to trade and which have considerable legal force. We then turn to look at the difficulties facing policies which are designed to fulfil social democratic goals and which mostly entail positive integration.

The European as a constraint on social democracy

In examining how EU policies might constrain social democratic economic policies we should note a few characteristics of that policy and how that policy has changed. Traditional social democracy's economic project is one which accepted the role of private enterprise, the market and of openness but recognized that there were shortcomings in these mechanisms which could be alleviated by public (generally state) intervention, not least in redistributing the gains which accrued from economic growth: along the state–market spectrum, traditional social democracy gave greater weight to the role of the state while along the equity–growth spectrum it gave greater weight to equity (see Figure 4.1). Thus government had a legitimate role in brokering deals between capital and labour, in providing a range of public and welfare services

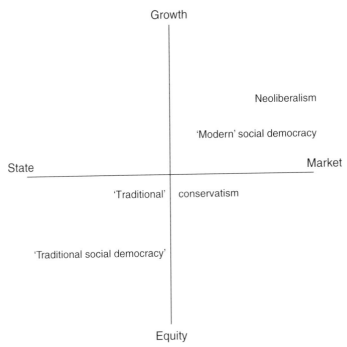

Figure 4.1   Classifying economic projects – ends and means

on the basis of progressive taxation system, in owning strategic industries and in managing trade and investment policies. These policies are not unique to social democracy of course – they are to a large extent characteristic of the postwar settlement across Western Europe – except perhaps in the degree to which they were pursued, the commitment to equity and the contribution of organized labour.

Much of this has been repudiated by the modernizing tendency in social democracy; it gives considerably greater weight to the market and more (though possibly not as much) to growth. If traditional social democracy came to terms with capitalism in the postwar period by redefining it, modernizing social democracy has come to terms with capitalism in the post-Cold War world by being redefined by it. As Figure 4.1 shows, modernizing social democracy has more in common with economic liberalism than traditional social democracy, while traditional centre-right policies have more in common with traditional social democracy than with either modern social democracy or economic liberalism.

How are these models affected by EU policies? As noted earlier, the corollary of the removal of trade barriers under negative integration is the agreement of member states to constraints upon their scope to manage their own economies. These commitments may be rather specific – the removal of a particular tariff or the liberalization of a particular industry – but they may be much more general, imposing wide-ranging and long-term commitments or restrictions upon governments. Here we examine three such policies: the competition rules, the Single Market programme and Economic and Monetary Union.

Competition policy

Competition policy – often known as anti-trust policy – is generally designed to prevent collusion or anti-competitive conduct among firms, thereby promoting competition and consumer benefits. A feature of the EU *acquis* since its inception, it was seen as an important mechanism to prevent primarily private restrictions on trade from replacing the publicly imposed tariffs and quotas which were to be removed in the common market.[54] At first sight it might be wondered why such a policy is problematic for social democracy since there does not appear to be an obvious incompatibility between the two:[55] competition policy aims to level the playing field and to ensure fairness in market access. Indeed at times trade unions and others have looked to competition rules as a way of reining in the power of business.[56]

Yet in practice social democracy has had problems with competition policy particularly in its European guise for two particular reasons. The first relates to the purpose of competition policy: as noted, it aims to provide a level playing field and to prevent abuses of the marketplace – in effect to create an efficient and undistorted market. Strictly speaking, competition policy is not concerned beyond that goal – the fairness it addresses is that of equality of opportunity rather than of outcome. Indeed, attempts to tackle fairness in a broader sense may prove to involve significant market distortions (for example, through permitting firms to control a market, thereby maintaining higher prices which permit higher salaries for the workforce). Similarly, an open and efficient market may have adverse social consequences which are problematic to social democracy (for example, by forcing local firms to close as a result of lower cost suppliers entering the market).[57]

The other problem for social democracy is the nature of the constituency to be served by competition policy – the consumer. Traditionally, there has been a strong producer bias in social democracy, bringing together business and labour because it has equated the producer interest with employment. Although some on the Left have occasionally highlighted the consumer interest in the past, it is only recently that social democracy has discovered the consumer. This has been particularly true in the UK, where it is precisely the pro-consumer nature of competition policy that has made the latter an attractive policy to 'New Labour'.[58] While competition policy is an important mechanism for modernizing social democrats, it is more problematic for traditional social democrats.

While these tensions can be managed in a national context – essentially by the invoking of the 'national interest' to override the decisions of regulatory agencies – they are more problematic in the EU since European competition policy is aimed at much at governments as it is at firms and is backed up by significant legal powers.[59] The maintenance by governments of special arrangements for firms or the non-application of national anti-trust rules or, most importantly, the provision of state aids are all subject to Community rules and can be judged to be anti-competitive. Thus aid to maintain industries in decline may be deemed to be contrary to the state aids rules while special treatment for particular services (where general obligations are pursued in exchange for privileged market positions) may also be seen as anti-competitive.

One should not overstate the conflict here. For much of the EU's history, competition policy has been applied quite sparingly – it was not fully applied until the end of the 1970s. Even in the recent past the bulk of cases are passed by the EU authorities, not least because the rules have embodied some important exemptions and derogations.[60] More generally there has clearly been a considerable sensitivity towards the exercise of the policy. Nor is competition policy purely problematic for social democrats – all governments subsidize or preside over anti-competitive markets and some of the most notable conflicts between the Directorate General for Competition and member states have been with governments of the centre-right. Even so, while modernizing social democrats seem at ease with competition policy, others have been less convinced of its value, seeing the destructive potential of market forces, and have opposed the constraints it imposes (see below on countervailing policies).

Single Market

In recent years, European competition policy has been closely bound up with the goal of a Single Market either as a means of prising open markets where restrictive practices have been the norm in the past or as the mechanism for policing the market once the rules are in place (for example, in the post-liberalization utility markets). However, there are distinctive dimensions to the EU Single Market programme which potentially raise problems for social democracy. Although an objective of the European Union from the Treaty of Rome, it was not until the 1980s that a concerted attempt was made to 'complete the internal market' . The programme set out in the Cockfield Report – the blueprint for the '1992' programme – highlighted the following goals: removal of restrictions on public procurement, harmonization of indirect tax regimes and a new approach to technical standardization.[61] While each aspect of the programme has been controversial with at least some member states, social democrats have been particularly concerned about the first element. The issue of procurement liberalization has been controversial since, in the past, preferential government purchasing policies have been a mechanism of regional, industrial and, most importantly, employment policy.[62] Replacing such preferences with cost-driven and objective criteria limit governments' discretion, removing another of the levers which they have had to pursue redistributive policies.

However, it is in the application of the principle of the single market to previously protected sectors that the ramifications for social democracy have been most serious, risking an unravelling of national compromises around the regimes governing particular economic sectors. This is clearest in the utility industries or *services publics* (in French), the latter term conveying the special nature of these sectors. They were often used to underpin a range of social obligations (universal service provision, equality of treatment, job creation, etc.). As has been seen in countries where liberalization has already taken place, the effect of competition can be to unravel many of these broader social obligations, for example the provision of uniform pricing underpinned by a system of cross-subsidies, or the maintenance of high levels of staffing to provide skilled jobs in underdeveloped areas.[63] EU liberalization, while containing some provisions to mitigate the effects of competition or to phase in the changes, can be expected to have a similar effect (see below).[64]

Economic and Monetary Union

Taken together, competition policy and the Single Market place real constraints upon the ability of government to use policies for other purposes. Whereas, historically, governments could subsidize or use preferential policies to support employment or development objectives, it is now much more difficult to pursue such objectives through policies which might have the effect of distorting the market. Of course, it could be argued that governments should pursue such goals not by subterfuge, but by explicit and transparent policies: if a subsidy is to be given, it is argued, then it should be a visible and justified subsidy. Yet the scope for pursuing such policies is limited by the third area of European policy-making – EMU.[65]

At first glance the paths towards the single currency and a social democratic Europe do not seem to conflict. The loss of a currency should not preclude governments from pursuing their own policy choices. Yet in practice the loss goes much deeper into national autonomy than the right to print banknotes. The requirements for EMU (both the convergence criteria which were a prerequisite for membership and the stability pact which governments have to observe inside the Eurozone) imposed a variety of constraints upon governments' macroeconomic policies, particularly the ability to borrow and run large fiscal deficits.[66] Both were historically characteristics of traditional social democracy and their loss has been seen as one of the most important constraints on centre-left governments. Moreover the principle of central bank independence – the aspect of EMU which is designed to ensure the credibility of the currency by removing it from short-term political pressures – prevents governments from using interest rates as a tool of economic management.[67] The effect of these factors might be less damaging for social democratic strategies if the remit of the central bank was designed to take account of growth and employment. However, not only is the main concern with the control of inflation, but the bank itself has called for economic changes in labour regulation and welfare provision which are again hard to reconcile with a traditional social democratic agenda.[68]

Reorienting the European Union in social democratic directions

So far we have considered the ways in which the thrust of EU policies serves to limit the ability of member states to manage their economy, particularly if those policies are broadly social democratic. However, is it not possible for those states to work together to reorient those rules or at least mitigate their effects? The coincidence of so many centre-left governments coming to power at the same time and and – for a time – a similarly constituted European Parliament should have provided an opportunity for such policies to develop. Moreover, are there not aspects of the EU *acquis* which are 'social democratic' or which could be enhanced? As we will see, however, the institutional barriers to making alternative policies or to redeveloping existing ones are considerable, combining the general difficulties of pursuing positive integration with those of conducting partisan politics in the EU.

In examining the scope for remaking the EU as a social democratic project we can distinguish between two types of policy – compensatory and countervailing. Compensatory policies are those which ameliorate the effects of an open market. The most common of these are various redistributive programmes which operate through the fiscal system. There may also be legal protections, rules which convey rights on workers or citizens against the effects of a free market. Although the former have the higher profile the latter have become increasingly important in a redefined social democracy. Countervailing policies are those which assert (or defend) a different model of development. They seek to remake aspects of the system rather than mitigate its effects. Although they are rarely designed to 'transform' the system as a whole, countervailing policies could serve to limit economic liberalism.

Such policies are not unique to social democracy, of course. We regard them as 'social democratic' only in so far as they align well with social democratic values – many of the policies have been introduced by non-social democratic parties and have featured in the postwar programmes of most governments. Yet it could be argued that the wider diffusion of such policies is a function of the factors which favoured the development of social democracy and were a response to the existence of a social democratic option—the threat of the Left was enough to persuade other parties to incorporate their policies.[69]

It is difficult to delineate precisely between compensatory and countervailing policies: an extremely redistributive regional policy or a wide-ranging social policy could have more effect than an amendment to the competition rules. Even so the distinction is a real one, particularly when we consider how such policies are made. For the purposes of this analysis compensatory policies tend to be developed from within the existing *acquis* (i.e. through the proposal of legislation, which then is agreed through the established decision-making procedures), while countervailing policies would require more substantial changes such as a treaty amendment: it is hard to identify a countervailing policy initiated at the legislature level (see Figure 4.2). This is not a perfect association – a number of compensatory policies have required constitutional changes to be implemented (for example, the Social Chapter, Cohesion Policy, Employment Policy) – but the fit between each pair is quite close.

		Nature of Policy Initiative	
		Compensatory	Countervailing
Nature of Legal Change	Legislative	Social policy, Regional policy	
	Constitutional	Social Chapter, cohesion policy	Industrial policy

Figure 4.2 The nature of EU policy changes

Compensatory policies

Budgetary policies

As in any system, the EU budget is at the core of most compensatory policies. As the main vehicle for the direct redistribution of resources it can be used to moderate disparities in income between regions and member states, more or less in line with social democratic concerns for social justice and equity and to alleviate the effects of a more open economy. The original ECSC budget was designed to cushion the blow of restructuring the coal and steel industries, while the EEC budget was mainly concerned with stabilizing agricultural markets and, later, providing resources to poorer member states and regions through the structural and cohesion funds.[70] The budget underpins many of the other compensatory policies which we examine here. As such they can be seen as very mildly 'social democratic', helping the groups and communities that lose out or gain less from the free market in goods and services. Moreover the patterns of decision-making on the budget, especially the 'trialogue' between Commission, Council and Parliament, could be amenable to partisan shifts such as the present social democrat turn.

Yet in practice there are severe limits to portraying the EU budget as an embryonic welfare state. Partly these are institutional limits, given that much of the budget is already earmarked, and the complexities of negotiating the budget (which in practice require a consensus rather than a partisan approach, given the scale of majorities required for agreement). But perhaps more important is the financial limit – the EU budgetary revenues are equivalent to approximately 2 per cent of EU GDP, compared with 50–60 per cent in most industrialized countries. Although such large national budgets might obviate the need for redistribution at the EU level, the limited scope of the budget at the EU level does limit the potential for more compensatory policies. Indeed, one might question just how redistributive the EU budget is: roughly half of resources are still devoted to agriculture (albeit down from close to 80 per cent in the past) and the nature of the beneficiaries casts doubts on the degree of solidarity involved in the redistribution. Other compensatory policies, such as the structural and cohesion funds, are potentially more redistributive, but many argue that in practice the schemes are often of benefit to the better-off in poorer member states (resources being given to better developed regions such as larger cities rather than to the poorer periphery) or benefit richer regions by opening up those markets to competition (as a result of improved infrastructure).[71]

In any case, there appear to be limits to the solidarity of EU citizens – governments in rich countries are increasingly reluctant to fund poorer member states. If the national progress of social democracy has been halted by tax revolts, the potential for similar movements (combined with Euroscepticism) is likely to place a brake on growth in the EU budget. Indeed, if anything, the pressures are for a reduction in the scale of the EU budget than for any increase. These political constraints compound the problem of using the budget to make the EU more 'social democratic'.

Social policy

Financial resources are not the only policy mechanism, even in social democratic programmes. The potential of the rule of law – regulation – to change societies has been seized by the centre-left perhaps more than others, reflecting perhaps the experience of the American Liberal Left to use social regulation as a vehicle for civil rights and affirmative action.[72] Regulation, moreover, is administratively attractive because it shifts the burden of compliance from government to firms: the policies are not costless, but it is not government that has to fund them. Social regulation straddles the realms of industrial relations and welfare provision, providing a series of rights in the workplace and rights to work. As such it constitutes an important updating of the social democrat canon, and is even attractive in some circumstances to the most modernizing of social democrats.[73]

Social democrats – and particularly the labour movement – have placed a great deal of hope in the development of EU social policy.[74] This, it has been argued, has been one of the key areas where European legislation can make a difference for the traditional constituencies of the Left. Indeed it was to serve as a calling card for Jacques Delors and others in seeking the support of trade unions and other social movements, particularly as the Single Market programme was coming into force.[75]

Yet the roots of European social policy date back to the beginnings of the EC – in provisions to incorporate gender equality which were designed to calm the concerns of the then French government – and the orientation is strongly defended in some corners of the Commission as well as in member states and the Parliament. Moreover, since the Social Charter, the encouragement of negotiations between the 'Social Partners' (a form of 'EuroCorporatism') and the inclusion of the Social Chapter in the Maastricht Treaty the policy has become a fixture in the EU's agenda.[76]

Yet the outcomes of EU social policy have been modest, not least because some member states (even some governments of the Left) have been wary of too extensive a European policy in this area, fearful that it would alienate business. This ambivalence has been further reflected in patchy implementation of the legislation (with the UK in particular adopting a minimalist approach to adopting measures such as the working hours directive). Moreover, there has been a tension between social policy and economic liberalization. This became acute in the early 1990s over the issue of 'social dumping' – trade unions and some governments accused other governments of using weak labour regulations to attract investment, who in turn defended their actions as 'flexibility'. The issue framed the debate in the Delors White Paper on 'Growth, Competitiveness and Employment'[77] and has continued to do so ever since.

Trade policy

In the 1970s and early 1980s trade policy was often deployed as a way of responding to concerns of the effects of industrial restructuring. To the extent that constituencies of social democracy were under threat from external competition, the adoption of protectionist measures was a prime mechanism and a focus for lobbying. Managed trade had been a hallmark of left policies for much of the period until the 1980s. Indeed, at some points, the problem for the EU was as much one of managing trade relations between member states as between Europe and the rest of the world. In some member states, left social democrats – and those to the left of social democrats – wanted selective (i.e. extensive) protection against all imports, regardless of their Europeaness.[78]

Over time, however, one could claim that – as with other elements of social democracy – such protectionist impulses have been eroded by the experience of government and an incremental embrace of liberalism. Indeed, for small social democrat states, free trade has long been an undisputed policy commitment.[79] For the most part, therefore, one would have to regard trade policy as a relatively unimportant dimension of social democracy, despite the considerable potential of the EU in this area. While it should not be written off, particularly as the process of multilateral trade liberalization exposes the economic effects of social compromises necessitating political responses, it appears that social democracy as a whole (and not just the modernizers) have accepted the efficacy of free trade.

Countervailing policies

While the pursuit of particular policies may reflect a variety of political calculations and pressures it is clear that some member states have hoped to trump the economically liberal orientation of European integration by seeking the inclusion of new treaty provisions. Given the nature of EU decision-making, particularly the role of the Commission and the importance of a legal basis for policies, the only way to refocus the EU is to have competing principles recognized in the structure by obtaining constitutional changes (particularly vis-à-vis the operation of competition policy). Thus countervailing policies have tended to require treaty amendments. However, if such moves are designed to overcome the institutional inertia of existing decision-making procedures, the obstacles to securing changes in an IGC context are even greater: a single state can veto any proposal. In some cases, moreover, the initial countervailing intent may be hijacked and reversed; the employment chapter was, for example, originally intended to serve as a commitment to full employment, in some respects balancing the anti-inflationary remit of EMU. In practice, however, it became a vehicle for pursuing labour flexibility. Overall therefore the record of such reforms has been very modest.[80]

Industrial policy

A case in point was the addition of an industrial policy article in the Maastricht Treaty. Industrial Policy has been one mechanism whereby social democratic governments (and others) have sought to facilitate the restructuring of their economies and foster national competitiveness. While arguably as old as the modern nation-state, the high point (or nadir, depending on perspective) of industrial policy was the 1960s and 1970s as European governments sought variously to 'pick winners' and protect losers.[81] Such policies fell out of favour in most European states in the 1980s and 1990s, not least, though not only, because of the pressure of other EU policies.[82] This was driven by the Belgian and French governments whose conflicts with the Commission on a number of competition cases had convinced them that a formal recognition of the legitimacy of industrial policy was required to counter such decisions. However it became clear that their aims were not widely shared either in the Commission or amongst member states. A Commission restatement of industrial policy, published in 1990, was very far from the *dirigisme* of its own historical approach, taking a relatively minimal approach.[83] In the IGC itself, moreover, the provision that was finally agreed very explicitly hedged a rather weak commitment to industrial policy with the proviso that competition policy prevail.[84] The article has scarcely been invoked since.

Public utilities

In the Amsterdam negotiations the French and Belgian governments again attempted to rein in competition policy this time as it affected the public utilities. These had been organized as natural monopolies and had been a means of pursuing a variety of industrial, regional and social policy objectives. The liberalization policies championed by the Commission threatened to overturn these achievements by transforming monopolies into competitive markets. At the same time as resisting specific measures, some member states sought to dampen the Commission's powers, most notably its ability to impose rules directly (through Article 86, formerly 90), and to include a Public Service charter.[85] However, lack of support from other member states meant that the changes were scaled down. After much debate and pressure (particularly from the PES) – and the publication of a Commission report on services of general economic interest[86] (as well as the incorporation of universal or public service derogations into most of the legislation for liberalizing utility services) – a much more limited commitment was included in the amended Treaty (under Article 7).[87]

Conclusion

Overall, therefore, it appears that the economic liberalism of the EU impinges upon social democratic policies quite severely while attempts to counter or mitigate that influence have been much more modest in their impact. We have highlighted the institutional character of the EU as tilting the policy playing field – locking in member states to the prevailing values of the Treaties and setting high hurdles for any reorientation of those values. However, a number of questions remain concerning the source of the constraint upon social democracy and the scope for social democrats to counter those constraints.

Are the constraints upon social democracy a result of European integration? Many would question whether the constraints faced by member states are purely or even primarily European, highlighting the impact of globalization on national economic policies. Other chapters in this book explore the nature of globalization for social democracy and there is no doubt that it has had a real impact. Indeed globalization has a major symbolic significance for social democrats: while traditional social democrats have bemoaned it as force for closing off policy options (though a few sceptics have cast doubt on how far this is so[88]), modernizers have regarded it as an opportunity to reform economic practices and enhance competitiveness. From this vantage point the EU is variously regarded as either a catalyst or an obstacle to globalization, but a part of a much bigger process. However, as this chapter has shown, European integration involves member states committing themselves to a much more robust set of rules than those which might be regarded as framing globalization (WTO, IMF, etc.). Moreover, in the detail of reforms, the imprint of the EU is much clearer than that of global pressures. Finally, even if globalization and EU liberalization are, for the moment, mutually reinforcing policies, there is more scope for regulating global forces at the regional level than there is at the global level, however remote that prospect may appear at the moment.

Indeed, does the remoteness of that prospect reflect an inability of governments to change the rules or an unwillingness to do so? There is no doubt that the institutional constraint is a real one, not just in terms of the 'locked in' nature of the commitments, but also because of the interplay between the three legislating bodies, the member state governments (as represented in the Council of Ministers), the European Parliament and the Commission. Of the three, it appears that the Party of European Socialists (the grouping of members of the European Parliament belonging to the centre-left) is the most cohesive, voting on partisan lines on a regular basis.[89] The problem is, however, that for the Parliament to make a difference it has to secure an absolute majority for its position, a condition which requires the various groups to seek consensus. Moreover, while the PES has worked quite cohesively, social democrats in national settings have been less able to cohere around a centre left agenda for the EU. As we have shown attempts by the leadership of the centre left governments to 'caucus' and refocus the policy agenda have been somewhat ineffective. The Commission is of course non-partisan, but its technocratic perspective is informed by a liberal economic orthodoxy, which with its considerable powers of proposal effectively sets the agenda.

Yet it is not clear how far the member states in particular are seeking to overcome this bias. For all the ideological predispositions and institutional constraints of the EU policy process, the very limited impact of social democracy on a European scale may be due to the choices of the governments themselves. Across the EU (and beyond) social democratic politicians have appeared increasingly ambivalent towards their traditional values and constituencies. Viewed in this way we might wonder whether those governments have preferred to invoke the EU constraint as a means of shifting away from old responsibilities and/or modernizing national debates.[90]

Equally, the national setting itself may also explain the failure to transform the EU. European social democracy has never been very true to its internationalist ideals and this may be reflected in the lack of effective mobilization on a European scale. The primary arena for these parties has been a domestic one and this has shaped attitudes and approaches to integration more than any shared ideology. Indeed, the overall shape of EU politics seems informed as much by national tactics, predispositions and values as by partisan ones (if not more). In discussing the reactions of member states to EU policies it is noteworthy how the rather divergent responses of apparently like-minded governments across the EU contrasts with significant continuities over time within countries notwithstanding changes in regime. Thus the response of centre-right governments in France does not differ that much from those of centre left while in the UK the differences in approach to liberalization between the Thatcher, Major and Blair governments are relatively small. If so we should expect ideological commonalities between countries to be overwhelmed by a range of organizational and cultural factors ranging from the autonomy of state machinery and the presence of important veto groups to the models of capitalist accumulation.

Of course, over time the integration process will intensify interactions between politicians, officials, interest groups and other social actors. As a result it may be not only that decisions are taken at the EU level but that a system of 'EU politics' emerges that transcends national ones. Within that arena an authentic partisan logic may develop, opening up the possibility for social democracy or other ideologies to influence the character of EU governance. In the meantime however the very nature of social democracy is changing and it is debatable whether a modernized and Europeanized form of social democracy will have anything distinctive to bring to such an EU polity.

Notes

1   See J. G. Ruggie, 'International Regimes, Transactions and Change: Embedded Liberalism in the Postwar Economic Order', *International Organisation*, 36:2 (1982), 379–415.

2   These institutional aspects of the EU are outlined in P. Pierson, 'The Path to the European Integration – A Historical Institutionalist Analysis', *Comparative Political Studies*, 29:2 (1996), 123–63.

3   On the nature of the EU as a political system, see S. Hix, *The Political System of the European Union* (London: Macmillan, 1999); and B. Laffan, R. O'Donnel and M. Smith, *Europe's Experimental Union* (London: Routledge, 1999).

4   On the earlier phase of regionalism, see J. Nye (ed.), *International Regionalism* (Boston: Little, Brown, 1968).

5   On the nature of the new regionalism, see C. F. Bergsten, 'Open Regionalism', *World Economy*, 20:5 (1997); and A. Gamble and A. Payne (eds.), *Regionalism and World Order* (London: Macmillan, 1996).

6   A thorough history of the EU is provided in D. Dinan, *Ever Closer Union?* (London: Macmillan 1999). On current developments in the politics and policies of the EU, see H. Wallace and W. Wallace (eds.), *Policy Making in the European Union* (Oxford: Oxford University Press, 2000). A recent account of the legitimacy issue is provided in D. Beetham and C. Lord, *Legitimacy and the European Union* (Harlow: Longman 1998).

7   For a wide-ranging review of the intellectual history of integration, see F. Machlup, *A History of Thought on Economic Integration* (London: Macmillan, 1977). The core integration debate in economics has been over the impact of integration on international trade and whether it is trade creating or trade diverting, see J. Viner, *The Customs Union Issue* (New York: Carnegie, 1950); B. Balassa, *The Theory of Economic Integration* (London: Allen and Unwin 1961); and P. Robson, *The Economics of International Integration* (London: Allen and Unwin, 1998).

8   On the problems of earlier integration projects, see Gamble and Payne, *Regionalism and World Order*.

9   The idea of negative and positive integration was first outlined by Tinbergen, see J. Tinbergen, *International Economic Integration* (Amsterdam: Elsevier 1954). On the political implications of these different modes of integration, see J. Pinder, 'Positive Integration and Negative Integration: Some Problems of Economic Union in the EC', *World Today*, 24 (1968), 88–110.

10 F. Hayek, 'Economic Conditions of InterState Federalism', in *Individualism and Economic Order* (London: Routledge, 1949), 267.

11 See, for example, M. Mazower, *Dark Continent* (London: Penguin, 1998); and P. Gourevitch, *Politics in Hard Times* (Ithaca, NY: Cornell University Press, 1986).

12 Ruggie, 'International Regimes'.

13 See, for example, J. Ikenberry, 'Rethinking the Origins of American Hegemony', *Political Science Quarterly*, 104:3 (1989), 375–400; A. W. Lovett, 'The United States and the Schuman Plan: A Study in French Diplomacy 1950–2', *Historical Journal*, 39:2 (1996), 425–451; J. Gillingham, *Coal Steel and the Rebirth of Europe, 1945–1955: The Germans and the French from Ruhr Conflict to Economic Community* (Cambridge: Cambridge University Press, 1991).

14 On the intentions of the original architects of integration, see F. Duchêne, *Jean Monnet: First Statesman of Interdependence* (New York: Norton, 1994); and H. Young, *This Blessed Plot* (London: Macmillan, 1998). More sceptical views of their importance can be found in A. Milward, *The European Rescue of the Nation-State* (London: Routledge, 1992).

15 On the details of the Coal and Steel Community, see W. Diebold, *The Schuman Plan: a Study in Economic Cooperation 1950–9* (New York: Praeger, 1959); and D. Spierenburg and R. Poidevin, *The History of the High Authority of the European Coal and Steel Community* (London: Weidenfeld, 1994). The *dirigiste* aspect was arguably less obvious in the case of the European Economic Community, however.

16 See the historical account in Dinan, *Ever Closer Union?*

17 See E. Haas, *The Uniting of Europe: Political Social and Economic Forces* (Stanford: Stanford University Press, 1968); and Young, *This Blessed Plot*.

18 See, for example, L. Lindberg and S. Scheingold, *Europe's Would-be Polity* (Englewood Cliffs, NJ: Prentice Hall, 1970); and J. Richardson, 'Policy-making in the EU: Interests, Ideas and Garbage Cans of Primeval Soup', in J. Richardson (ed.), *European Union: Power and Policy-Making* (London: Routledge, 1996).

19 As one left-wing critic of the EU, Stuart Holland, noted, the founders of the EC drew upon a prevailing ideology of liberal capitalism, 'the self interest of enterprise should be harnessed in the public interest through a liberalization of trade capital and labour movements'. S. Holland, *UnCommon Market Capital Class and Power in the European Community* (London: Macmillan 1980), p. 4. See also K. Featherstone, *Socialist Parties and European Integration* (Manchester: Manchester University Press, 1988) on the particular attitudes of different parties towards the EU over time.

20 On the reasons for this interaction, see D. Cameron, 'The Expansion of the Public Economy: A Comparative Analysis, *American Political Science Review*', 72:4 (1978); D. Rodrik, 'Why Do More Open Economies Have Bigger Governments?', *Journal of Political Economy*, 106: 51 (1998); and G. Garrett, *Partisan Politics in the Global Economy* (Cambridge: Cambridge University Press, 1998).

21 The issue was crystallized during the Luxembourg crisis and compromise of 1965/6 which instilled the principle of unanimity in Council of Ministers decision-making. On the general issue of the reassertion of member state control, see S. Hoffmann, 'Obstinate or Obsolete? The Fate of the Nation-State and the Case of Western Europe', *Daedalus*, 95 (1966).

22 For an assessment of the EU progress at the end of this period, see H. Wallace, W. Wallace and C. Webb (eds), *Policy Making in the European Communities* (London: Wiley, 1983); and for a hindsight view, see R. Keohane and S. Hoffmann, 'Institutional Change in Europe in the 1980s', in R. Keohane and S. Hoffman (eds.), *The New European Community: Decisionmaking and Institutional Change* (Boulder, CO: Westview 1991). Of course, the problem was not only apparent in the context of integration but in industrialized democracies more generally. See R. Keohane, 'The Crisis of Embedded Liberalism', in J. Goldthorpe (ed.), *Order and Conflict in Contemporary Capitalism* (Oxford: Clarendon Press, 1982).

23 See Gourevitch, *Politics in Hard Times*; 1986 and D. Sassoon, *One Hundred Years of Socialism* (London: I. B. Tauris, 1996). On the debates on the Left on

one particular contentious issue – nationalization – see F. McGowan, 'What is the Alternative? Labour and Public Ownership', in M. Bishop, J. Kay and C. Mayer (eds.), *Privatisation and Economic Performance* (Oxford: Clarendon Press, 1995).

24   A. Moravcsik, 'Negotiating the Single European Act', *International Organization* 45 (1991). One should not overstate the degree to which neoliberalism was embraced – it could be argued that the French and German shifts were more symbolic than substantial.

25   On the nature of the Single Market, see P. Cecchini, *The European Challenge* (Avebury: Wildwood, 1988); and L. Tsoukalis, *The New European Economy Revisited* (Oxford: Oxford University Press, 1997).

26   See W. Sandholtz and J. Zysman '1992 – Recasting the European Bargain', *World Politics* 42 (1989) on the reasons for the Single Act and the changes introduced. An account of Delors' leadership of the Commission is given in G. Ross, *Jacques Delors and European Integration* (Oxford: Polity, 1995). More generally, accounts of the dynamics of the Court and Commission, see K. Alter, 'Who are the "Masters of the Treaty"? European Governments and the European Court of Justice', *International Organization*, 52:1 (1998); and M. Cini, *The European Commission: Leadership, Organisation and Culture in the EU Administration* (Manchester: Manchester University Press, 1996).

27   On the causes of EMU, see W. Sandholtz, 'Choosing Union – Monetary Politics and Maastricht', *International Organization* 47:1 (1993); and K. Dyson and K. Featherstone *The Road to Maastricht* (Oxford: Oxford University Press, 1999).

28   The elaboration of European Social Policy was the most important policy development, see J. Grahl and P. Teague, 'Economic Citizenship in the New Europe', *Political Quarterly*, 65 (1994); and P. Lange, 'Maastricht and the Social Protocol: Why Did They Do It?', *Politics and Society*, 21:1 (1993).

29   Commission of the European Communities, *Growth, Competitiveness, Employment – the Challenges and Ways Forward into the 21st Century* (Luxembourg: OOPEC, 1993); and European Council, Summit Conclusions – Lisbon 2000.

30   This section draws heavily upon Kevin Featherstone's (*Socialist Parties*) historical analysis of socialist attitudes to European integration. The historical evolution of social democratic views on integration in Germany, France and the UK are covered in W. Patterson, *The SPD and European Integration* (London: Saxon House, 1974); B. Criddle, *Socialists and European Integration: A Study of the French Socialist Party* (London: Routledge & Kegan Paul, 1969); and Young, *This Blessed Plot*. See also Sassoon, *One Hundred Years of Socialism* on the overall history of European social democracy in this period.

31   A Moravscik, *The Choice for Europe: Social Purpose and State Power from Messina to Maastricht* (London: UCL, 1999).

32   Holland, *UnCommon Market*; Young *This Blessed Plot*.

33   The Party's commitment to leave the Common Market was symptomatic of a wider radicalism which cast doubt on its governability.

34   On developments within socialist parties in this period, see Sassoon, *One Hundred Years of Socialism*.

35   On the changing nature of Spanish socialism and the role of Europe in that transformation, see V. Navarro, 'The Decline of Spanish Social Democracy 1982–1996', *Socialist Register* (1997); A. Recio and J. Roca, 'The Spanish

Socialists in Power: Thirteen Years of Economic Policy', *Oxford Review of Economic Policy*, 14:1 (1998).

36   In some ways these conversions matched the earlier shift in German policy at Bad Gödesburg – see Patterson, *The SPD and European Integration*; and Featherstone, *Socialist Parties and European Integration*.

37   On the background to the shift in French economic policy see P. Hall, 'The Evolution of Economic Policy under Mitterrand', in G. Ross, S. Hoffman and S. Malzacher (eds.), *The Mitterrand Experiment* (Oxford: Polity, 1987); and G. Ross, 'The Euro, the French Model of Society and French Politics', *French Politics and Society*, 16:4 (1998).

38   On the contemporary varieties – Left and Right – of 'Euroscepticism', see P. Taggart, 'A Touchstone of Dissent: Euroscepticism in Contemporary West European Party Systems', *European Journal of Political Research*, 33:3 (1998).

39   S. Hix and C. Lord, 'A Model Transnational Party? The Party of European Socialists', in D. Bell and C. Lord (eds.), *Transnational Parties in the European Union* (Aldershot: Ashgate, 1998); and R. Ladrech, 'Social Democratic Parties and EC Integration', *European Journal of Political Research*, 24 (1993).

40   On the differences between economic systems, see P. Hall, *Governing the Economy* (Oxford: Polity 1986); M. Albert, *Capitalism against Capitalism* (London: Whurr, 1993), D. Coates, *Models of Capitalism* (Oxford: Polity, 2000); and C. Crouch and W. Streeck (eds), *Political Economy of Modern Capitalism* (London: Sage, 1997).

41   On the nature of the changes adopted by New Labour, see P. Mandelson and R. Liddle, *The Blair Revolution: Can New Labour Deliver?* (London: Faber, 1996); and S. Driver and L. Martell, *New Labour: Politics after Thatcherism* (Cambridge: Polity, 1998). Of course, it could be argued that the UK's historical 'Anglo-Saxon' pattern of capitalism predisposed politics to a more neoliberal model. See F. McGowan, 'The Exception Becomes the Rule: British Economic Liberalism and European Integration', mimeo, 2000.

42   On the nature of 'Blairism' *vis-à-vis* the EU and the persistence of national concerns and traditions see Young, *This Blessed Plot*.

43   *Le Monde*, 6 June 1997; *Financial Times* 7 June 1997.

44   K. M. Johansson, 'Tracing The Employment Title in the Amsterdam Treaty', 6:1 (1999).

45   The conference was not attended by the French prime minister. See *Le Monde*, 23 September 1998.

46   *Financial Times*, 23 October 1998.

47   *Financial Times*, 25 November 1998.

48   *Financial Times* 9/10 June 1999; *Le Monde*, 10 June 1999.

49   *Financial Times*, 9 November 1999.

50   Indeed, all along there has been some debate about just how far apart the two countries are in substance rather than rhetoric. See *Financial Times*, 2 October 1998; and *Economist*, 12 February 2000.

51   On the divergent policy signals from Germany, see *Economist*, 8 July 2000.

52   See European Council, 2000. There was none the less some French opposition to the calls for further liberalization *Financial Times*, 23 March 2000.

53   Essentially governments are seeking to render their policy commitments credible. The idea has been most elaborated in the context of monetary policy, see F. Giavazzi and M. Pagano, 'The Advantage of Tying One's Hand:

EMS Discipline and Central Bank Credibility', *European Economic Review*, 32 (1988). For a similar explanation of the willingness of governments to submit to a supranational legal order and European regulation, see G. Garrett, 'The Politics of Legal Integration in the European Union', *International Organization* 49:1 (1995); K. Gatsios and P. Seabright, 'Regulation in the European Community', *Oxford Review of Economic Policy*, 5:2 (1989).

54   On the early history of competition policy in Europe and the political struggles surrounding its introduction in member states, see H. Dumez and A. Jeunemaitre, 'The Convergence of Competition Policies in Europe: Internal Dynamics and External Imposition', in S. Berger and R. Dore (eds.), *National Diversity and Global Capitalism* (Ithaca: Cornell University Press, 1996), V. Berghahn, *The Americanisation of West German Industry* (Leamington Spa: Berg, 1986); and G. Majone, *Regulating Europe* (London: Routledge, 1996).

55   After all the roots of the policy lie in the attempts by the populist movement of late nineteenth-century America to rein in the power of big business. On the history of anti-trust, see W. Comanor et al. (eds.), *Competition Policy in Europe and North America: Economic Issues and Institutions* (London: Harwood, 1990).

56   In the UK, for example. See H. Mercer, *Constructing a Competitive Order: The Hidden History of British Antitrust Policies* (Cambridge: Cambridge University Press, 1995).

57   On the general thrust of European competition policy see the Commission's *Annual Report on Competition Policy* (Luxembourg: OOPEC, various). For overviews, see P. Montagnon (ed.), *European Competition Policy* (London: RIIA, 1990), L. Brittan, *Keeping the Playing Field Level* (London: Brasseys 1992); and M. Cini and L. McGowan, *European Competition Policy* (London: Macmillan, 1998).

58   For an account of how the Labour Party adapted its policies in this area, see F. McGowan, 'Labour's New Competition Policy – Market Forces and Public Interests', *Renewal*, 3:4 (1995).

59   F. McGowan, 'Competition Policy: the Limits of the Regulatory State', in Wallace and Wallace, *Policy Making in the European Union*.

60   Ibid.

61   Commission of the European Communities, *Completing the Internal Market* (Luxembourg: OOPEC 1985).

62   Tsoukalis, *The New European Economy Revisited*.

63   F. McGowan, 'The Consequences of Competition', *Revue des Affaires Européenes* (1994).

64   While modernizers have often backed utility liberalization, there are signs that there are political limits to this support. The Commission's plans to open postal services to competition have been opposed by the British government joining the more consistently hostile French. This apparent contradiction is explained by the government's fear that liberalization would lead to the closure of many rural post offices with adverse consequences in Middle England. See *Financial Times*, 30 May 2000.

65   If competition policy is complementary to the Single Market, then EMU is the logical progression of the Single Market since the final obstacle to the latter is the absence of a single currency. See, for example, Commission of the

European Communities, *Annual Report on Competition Policy* (Luxembourg: OOPEC, 1998).

66 Ross, 'The Euro'; Garrett, *Partisan Politics in the Global Economy.*

67 L. Tsoukalis, 'Economic and Monetary Union', in Wallace and Wallace, *Policy Making in the European Union*

68 See, for example, W. Duisenberg, 'Introductory Statement at the High Level Forum', Brussels, 15 June 2000. See also Commission of the European Communities, *Recommendations for the 2000 Broad Guidelines of the Economic Policies of the Member States and the Community* (Brussels: Commission of the European Communities, 2000).

69 Sassoon, *One Hundred Years of Socialism.*

70 D. Allen, 'Cohesion and the Structural Funds', in Wallace and Wallace, *Policy Making in the European Union.*

71 A. Amin and J. Tomahey, 'The Challenge of Cohesion', in A. Amin and J. Tomahey (eds.), *Behind the Myth of European Union: Prospects for Cohesion* (London: Routledge, 1996). For a more technical critique, see P. Martin, 'Are European Regional Policies Delivering?' EIB Papers 4:2 (1999).

72 For one – positive – account of the potential of social regulation, see C. Sunstein, *After the Rights Revolution: Reconceiving the Regulatory State* (Cambridge, Mass: Harvard University Press, 1990).

73 On the nature of regulation in the EU, see G. Majone, *Regulating Europe* (London: Routledge, 1999). It should of course be noted that some modernizing social democrats, sensitive to business lobbies' criticisms are also suspicious of regulation as a source of red tape, see *Financial Times*, 7 August 2000.

74 Lange, 'Maastricht and the Social Protocol'.

75 Ross, *Jacquos Delors.*

76 S. Leibfreid and P. Pierson, 'Social Policy' in Wallace and Wallace, *Policy Making in the European Union.*

77 Commission, *Growth, Competitiveness, Employment.*

78 Featherstone, *Socialist Parties and European Integration.*

79 E. Huber and J. Stephens, 'Internationalization and the Social Democratic Model', *Comparative Political Studies*, 31:3 (1998) argue that it was not free trade but the free movement of capital that undermined social democracy.

80 K. M. Johansson, 'Traung the Employment Title: Uncovering Transnational Coalitions', *Journal of European Public Policy*, 6:1 (1999).

81 On earlier ideas of industrial policy, see A. Shonfield, *Modern Capitalism* (Oxford: Oxford University Press, 1965); and W. Grant, *The Political Economy of Industrial Policy* (London: Butterworths, 1982). For an account of earlier attempts at developing an EU industrial policy, see M. Hodges, 'Industrial Policy', in Wallace, Wallace and Webb, *Policy Making in the European Communities.*

82 In August 2000 the British Industry Minister Steven Byers outlined a major reassessment of his Department's role, stressing 'activism' over 'interventionism', see *Financial Times*, 4 August 2000.

83 Commission of the European Communities, *Industrial Policy in an Open and Competitive Environment* (Brussels: Commission of the European Communities, 1990).

84 *Agence Europe*, no. 5611, 18 November 1991; no. 5627, 11 December 1991.

85   M. Ross, 'Article 16 EC and Services of General Interest: From Derogation to Obligation', *European Law Review*, 2S:1 (2000).

86   Commission of the European Communities, *Services of General Economic Interest in Europe* (Brussels: Commission of the European Communities, 1996).

87   The idea of such a charter was revived in 2000 by the European Trade Union Confederation in a bid to have these provisions strengthened at the Nice IGC.

88   For a critical views of the impact of globalization upon state strategies, see P. Hirst and G. Thompson, *Globalisation in Question* (Cambridge: Polity, 1996); L. Weiss, *The Myth of the Powerless State* (Cambridge: Polity, 1998). An earlier sceptical view of the constraints on the Left is provided in G. Garrett and P. Lange, 'Political Responses to Interdependence: What's Left for the Left?', *International Organization*, 45:4 (1991).

89   Hix, *The Political System of the European Union*.

90   On the extent to which governments have sought to redefine their role, see T. Notermans, 'The Abdication from National Policy Autonomy: Why the Macroeconomic Policy Regime has Become so Unfavorable to Labor', *Politics and Society*, 21:2 (1993); and J. Moses, 'Abdication from National Policy Autonomy: What's Left to Leave', *Politics and Society*, 22:3 (1994).

5
Social Democracy in Britain? New Labour and the Third Way[1]

Nick Cowell and Phil Larkin

The Third Way has become established as the description of New Labour's politics,[2] but what exactly this entails as a modernized form of social democracy is still far from clear. How much guidance the concept offers for future policy is also problematic. From the start this latest revisionist tendency had defined itself largely in the negative sense of what it is not. It is not the old Left as portrayed in a class-oriented, trade union-dominated, dogmatic approach of tax-and-spend that failed to recognize the realities of the modern world. Neither is it a slavish acceptance of free market, 'red in tooth and claw' neoliberalism and the social divisiveness that came with Thatcherism. The New Labour interpretation of Labour's own recent history revolves around images of former Labour governments as upholders of punitive taxation levels to support high levels of public spending, and yet at the same time presiding over inefficiency in public services and an uncompetitive private sector. Both were seen as subject to industrial strife that culminated in the Winter of Discontent in 1978–9. In contrast, New Labour portrays itself as a party that has come to terms with this past and has now moved on, not automatically rejecting what Thatcherism has done, but not necessarily endorsing all that it entailed either, leading Driver and Martell to label New Labour as 'post-Thatcherite'.[3] In addition, though, it can be seen that it is also a response to Labour's last experience of government and the divisions that became apparent then. We will first examine these factors within the context of Labour's history and recent experiences in Britain. This will show that whilst New Labour is the product of adjustments to European and global socio-economic conditions it is also the product of specifically British factors. In considering the concept of the Third Way we will see how the style and tone adopted is a response to the combination of the legacy of Thatcherism, the inheritance of its own past, and a perception of contemporary British and world conditions. We then go on to consider how the Third Way has been contested as the pan-European model for social democracy. Its largely lukewarm response at the European level reflects the fact that whilst social democratic governments are subject to a number of the same significant international constraints, domestic factors play a key role in shaping national social democratic agendas and the way in which they are put forward.

The Third Way in Britain

In terms of its positive statements of intent, New Labour claims to want to marry the New Right's concern for economic efficiency and enterprise with an invocation of long-standing ethical concern of British socialists and social democrats for social justice. In a speech by Tony Blair to the Socialist International conference in 1999, he identified the twin concerns of an emerging Third Way in politics:

> The world over, there is a debate underway about the future of the left. It is whether we are able to set out a vision for the left that can combine our traditional emphasis on social justice with the necessities of the new economy of the 21st century; whether we can stand for fairness and enterprise.... What I have called the Third Way but in reality is modernized social democracy, is to become the champions of change, managing change in a way that overcomes insecurity and liberates people, equipping them to survive and prosper in this new world.[4]

New Labour has explicitly accepted changes in sociological and economic perspectives. Sociologically, New Labour has accepted that the class structure in Britain has changed. The working class is shrinking and the middle class expanding, and there is a developed underclass of people in families without work. For those who are in employment, the nature of work and the pattern of occupations has changed to much more short-term, insecure work that requires greater flexibility for adjustment of skills and services available, both by employee and employer. Women have entered the workforce in greater numbers and are congregated in the less secure, lower-status jobs. The nuclear family is becoming one of a number of different family structures, but stable relationships are still seen by New Labour as the bedrock of a stable society. All these changes are seen as having taken place within an increasingly globalized market economy that has reduced the scope of governments to intervene effectively in the economy. The government's failure to be able to prevent BMW's dissection and disposal of the dismembered parts of Rover is cited as just one example of the futility of trying to act the part of King Canute trying to stem the tidal flow of economic change on an international scale. This is the modernized world that first the Labour Party and then Britain has to come to terms with, it is argued. On the other hand, New Labour's continual statements about the reduction of an individual state's ability to affect decisions of multinational corporations may have themselves contributed to the likelihood that these organizations will ignore the government in their calculations.[5]

In terms of ideology it is claimed that these changes have rendered social democracy in its traditional Keynesian, welfarist form obsolete. New Labour has then been searching for an ideological basis that provides a coherent theme to policy but that avoids hostages to fortune and remains flexible enough for an uncertain and changing world. The Third Way motif is the latest attempt to fulfil this role of 'big idea'. It follows on from the short-lived flirtations with stakeholding (apparently abandoned due to its association with the more interventionist agenda of Will Hutton[6]) and communitarianism (apparently influenced by the work of Amitai Etzioni[7]). But through these changes of label there have been certain themes that have remained dominant. Blair has emphasized social inclusion as his central tenet and this nominally provides a contrast with the avowed egalitarianism of earlier Labour approaches:

> The promotion of social justice was sometimes confused with the imposition of equality of outcome.... The means of achieving social justice became identified with ever higher levels of public spending regardless of what they achieved or the impact on the taxes required to fund it.[8]

The economy

In reality this emphasis on social inclusion does not mark as significant a break from the social democratic agenda of old Labour, or at least variations of it,[9] as is suggested. However, what is significant with New Labour is the separation of the concept of social inclusion from the structure of the economy. New Labour have accepted an argument that has been proposed by some in the party since the Revisionists of the 1950s that the ends and means of party policy should be considered separately. In this perspective, nationalization was seen as a means of achieving economic aims rather than being an aim in its own right. If nationalization no longer seemed the best way to achieve these aims, then it could be replaced by other means. Significantly, Blair used this ends/means distinction in pushing through the change to Clause IV of the party's constitution, which had nominally committed the party to the public ownership of the means of production.[10] Under New Labour's response to the modern economy, the market, modified by means of regulation, has replaced ownership or direct state provision. Nevertheless, this acceptance of the market is not an acceptance of a neoliberal or Hayekian faith in the spontaneous harmony of the market, but does believe that through benign regulation market forces can be channelled in socially acceptable directions.

At the macroeconomic level the broadly Keynesian approach of previous postwar Labour administrations has been replaced by an economic strategy that accepts elements of the neoliberal approach, but seeks to regulate it to a greater extent than free-market supporters would prefer. The paper on the Third Way published jointly under the names of Blair and Schröder stated that:

> In the past social democrats often gave the impression that the objectives of growth and high unemployment would be achieved by successful demand management alone. Modern social democrats recognise that supply side policies have a central and complementary role to play.... The aim of social democratic policy is to overcome the apparent contradiction between demand- and supply-side policies in favour of a fruitful combination of micro-economic flexibility and macro-economic stability.[11]

The party's economic approach had been gradually moving in this direction throughout the late 1980s and early 1990s under the influence of John Smith, Gordon Brown and their adviser, John Eatwell. New Labour has built on these moves so that there is now little place for budget deficits, with Gordon Brown's 'Golden Rule' stating that 'the government will only borrow to invest, public debt will remain stable and the cost effectiveness of public spending must be proved...'.[12] Fiscal prudence and balanced budgets have become the new orthodoxy of Labour economic policy aimed at achieving long term macro-economic stability. Control of inflation rather than unemployment has been the main focus, but there has still been more emphasis on the government's ability to influence employment levels than was seen under Thatcherism. Whilst Labour governments had previously been prepared to reverse their full employment policies when inflation or balance of payments problems arose in the economic cycle, the overt assumption was that they would return to centre stage after temporary remedial action. New Labour has concentrated more on providing a stable economic environment, in which control of inflation has been prioritized, as the backdrop to creating the conditions that will encourage a gradual climb towards a high and stable level of employment. This has also included a cautious attempt to embrace the advantages of membership of the European Union, if and when public opinion can be seen to be reasonably favourable. The economic strategy aims to improve the quality and quantity of investment in Britain, based on the assumption that an increase in the amount of money invested and the terms on which it is invested is dependent on the long-term stability of the British economy.

A further key element of the supply-side economic strategy is labour market reform, aimed at encouraging microeconomic flexibility. Whilst the influence of the social justice element has been seen in the acceptance of the European Social Chapter and the introduction of the minimum wage, both have been at levels that would not risk restriction of labour market flexibility. Thus much has been made of retraining opportunities as the basis for full employment, again on the assumption that a better trained and more flexible workforce will be a further enticement to investment, modernization and job creation. As mentioned earlier, however, the key element that is meant to marry together the concern for economic efficiency with the concern for social justice is the attempt to link welfare provisions to work in a more integrated way than before. This was another area that was well under way before Blair became leader, and the fundamental position was summed up in the report of the Commission on Social Justice established by Blair's predecessor, John Smith.

The Commission's finding was that the mass unemployment that contributed so much to poverty was a symptom of the failure of Britain's economy to compete in the world market. A lack of sufficient and appropriate skills amongst the workforce was an important factor in this failure. This had thrown many into dependence on welfare and the existing benefit rules included several disincentives to work because the loss of benefits on returning to work could result in the creation of a poverty trap. The recommended solution was to change the emphasis of the welfare state 'from a safety net in times of trouble to a springboard for economic opportunity'.[13] The Commission suggested that a 'welfare-to-work' environment had to be built in which the poverty caused by unemployment would be attacked mainly by removing the disincentives; increasing the marginal net rewards for work over benefits; improving access to training; and helping people to find jobs:

> [T]hese strategies for economic prosperity do not only generate the wealth on which social justice depends; in themselves they constitute elements in any plan for social justice.[14]

Welfare provision is increasingly being tied to the obligation to take available work even if outside of one's previous trade or unsatisfactory in other ways:

> Part-time work and low-paid work are better than no work because they ease the transition from unemployment to jobs.[15]

Retraining for alternative careers has also become a stipulation for continued receipt of full benefit. In the spring of 2000 Brown and Blair were emphasizing the point that as there were then 1 million vacancies in the economy and as officially recognized unemployment was almost down to 1 million, then nobody had the justification to claim that there was not a job available for them. The maintenance of job opportunities and the improvement of investment potential has thus replaced the earlier Keynesian emphasis of expansion of demand.

There have been various analyses of this shift away from the mixed economy, Keynesian economics and the Beveridge style welfare state. It has been seen as an 'accommodation to Thatcherism' and a Downsian attempt at electoral 'catch-up'.[16] There is, however, clearly more underlying this change of direction. There have been significant attempts to change the direction of Labour Party policy throughout the postwar years, but each of these has to be seen in the light of the conditions of the time. The social democratic Revisionists of the 1950s and 1960s thought that the worst elements of interwar capitalism had been eradicated by the welfare state and the use of Keynesian techniques to manage the economy at full employment levels.[17] This came to be seen as an overoptimistic evaluation of economic prospects. In the 1970s and early 1980s the Left of the party promoted an Alternative Economic Strategy based on the analysis of the rise of a *meso-economy* of multinational corporations able to circumscribe established economic controls of national governments.[18] From a different perspective New Labour has also accepted that increased globalization of capitalist production and finance has rendered the Keynesian approach obsolete because any attempt to unilaterally reflate the economy will result in a prompt flight of capital towards economies that are seen to adopt harder lines on inflation control. Whilst specific issues, such as the need to present a low taxation stance, are still clearly affected by the legacy of Thatcherism, there are clearly many responses to contemporary conditions within this latest change in Labour Party policy. It is more than mere catch-up politics, it is also a recognition that 'every part of its postwar social and economic strategy [was] undermined'.[19]

Social justice

Previous employment policies have been seen as being based on assumptions that no longer apply in the British economy. The world of old, Fordist employment dominated by males entering at the age of 16 and remaining in a similar line of work until retirement has been contrasted by Blair and Brown to a post-Fordist economy with flexibility required by men and women to maintain employment in several different types of work under rapidly changing conditions.[20] In this scenario entire trades or professions can become redundant in a short space of time. Keynesian reflationary policies can have only little impact in the short term; retraining and other supply-side measures become the key to sustaining employment opportunities. Long-term macroeconomic stability has been the target to be reached by the combination of providing the necessary flexibility in the labour market together with sound finance to control the government's budget.

This perception of the changed economic conditions has had a substantial effect on the way New Labour can address its concern for social justice. As we have seen some aspects of the welfare policy have been regarded as just as outmoded as the economic. The unemployment benefit system in particular was seen as having been designed to provide assistance to the frictionally unemployed rather than as a provision to cope with either mass unemployment or long-term unemployment. The 'New Deal' is essentially a short-term intervention reorienting welfare towards an era of flexibility.

New Labour's 'new social democracy' and the issue of social justice has been presented in terms designed to be unthreatening to middle class voters. However this has been the cause of considerable disquiet amongst its 'traditional' supporters. The New Labour government will have to maintain a careful balancing act to avoid too many adherents of the traditional ethos becoming disillusioned enough to endanger levels of electoral support. The budget of March 2000, for example, was widely interpreted as a move to stem the disaffection of traditional voters by re-emphasizing concern for core welfare state components of health and education, whilst also offering some redistributional help by way of changes to disposable income of the poorer sections of society. This latter aspect of the 2000 budget was, however, an underplayed aspect of all but the first of New Labour's budgets. Its reluctance to be portrayed in any way that was reminiscent of the caricature of 'Old Labour' has prevented them from pointing out the achievement of modest levels of redistribution that have occurred after the first budget. The income data produced by the Office of National Statistics for 1998–99 showed a continuation of the trend towards a widening of the gap between rich and poor. As minimum wage and working families tax credits started to take effect though the Institute for Fiscal Studies analysis of the cumulative effects of the first four budgets showed that the poorest ten per cent of the population had experienced an average 9 per cent increase in weekly income as a result of the fiscal changes under New Labour. The next poorest decile had gained over 8 per cent and each successive decile had gained less with the top two deciles showing only the slightest of losses (less than 1 per cent). The analysis also shows that the redistribution was targeted towards families with children (with or without a working wage). Although pensioners had made some gains (4 per cent for singles and 2 per cent for couples), the largest gains were made by couples with children but with no wage (10 per cent), with single parent families a little behind (over 6 per cent).[21]

Gordon Brown reluctantly admitted the redistribution in an interview on BBC Radio 4's Today programme, but immediately connected it to New Labour's twin concerns:

> We're redistributing to entrepreneurs by the capital gains tax cut.... We're putting money into entrepreneurs, we're putting money into tackling child poverty. We're giving a balance that is right, so there is fairness and enterprise in our society.

He went on to excuse the redistribution by pointing out that because of the growth in the economy 'There is nobody suffering from what we are doing.'[22]

This redistribution and increased spending on health and education services did take place during a time of economic improvement in the government's budget due to the buoyant economy. If New Labour were faced with a real recession, then it would show just how much emphasis was placed on social justice rather than sound finance. If 1950s revisionists were overoptimistic in their reliance on a growing full-employment economy to fund welfare then New Labour's policy seems fraught with the same problem. In constantly reiterating its modernized outlook, New Labour has contributed to the disaffection of some of the traditional supporters by seemingly ignoring its historic concerns. Significantly, the 2000 budget also included significant increases in health spending after disaffection expressed over another of the Labour's traditional concerns as the government cannot afford to lose too much of its traditional support in its pursuit of the middle ground.

The constitution

Domestically, the Third Way has not been uncontested as the way forward for social democracy in Britain. Opposition has apparently grown inside the Labour Party since the relative unity prior to the General Election victory of 1997. Events such as the resignation of junior minister Peter Kilfoyle, previously considered a Blairite loyalist, over the direction of government policy highlight the fact that the Third Way is not accepted uncritically on the social democratic Left. And yet both Blair and the Third Way seem in a relatively strong position and neither the party leader nor his programme face the sorts of organized threat from within the Party that previous leaders have been subject to. This can be attributed first to the absence of alternatives. Whilst some opposition to the general direction of policy has been clear there is no coherent alternative programme around which opposition can coalesce. Second, Blair has effectively secured control of the party organization and has been able to easily face down opposition through this.

Given the monopoly of Labour over left-of-centre party politics and Blair's apparent dominance over the party itself, it is legitimate to consider where the space for social democratic alternatives to emerge might be. The social and economic agenda of the Third Way is notable for its moderation and its comparative lack of radicalism to the extent that some consider it essentially a continuation of Thatcherism.[23] However, the constitutional agenda of New Labour, even if perhaps failing to live up to the promised radicalism, has amounted to the most significant constitutional reform of the postwar period with a devolved parliament in Edinburgh, an assembly in Wales and a devolved assembly and mayor in London (potentially seen as a forerunner of regional assemblies across England) as well as the reintroduction of regional government in Ulster.

The call for devolution away from the centralized state in Westminster has been pushed as part of the social democratic agenda since the 1970s.

At that time devolution was seen both as a way of providing a bulwark against the 'elected dictatorship' in Westminster and promoting a more pluralist, moderate politics than the adversarial model that was regarded as characterizing British politics at the time.[24] It was also seen as a component in the promotion of citizenship and the diffusion of the statist, paternalistic form that it was perceived that social democracy had taken in Britain prior to this.[25] Later, the pressure group advocating constitutional reform, Charter 88, gained significant support on the liberal–social democratic Left.

The New Labour constitutional reforms have in practice displayed a significant tension. On the one hand, there has been the obvious, if limited, diffusion of power away from Westminster. On the other hand, however, and mindful of the internecine in-fighting that so damaged the party's prospects in the 1970s and 1980s, these has been an attempt by Blair to maintain close control of the devolved assemblies. Given their geographical location in Labour heartlands (excepting Ulster), these assemblies were expected to be dominated by the Labour Party. Blair has tried to maintain this control over the assemblies through his grip on the party, with vetting of potential candidates for election to the assemblies and by trying to ensure that senior appointments are obedient to the party leadership.

However, this strategy has proved rather more problematic than was anticipated. 'Blair's man' Alun Michael was ousted as leader of the Welsh Assembly and replaced by Rhodri Morgan, the man that Blair had tried to keep from the post. And in the election for London Mayor, the official Labour candidate, Frank Dobson, was resoundingly beaten by the 'unofficial Labour candidate', Ken Livingstone, seen as a left-wing maverick opposed to Blair and the Third Way.

The implications of all this for Blair's Third Way agenda are unclear. Despite the fact that support for the Third Way agenda clearly cannot be assured throughout the devolved institutions, there does seem to be a lack of fully formed alternatives. As a result the Third Way 'fundamentals' of tight money and flexible labour markets may remain unchallenged. However, the Third Way has thus far been designed not to alienate middle-class voters who are seen as potential recruits to the Conservatives at the next election. This appears to have alienated much of Labour's 'traditional' constituency. If devolution has a short- or medium-term impact on the form that social democracy takes within the Labour Party, it may be that it reorients it back towards Labour's core support a little more rather than prompting wholesale change.

The Third Way in European context

The relationship of the Third Way to the European social democratic mainstream has become an area of significant debate.[26] With New Labour's apparent enthusiasm for greater EU involvement, and with so many of the governments of the EU members dominated by social democratic parties, the closeness of the Third Way agenda to that of these social democratic governments is key both for those who would like to see this 'social democratic moment' seized and used to bring about a reorientation of European politics in a more social democratic direction and for those who would like New Labour to end Britain's 'semi-detached' status in the EU and engage wholeheartedly with greater European integration. The chapter now turns to examine how the Third Way has faired as model for social democracy outside Britain and those other versions of social democracy that have been put forward as alternatives at the European level.

Noting, as we have, at least some continuity between what has become known as Old Labour and New Labour apparently adds grist to the mill of those who have argued that the Labour Party has always been at somewhat of a tangent from the mainstream of European social democracy. Even when Labour Party intellectuals sought to emphasize their credentials within the mainstream of social democracy their claims were dismissed.[27] The basis of this 'British exceptionalism' stemmed from Labour's unusual origins.[28] Unlike the continental social democratic parties, and despite lip-service paid to Marx by some sections of the party, Labour did not have its roots in any form of Marxist ideology. Labour was essentially founded by the trade union movement and as such it was guided by an untheoretical and rather defensive pragmatism compounded by a romanticized working-class 'ethos'.[29] Detailed discussion of the underpinnings of Labour beliefs amounted, in the words of former Labour minister Dick Crossman, to 'dangerous, Teutonic verbiage'[30] and, in the infamous words of Herbert Morrison, socialism could be considered what the Labour Party does. Such political theory as there was within the Labour Party was confined to its small but prominent middle class constituency and was derived more from reformist liberalism than socialism, often mediated through Christianity and its goal of fraternity and the bourgeois ethic of duty (as in the case of R. H. Tawney) or through technocratic managerialism (as in the case of the Webbs).

The modern-day manifestation of this British exceptionalism can be seen in recent debates about the future direction of trans-European social democracy. Tony Blair has been pushing a deregulationist, business-friendly model of Europe, generalized from his project for Britain[31] under the banner of the Third Way. Jospin, on the other hand, has been a notable opponent of this Third Way model. Schröder, after initially signing up to the Third Way (though perhaps in the face of French opposition), has apparently sought to distance himself from it. Other party leaders have not noticeably been lining up to support the Third Way initiative.

Jospin has been the most conspicuous opponent of the Third Way approach and he countered the Blair–Schröder document with a well-publicized publication of his own, *Modern Socialism*.[32] In *Modern Socialism* Jospin portrayed the *Parti Socialiste* (PS) as a party of modernization but argued that modernization needed to remain true to its radical, egalitarian traditions. By implication the Third Way is portrayed as a project of rootless modernization. This distinction is reflected in the titles of the publications. *The Third Way* apparently aiming to escape from historical associations and to transcend traditional ideological distinctions. *Modern Socialism* clearly aims to portray the PS as modernizing whilst remaining true to its traditions rather than moving beyond them.

One of the major points of divergence between 'Blairism' and 'Jospinism' has been over the role of the market. Jospin made it clear that the distinction between socialism and social democracy on the one hand and 'left liberalism' on the other lay in rejecting 'market society' whilst accepting the market. 'We are socialists,' he proclaims, 'and to be a socialist is to affirm that the political should take precedence over the economic.'[33] Whilst not explicitly attacking Blair (after all it is he, rather than Schröder, who has been the Third Way's main evangelist) it is clear that Jospin has been seeking to put 'clear red water' between himself and the rhetorical celebration of the market and private enterprise apparently at the heart of Blairism. Jospin still apparently aspires to the values of socialism and their realization through the state regulation of capitalism.

However, the divide between Blair and Jospin is perhaps not as straightforward as the different rhetoric might suggest. Blair has made much of the constraints under which parties of the Left must govern, and these constraints are much the same for all nations. First, economic growth is seen as a prerequisite of financing any form of redistribution or increasing government expenditure. In practice this may have always been the case, it is then no coincidence that the social democratic golden age of the 1950s and 1960s coincided with an era of unprecedented economic growth. However, with the changing nature of the class structure in western societies and the shrinkage of the industrial working class that provided the social democratic parties with their core constituency (at least in the Northern European variant of social democracy), the need to build cross-class support effectively rules out steeply progressive taxation.

In an era of globalization Blair argues that there are certain imperatives that social democratic parties must adhere to. This has meant financial probity underpinning monetary stability is a prerequisite, a starting point for social democrats in government, 'monetarism (in the sense of non-accommodating macroeconomic policy regimes) seems to have a necessary evil for social democracy'.[34] In the absence of this stability the government runs the risk of capital flight with the experiences of France in the early 1980s providing the defining example.

The requirement of this economic orthodoxy has important implications for social democratic governments. It apparently undermines the Keynesian route to full employment and it limits the amount of public money that can be spent on welfare provision – the two primary means of promoting egalitarianism. Consequently, full employment apparently has to come from labour market adjustment. The need to attract investment in a global era has pushed parties towards adopting flexible labour markets and apparently provides the most unsettling element of the new context.[35]

European integration has provided a further constraint on the social democratic room for manoeuvre. The Maastricht convergence criteria and, subsequently, the conditions for membership of European Monetary Union (EMU) pushed governments to adopt orthodox monetary policy and limited public expenditure. There are also criteria that limit governments' intervention in the domestic economy, in the form of subsidies to private companies for example. This institutionalization of the 'new revisionism'[36] at the European level has reinforced the perceived pressures of globalization limiting the role for an active, interventionist state. Interestingly, the social democratic parties have for the most part been enthusiastic about signing up to the continued deepening of European integration. The Scandinavians have been an exception to this where European policies have been considered a threat to the integrity of the welfare systems. Whilst for the most part the Scandinavian social democratic parties have chosen continued if slightly apathetic EU membership Norway voted not to join the Union. The other party showing equivocation about Europe has of course been Labour. Blair clearly sees Britain's future in Europe. Despite initially opting out of the Euro he has expressed a desire to join as soon as conditions are right. It might be suggested that he will consider the conditions to be right as soon as he thinks that the referendum on membership is winnable. Labour are clearly faced with an electorate and a press that are more hostile than their continental counterparts and so their restrained enthusiasm is understandable. Furthermore, despite (or perhaps because of) patriotism being the last refuge of a scoundrel, the Conservatives under William Hague have clearly put all their eggs in the Eurosceptic basket – a marked contrast to the right of centre parties on the continent. Labour clearly would have to modify their apparent enthusiasm to avoid polarising the electorate and allowing the Conservatives to succeed in their attempts to turn an election into a single issue one.

As a consequence of these factors the actual policies of Blair and Jospin, like those of almost all the social democratic parties, share central features and are not as strikingly different as the conflicting discourses might appear. In particular Jospin's PS has not broken fundamentally with the *désinflation compétitive* model of the 1980s. Despite the socialist rhetoric radical redistribution is a long-term aim rather than an immediate prospect, the PS remains committed to continued membership of the Euro, as noted a significant constraint on socialist radicalism, and the privatization programme in France under Jospin shows no fundamental discontinuity from that of the its right of centre predecessor under Juppé.[37] Even the apparently radical departure from the new revisionist agenda, the 35-hour week, can in fact be seen as an attempt to smuggle labour market flexibility into the French economy under the guise of regulation and social justice.[38] The attempt by the one party leader to play down their links with traditional social democracy and by the other to emphasize these links can be attributed to the need to appease the coalition partners on the Left in France and by the unfortunate associations that references to Labour's past tend to conjure up in the minds of the electorate and press. Added to this is the electoral system that allows Labour not only to form single-party government, a rare luxury for any social democratic party in Europe, but also to dominate the political competition on the left of centre. Having established control of the party the leader of the Labour Party effectively controls parliamentary politics from the left of the Conservative Party to the margins of the 'outside' left of Marxist fringe organizations and New Social Movements.

Similar components of this new revisionism can be seen throughout the social democratic governments. After an initial struggle with his first

Finance Minister, Lafontaine, Schröder has been pursuing significant spending cuts very much in keeping with the new revisionism. In Italy Massimo D'Alema's coalition government continued with Prodi's financial orthodoxy. Even in Sweden, the classic exemplar of a social democratic economy, and the SAP, the classic exemplar of a social democratic party, the new revisionist agenda can be seen with the emphasis on low inflation adopted by the Swedish Social Democrat leadership supplementing the existing emphasis on labour market flexibility.[39]

The Party of European Socialists Malmö declaration *Let's Make Europe Work!* also reflects this new approach.[40] Most of the central elements of New Labour's stated aims are contained within the document and the approach set out to realize these aims are also very similar to those adopted domestically by the Blair government. The new context of globalization and rapid change is made much of in the document as it is by Blair and Brown domestically. And the response of education and training to promote labour market flexibility within parameters set by the European social chapter and the minimum wage is also present.

> We want to improve the quality of work by investing more in research and education, by using new technologies to create new sectors of economic activity, by making working life more flexible and by reorganising working hour with the agreement of the social partners. In other words by investing more in human capital.[41]

There are, of course, some references to the aspects of the traditional social democratic agenda which New Labour has sought to downplay. References to the preservation of the 'mixed economy' in the document might imply that New Labour had signed up to a document advocating a significant project of renationalization whereas the party has been explicit in distancing itself from calls for public ownership and indeed has even proposed further privatizations such as the Post Office, Air Traffic Control as well as introducing private capital into the financing of the public infrastructure such as the London Underground. Furthermore, the reference to 'social partners' might suggest an element of corporatism which, given Labour's 1970s experience, the party might understandably be wary of.

However, too much should not be drawn from the broad similarities between New Labour's agenda and the Malmö declaration. The document was after all a collaborative effort and needed to be acceptable to all the member parties and as Puttnam noted, a narrow room for manoeuvre in the domestic political arena can strengthen the bargaining position at the international level.[42] As such the British reluctance to sign up to a document that might be portrayed as too 'Old Labour' and the general unpopularity of the idea of closer European integration would be likely to gain Blair concessions in the negotiations over the drafting of the document. The end product might then be expected to be somewhat more to the liking of Blair than it might otherwise have been. As we have seen, Blair has been vocal in his desire to see his Third Way adopted at the European level. Others have, however, sought a rather different approach at the European level. Jospin in particular, whilst implementing few radical policies domestically, has tried to challenge the imperatives of globalization at European level.

And with this in mind the actual similarities between the social democratic parties can easily be overstated. It is certainly true that the contemporary social democratic governments are moving in similar directions. They are facing similar constraints on the formation of their strategy and their scope for manoeuvre in office. The response to the perceived pressures of globalization have been to adopt orthodox monetary policy which limits public spending. This in turn places limits on the welfare state and on the possibility of job creation through Keynesian aggregate demand stimulation. These constraints have been institutionalized in the criteria governing membership of the Euro and accepted by the Party of European Socialists. But despite the similar response to these pressures in terms of labour market flexibility and macroeconomic orthodoxy the net effects can differ significantly between countries. These pressures may be similar but they are mediated through national factors. In this sense, then, the impact of labour market deregulation will be radically different in a highly regulated economy such as France from that in an already unregulated labour market such as Britain. The expansion of the Swedish welfare state may be over but it remains a more generous and comprehensive welfare state than that found in Britain.

Conclusion

New Labour cannot be considered as merely an accommodation to Thatcherism, nor even as a post-Thatcherite mixture of acceptance and rejection. Clearly the Thatcherite period was an important factor in shaping the social democratic response in Britain; nowhere else on the European continent had such a strong dose of New Right neoliberalism, and so the effect on social democracy was stronger in Britain than elsewhere in Europe. On the other hand, the Labour Party in Britain had 'modernized' less than some of the other European social democratic parties, and images of the last Labour government had been indelibly etched on the minds of those intent on regaining power within the party. The party had suffered from increasing tensions within its ranks, particularly in disputes between Left and Right, as well as between leadership and activists. The resulting split had threatened the viability of Labour as even the main opposition let alone as an alternative government. Together with another image of disunity and weakness that resulted from the trade union disputes in the 'Winter of Discontent', there was concern that the last Labour government might have become the last ever Labour government. It is unsurprising that so much adverse publicity changed the Labour leadership's views on the need for controlling publicity. The character assassination by the British press of Michael Foot in his period as leader could only have reinforced the recognition of the need to try to present a more positive image in what was a predominantly right wing sector of the media. The move to attract the centre ground of British politics and to 'spin' publicity to appeal to that sector was a consequence of these concerns as much as it was a reaction to Thatcherism. Finally, there was the matter of recognizing that the world had been changing rapidly and the need to adjust the ethos and doctrine to a globalized economy and changed class structure. With the dramatic collapse of communism in the Soviet Union and elsewhere, the loss of credibility of Keynesian economic techniques and the lack of support for the left-oriented policies of the 1983 manifesto, British social democracy had to present a modern policy programme that was created in the absence of any substantial power base on the left of the party.

However, national factors alone do not account for the shape of New Labour or its Third Way agenda. New Labour is moving in a similar direction to the other social democratic parties of Europe. This is because it is clearly responding to similar pressures as other parties with broadly similar aims. But these forces, whilst pushing in similar directions are inevitably filtered through nationally-specific factors which means that the immediate political agenda of social democratic parties will be rather more different than the blanket title of 'new revisionism' might suggest.

These domestic factors include the different institutional arrangements of the different countries. Lees, (this volume), suggests that the different constitutional arrangements of Germany and the UK can account for the more problematic status of the Third Way in German politics. Elsewhere, Esping-Andersen notes the importance of path dependency in welfare. Whilst all welfare states are responding to the pressures discussed above the way in which they are responding is guided by the existing welfare regime. [43]

The fact that the British electoral system allows the prime minister to govern without recourse to external coalitions is clearly significant. Provided the party leader can establish dominance of the party (a tall order, and more easily said than done, as the history of the party amply demonstrates) they have control of the parliamentary left of centre. Blair appears to have achieved this control more successfully than any other Labour leader since the Second World War. He has thus been able to push the Third Way agenda without need to trim to appease either external coalition partners or rival agendas within the party. There are certainly complaints about aspects of the Third Way including from sources that might have been expected to be reasonably sympathetic.[44] But these complaints do not amount to a coherent alternative approach and furthermore they lack a means to enter debates within the party given the tight rein kept on policy making by the Party elite.

These institutional factors can provide only part of the story and it is impossible to account for New Labour without reference to the party's postwar history. Thatcherism is clearly an important factor. Any social democratic party would find the prospect of governing after almost two decades of neoliberalism a very different prospect from following a Christian Democrat or Gaullist government. But that Thatcherism emerged in Britain but with no major comparable agenda on the continent is itself significant. Its immediate emergence was crucially affected by the British failure to manage corporatist governance effectively. British tripartism worked adequately at redistributing the proceeds of economic growth though with the attempts by the big unions to maintain differentials its egalitarian impact was marginal at best.[45] However, it proved unable to manage the pressure that emerged as the economy slowed in the 1970s. Industrial relations deteriorated until the Winter of Discontent, the importance of which in defining the shape and concerns of New Labour perhaps outweighed its genuine significance.[46]

But this failure to implement corporatism as successfully as a number of other social democratic parties is also significant. The arguments about British exceptionalism are overstated, not least because they overestimate the coherence and similarity of the other social democratic parties in Europe. However, it is true that Britain was less effective in implementing the social democratic agenda than were other countries regardless of the party in office. In this respect, whilst most of the elements of the 'classical' social democratic model were in place in Britain, they were less embedded. In this sense the British welfare state, whilst funded in a 'social democratic' manner quickly moved towards the more liberal models of the United States or New Zealand rather than that of Sweden.[47] Meanwhile Labour's record on corporatism is less good than the right-of-centre governments of West Germany. Its record on economic intervention is less good than the Gaullist governments of France over the same period. Even Keynesianism was used to depress employment in pursuit of low inflation in Britain.

The result of these factors is something that resembles the ideas of the revisionist wing of the party that has existed within the party from the 1930s. So New Labour emerged from a mixture of Labour's own history, a reaction to the Thatcherite experience in Britain, and as a response to the changing world conditions. Whether or not the Third Way is a sufficiently substantive concept to act as a guide for the development of future policy is more problematic. If the economy were to take a downturn there does not seem to be the means to maintain the balance between policies aimed at enterprise and those aimed at social justice. So far New Labour has operated under relatively advantageous economic conditions that have allowed a small degree of redistribution and increased expenditure on welfare in trying to meet their target to eliminate child poverty. Under less favourable economic conditions though, it is not clear that welfare-to-work would be sufficiently robust to counter pressures on rising unemployment. It is also doubtful that adherence to the principle of sound finance would leave much scope for increased welfare expenditure that becomes necessary in many areas in such times. So the Third Way of New Labour politics still awaits its most demanding test.

Notes

1 We are grateful to Stephanie Hoopes, Charlie Lees, Luke Martell and Neil Stammers for helpful comments on a draft of the chapter.
2 T. Blair, *The Third Way: New Politics for the New Century* Fabian Pamphlet 588 (London: The Fabian Society, 1998); For a more elaborate formulation by Blair's Third Way 'guru', see A. Giddens, *The Third Way: the Renewal of Social Democracy* (Cambridge: Polity, 1998)
3 S. Driver and L. Martell, *New Labour: Politics after Thatcherism* (Cambridge: Polity, 1998).
4 T. Blair, Speech to the Socialist International Conference (Paris, 8 November, 1999).

5   However, Garrett has argued that the social democratic state is not as impotent as this interpretation of its impact suggests. In particular its ability to control wage increases through corporatism, along with its role in providing education, training, and health care, can be attractive to globalized capital. However, as Wickham-Jones notes, given the slim likelihood that corporatism can actually fulfil this role in Britain it may be that Garrett is over-optimistic, at least in the British context. See G. Garrett, *Partisan Politics in the Global Age* (Cambridge: Cambridge University Press, 1998); M. Wickham-Jones, 'New Labour in the Global Economy: Partisan Politics and the Social Democratic Model', *British Journal of Politics & International Relations*, 2:1 (2000).

6   W. Hutton, *The State We're In* (London: Vintage 1996).

7   A. Etzioni, *The Spirit of Community: Rights, Responsibilities & the Communitarian Agenda* (New York: Crown, 1993).

8   T. Blair and G. Schröder, *The Third Way – Die Neue Mitte* (London: Labour Party and SPD, 1999).

9   There was, of course, no such thing as 'Old Labour'. Labour has always consisted of a notoriously 'broad church'. For discussions of the different divisions with the Party, see *inter alia* T. Bale, *Sacred Cows and Common Sense: The Symbolic Statecraft and Political Culture of the British Labour Party* (Aldershot: Ashgate, 1999); N. Ellison, *Egalitarian Thought: Retreating Visions* (London: LSE/Routledge, 1994); G. Foote, *The Labour Party's Political Thought*, 3rd edn (Basingstoke: Macmillan, 1997); P. R. Larkin, 'Revisionism & Modernisation in the Post-War British Labour Party' (University of Sussex D. Phil., 2000); A. Warde, *Consensus and Beyond: The Development of Labour Party Strategy since the Second World War* (Manchester: Manchester University Press, 1982).

10 In fact, it committed the party to 'common ownership'. However, in practice, this has tended to be public ownership.

11 Blair and Schröder, *Third Way.*

12 G. Brown, speech on 'Labour's Macroeconomic Framework' (London, 17 May 1995).

13 Commission on Social Justice, *Social Justice: Strategies for National Renewal* (London: Vintage, 1994), p. 1.

14 Ibid., p. 103.

15 Blair and Schröder, *Third Way.*

16 C., Hay, 'Labour's Thatcherite Revisionism: Playing the "Politics of Catch-Up"', *Political Studies*, 42: 4 (1994).

17 C. A. R. Crosland, *The Future of Socialism* (London: Jonathan Cape, 1956).

18 S. Holland, *The Socialist Challenge* (London: Quartet, 1975).

19 P. Q. Hirst, *After Thatcher* (London: Collins, 1989), 21.

20 For example, see G. Brown, 'The Crosland Memorial Lecture' (London, 12 February 1997).

21 The Institute for Fiscal Studies analysis was reported in, article by L. Elliott and M. Atkinson *The Guardian* (23 March 2000), 28.

22 Reported in the same article.

23 C. Hay, *The Political Economy of New Labour: Labouring Under False Pretences?* (Manchester: Manchester University Press, 1999); R. Heffernan, *New Labour and Thatcherism* (Basingstoke: Macmillan, 2000).

24 See S. Finer (ed.), *Adversary Politics & Electoral Reform* (London: Anthony Wigram, 1975).

25 See S. Williams, *Politics is for People* (Harmondsworth: Penguin, 1981).

26 See *inter alia* B. Clift, 'New Labour's Third Way and European Social Democracy', in S. Ludlum and M. J. Smith, *New Labour in Power: Ideology, Party and Policy* (Basingstoke: Macmillan, 2000); M. E. Goes, 'The Sinatra Doctrine for European Social Democrats: Why the Continent Rejects Blair's Third Way', *Acqua Terra* (Autumn 1999).

27 See D. Wincott, 'Crosland, European Social Democracy and New Labour', in R. L. Leonard (ed.), *Crosland and New Labour* (Basingstoke: Macmillan/The Fabian Society, 1999).

28 M. Wickham-Jones, 'An Insular Party? Labour's Century in Comparative Perspective' *Renewal*, 8:1 (2000).

29 H. M. Drucker, *Doctrine and Ethos in the Labour Party* (London: Allen & Unwin, 1979).

30 R. H. S. Crossman, 'Towards a Philosophy of Socialism', in R. H. S. Crossman (ed.), *New Fabian Essays* (London: Dent, 1952), p. 4.

31 Such as it is his, Gordon Brown having been at least as responsible for the evolution of what we might now call Blairism.

32 M. Jospin, *Modern Socialism*, Fabian Pamphlet 592 (London: The Fabian Society, 1999).

33 Ibid., 1.

34 T. Iversen, 'The Choices for Scandinavian Social Democracy in Comparative Perspective', *Oxford Review of Economic Policy*, 14:1 (1998) 72–3.

35 After all the German SPD was never reliant on Keynesianism. The Bundesbank remained committed to the maintenance of low inflation throughout the postwar years.

36 D. Sassoon, *One Hundred Years of Socialism: The West European Left in the Twentieth Century* (London: Fontana, 1997).

37 F. Lourdon, 'The Logic and Limits of '*Désinflation Compétitve*', *Oxford Review of Economic Policy*, 14:18 (1998).

38 The 35-hour week is being 'averaged' over the year allowing the 35-hour limit to be exceeded when necessary. This has meant longer holidays but the cost of this recouped by larger firms through the greater productivity made possible by the greater flexibility (though Jospin dislikes the capitalist overtones of 'flexible' labour markets, preferring the terms 'supple'). However, this 'temporal' flexibility should be distinguished from wage or external flexibility. D. Lawday, 'NS Profile: Martine Aubry', *New Statesman* (14 February 2000) 18–19.

39 J. Vartiainen, 'Understanding Swedish Social Democracy: Victims of Success?', *Oxford Review of Economic Policy*, 14:1 (1998).

40 Party of European Socialists *Let's Make Europe Work!* <http://www.pes.org/english/frames4.htm>.

41 Ibid.

42 R. Puttnam, 'Diplomacy & Domestic Politics: The Logic of Two-Level Games', *International Organization*, 42:3 (1988).

43 G. Esping-Andersen, *The Social Foundations of Postindustrial Economies* (Oxford: Oxford University Press, 1999); see also P. A. Hall, *Governing the*

Economy: The Politics of State Intervention in Britain and France (Cambridge: Polity, 1986).

44   See A. Gamble and A. Wright, *The New Social Democracy* (Oxford: Blackwell, 1999), for example.

45   In Britain tripartism was largely seen as a crisis measure to control the rapidly accelerating inflation of the 1970s through the implementation of prices and incomes policies. As such its impact on the redistribution of income was 'both uncertain and short-lived'. R. F. Elliott and J. L. Fallick, Incomes Policies, Inflation and Relative Pay: An Overview', in R. F. Elliott and J. L. Fallick, *Incomes Policies Inflation and Relative Pay* (London: Allen & Unwin, 1981), 260.

46   C. Hay, 'Narrating Crisis: The Discursive Construction of the "Winter of Discontent"', *Sociology*, 30 (1996).

47   G. Esping-Andersen, *The Social Foundations of Postindustrial Economies* (Oxford: Oxford University Press, 1999).

6
Dutch Social Democracy and the Poldermodel[1]

Christien van den Anker

Introduction

A critical discussion of social democracy is highly relevant at the present moment for at least five reasons. First, the idea that the world has changed significantly and that we now live in an era of globalization raises questions with regard to social policies and the social democratic tradition.[2] Globalization is often regarded as a constraint on the social policies that are traditionally identified with social democratic governments, since companies are believed to be more able and willing to move production away to locations with less legally protected social and economic rights. Therefore, social democracy needs to rethink and does, its view on the desirable and feasible role of the state, and its economic and social policies in an era of globalization. Social democratic parties need to establish what has changed and what implications this has for their party programmes and government policies. In addition to restricting national policies by allowing capital to flow more freely between countries, globalization also implies that there is a greater need for social policy (national and international) to soften the blows of a global market economy. Yet, simultaneously, social democracy needs to establish whether the traditional methods of redistribution are still feasible in a globalized world. National models of redistribution relied on a welfare state, which has come under fire in recent years. The international efforts to redistribute income via development aid have also been subject to critical discussion. This means social democracy needs to re-evaluate its programme in terms of its effectiveness in one nation-state and it needs to look into possibilities for global regimes that regulate global capitalism and protect those who cannot participate in the labour market. Another aspect of globalization is the transformation towards service economies that are knowledge-based and require flexible attitudes to training and skills. In the Nether-lands the coalition government in which the social democratic party has a majority has introduced a new model of education in response. The new set-up aims at individualization of learning strategies, flexibility in choice of subjects and independent learning to prepare for lifelong learning in the newly flexible labour market.[3] Therefore, a critical academic assessment of social democratic circles seems timely in the light of the present perceived trend towards globalization of the eco-nomy. Intensified debates in the social democratic tradition about its ability to regulate the effects of global capitalism are helpful sources for such an assessment. A central question to be discussed in this chapter is therefore what the implications are for (Dutch) social democracy of the globalization of capitalism and other aspects of the globalization process.

The second reason that an assessment of the social democratic trad-ition is relevant at the present moment is the fact that the end of the Cold War has been claimed to herald a victory for neoliberalism, and not for social intervention in markets by the state. The increasing poverty and inequality that are the result of neoliberal government policies worldwide require urgent answers from social democrats, who are unfor-tunately easily dismissed in the present climate if they sound too much like socialists. Liberal democracy is said to be spreading worldwide, but serious thinking needs to be done about whether any democratic polit-ical system can be effective if the market is not curtailed by a social democratic model of government intervention. A discussion is also needed about the commitment of social democracy to the liberal demo-cratic model. The lack of participation in national party politics and a lack of voters turning out for local and national elections is a problem for social democracy since traditionally it has given a voice to people committed to a fairer division of resources and opportunities in society. If social democratic parties get into government but lose support from the grassroots, then they will have sacrificed the principle of emancipa-tion of the disadvantaged they historically stood for. With the growth of the middle-class, social democratic parties have moved away from their traditional membership of mainly working-class people towards a more middle class membership base. This raises the issue of solidarity with working-class and non-working people. In addition, internal party democracy has undergone changes in most European social democratic parties. In the Netherlands, for example, the changes in party demo-cracy have been in favour of a geographically and functionally restricted group, including people in the party bureaucracy who are living in the densely populated areas covering the big cities in the West and excluding local party members elsewhere. Therefore, democracy and participation need to be on the agenda in an era when a neoliberal emphasis on markets, individuals and private entrepreneurship makes solidarity seem unfashionable, as it is easily associated with the bankruptcy of communism in the former Soviet Union and Eastern Europe. A second central question to be addressed in this chapter is, therefore, whether or not the end of the Cold War necessarily implies a shift to the right for social democracy. This question raises the issue of whether the radical social democratic strategies of (among others) the Dutch social democratic party in the 1970s have had counterproductive results and should be revised independently of the 'historic victory of liberalism'.[4] It also raises the issue of participation and internal party organization as parts of a model of democracy that promises to be more radical than the traditional liberal democratic model.

Third, western liberal societies have been changing in nature since the end of the Second World War, and especially since the late 1960s. Common trends in these types of societies are increased individualization, a decrease in the number of members of households, less acceptance of authority and more emphasis on choice of lifestyle. Partly in response to those processes there is also an increased emphasis on identities and communities and therefore discussion of government initiatives to resolve problems of exclusion and the challenges posed by increasingly multicultural societies. Social democracy has had to revise its traditional model of nuclear families as the basis of households as well as the traditional model of male breadwinners and female carers who worked part time at the most. With women participating increasingly in the labour market, childcare, care of the elderly and voluntary work in schools, libraries and churches are becoming areas where policy is needed. The Dutch government is currently designing legislation aimed at creating the opportunity for all adults in a household to work part-time and for all to have access to leave for care or study purposes at different times in their career. With the development of post-material concerns about the environment and the rat race, policy needs to be developed to incorporate these concerns. And with the decline in moral and spiritual guidance from the traditional mainstream churches and the unions, policy needs to be rethought with regard to moral education and the legitimate interference in private lives by the state. A recent example of a debate sparked off by the changing and multicultural nature of society is a discussion on whether or not abortion should be freely available to families of ethnic minorities in the Netherlands who want to have abortions based on a preference for a male child.[5]

A central question to raise in the assessment of current trends in social democracy in the Netherlands is therefore whether it takes these socio-logical changes seriously enough to revise and introduce policy. A related issue to comment on is whether a social democratic strategy of government should include measures to counteract negative conse-quences of sociological changes. And if this is considered to be desirable, is there evidence that the government can influence these trends effect-ively? If it is possible for the government to shape the process of change, then is the current government doing so effectively?

A fourth reason for evaluating the social democratic tradition is that European social democratic parties did well in recent elections and are now (2001) in government in Britain, France, Germany, Italy and Sweden. In the Netherlands, the country this chapter focuses on, the social democrats are the largest party in a coalition government. Several topics for discussion can be distilled from the electoral success of European social democratic parties. First, an assessment is needed of the most radical shift in social democratic direction since the Second World War. The Third Way, *Die Neue Mitte* and the Poldermodel were all innovations of the previous electoral strategies and ideological pro-grammes of the social democratic parties. Their attraction to the current electorate has been shown but both their success in practice and their normative foundations need to be interrogated. It has been argued that the 'new' social democracy has shifted to the Right as a requirement for electoral success in a neoliberal age of globalization. If there is a shift to the Right in 'new' social democracy, then the inevitability of this move needs to be questioned.

Another issue raised by the electoral success of several European social democratic parties is whether or not the strategy of the EU as a whole moves into a social democratic direction under some conceptions of social democracy. The process of European integration under social democratic leadership presents another relevant context for a critical review of social democratic policy-making. The various European trad-itions of social democracy pull in different directions. A discussion of the respective influence of the different social democratic directions within Europe on a common European social policy should be an important part of the current agenda of political reflection in social democratic and academic circles. Initial debates are being held between European social democratic parties and think tanks. Although a common European social policy has not emerged yet, identifying recent changes in policy on a national scale in answer to European integration, globalization and the end of the Cold War may be helpful in working towards it.[6]

So central questions emerging in the context of the recent European electoral success of social democratic parties include first, an assessment of whether a general shift to the right has occurred and, if so, whether this shift is necessary for electoral success; and second, the possibility of a common European social democratic policy needs to be assessed. One way in which this chapter addresses these questions is by discussing the feasibility of exporting the Dutch Poldermodel as a basis for a common European social and economic policy.

Fifth, the economic growth experienced generally across Europe creates opportunities for social democracy to realize its objectives to achieve a more just society. In the Netherlands this context is explicitly recognized by the leadership of the social democratic party (PvdA). This led to the publication of a document, *Kracht en Kwaliteit* (Strength and Quality), in which the PvdA sets out its objectives for the next period.[7] The document is a response to three phenomena. First, there is an urgent need to modernize in order to compete successfully in the global economy; second, all the talents of people in society should be made to use in the new knowledge economy; and third, there is a widespread call for a more fair distribution of the new wealth. This recent trend of a growing economy (the Dutch economy has outperformed the expectations in the annual budget every year since 1994) and the consequent explicit formulation of priorities in the Dutch social democratic party provides an excellent context for a reassessment of the 'new social democracy' in the Netherlands. It also provides a further basis to compare European social democracies in relation to their priorities in allocating new resources to areas of investment and spending.

All five contexts of change have influenced the present debate on social democracy and constrain the possibilities for social policies to handle these changes effectively. The central questions for discussion in this book are all, in some way or other, related to a contemporary assessment of social democratic strategies of governance under the present global, regional and socio-cultural circumstances. But they also leave room for an assessment of social democratic policies in their own terms. In this chapter, I will discuss the 'transformation in progress' initiated by the Dutch social democratic party and evaluate its relationship to the wider developments described above.[8]

This chapter is structured in the following way. The first section addresses the domestic contextual factors underpinning rethinking of social democracy in the Netherlands. This is followed by a discussion of what social democracy stands for in the Netherlands at present. Here the shift away from the social democratic tradition of building a welfare state beyond the minimum provision and towards the more market-oriented Poldermodel will be presented.

In the third section some of the criticisms of this model are addressed and an assessment is made of how complete the shift towards more market-oriented policies is. Finally, this chapter will look at how much commonality or difference there is between the Dutch social democratic tradition and other national traditions and political systems in the European Union. In this context, the possibility of developing an integrated European social democratic vision is discussed and the possibility of exporting the Dutch model of social policy, the so-called Poldermodel, to the European level is considered. One comment that is often heard is that European social democratic parties have moved closer to their neoliberal opponents in order to capture the support of the middle classes, who may just as easily move towards a more economically neoliberal policy preference. But is this equally the case for social democratic traditions in different countries?

In my conclusion I present some reflections on the impact of globalization, the end of the Cold War, Europeanization, economic prosperity and (post)-modernization on the changing direction of Dutch social democracy.

The Dutch historical and political context

According to Esping-Andersen, social democracy is premised on two assumptions. 'The notion of a social democratic "road to power" is based on the assumption that class formation under democratic parliamentary conditions can provide the strength and solidarity needed to transform capitalism. It is also premised on the assumption that electoral politics and reformist accomplishments will enhance social democracy's progress.'[9] Esping-Andersen also notes that

> Social democracy, then, distinguished itself by the decision to subordinate class purity to the logic of majoritarian politics. . . . Whereas the vanguard party only admits recruits who are willing to adhere to its manifesto, the social democratic party is prepared to realign its program in response to current requirements for alliance formation.[10]

Social democracy in the Netherlands fits in with this description of social democracy and it can be used to distinguish the Dutch social democratic from the communist and socialist parties. In 1918 the social democratic leader Troelstra proclaimed the Dutch revolution. After its failure, the internal debate on legitimate means of politics was intensified.[11] The Dutch social democratic party (SDAP) was one of the first socialist parties in Europe to abandon Marxist revolutionary theory and to advocate a mixed economy. This was explicitly incorporated in the 1937 party manifesto. The electoral strategy was aimed at incorporating the middle class. The social democratic party therefore became a broad people's party even before the Second World War.[12]

The formation of the Partij van de Arbeid in 1946 was a further key historical moment in this respect. The foundation of the Partij van de Arbeid (PvdA) was as a party that would break through the 'pillarization' (*verzuiling*) of society. Pillarization is a concept used to describe the historic situation in the Netherlands where people of different (religious) persuasion belonged to organizations of their own kind. For example, Catholics would vote for the Catholic People's Party (KVP), belong to a Catholic Church, read a Catholic newspaper, listen to the Catholic radio broadcasts and send their children to a Catholic school. Socialists would vote for the social democratic party, read the socialist newspaper, belong to a socialist union and send their children to a secular school. Although the respective 'pillars' segregated people in their daily lives, there was cooperation at the top. Pillarization created a structure of authority in which people followed the leaders in their own 'pillar', yet the leaders negotiated political deals at the top of the organization.[13] The establishment of the PvdA was revolutionary in this historical context. Catholic and socialist leaders had started talking to each other and had worked out a plan to bring together progressive elements in the Catholic party with the social democrats. This was a breakthrough of 'pillarization' but it was also a breakthrough of the traditional constituency of the socialists as working class. The new party welcomed people from non-working-class backgrounds and it accepted people with a confessional or liberal background. The PvdA has succeeded in attracting middle-class voters and most members of the party now view themselves as middle-class.[14] However, the big influx of Catholic voters the founders of the PvdA hoped for, has not happened. Instead a, general trend away from religion has reduced the membership numbers of the Catholic and Protestant parties: they are now combined into one large Christian-Democratic party (CDA).

In 1994 the PvdA formed a coalition with the conservative liberals and radical democrats. The neoliberal Christian Democrats were left out of government for the first time in 80 years. The coalition is called 'Purple'

(*Paars*) since the colours of the three parties in the coalition add up to purple when mixed. The support for Purple is strong. This is mainly due to the success of the government in reducing unemployment and securing economic growth. In recent government research evidence has been found that the Netherlands is doing better than its European counterparts as well as the United States and Japan in those respects. In addition to the Anglo-Saxon and Rhineland model of social policy, the Netherlands has put itself on the map by what is called the Poldermodel. This model has been hailed in the foreign press and Dutch ministers have suggested it be adopted in other European states, too. Some even speak of a Dutch miracle, especially taking into account the high unemployment figures in the Netherlands in the mid-1980s.[15] In 1998 the Purple coalition won the elections convincingly and the so-called 'Purple II' cabinet will pursue roughly the same policies as its predecessor.

Recently, the social democratic party has moved away from their version of a welfare state and views Keynesianism as no longer feasible in the current economic circumstances. According to some commentators, they were late in moving away from ideological dogmatism about the welfare state and were unelectable as a government party until they did so. As recent converts, however, they are being accused of going over the top in following the 'prudent' neoliberal economic policies of cutting public expenditure and reducing taxes. The PvdA's turn away from its original ideological position of statist social and economic planning, as well as from its emphasis on radical income inequality, has been electorally rewarding. According to van Kersbergen,

> In social and economic terms, the PvdA now very much looks like a social democratic party that still stresses social justice and solidarity as its main values, but has lost its faith in the state as an omnipotent political agent and accepts the market as an efficient allocator of scarce resources, even if this means accepting a higher degree of inequality. Equality is increasingly defined in equal opportunities on the labour market.[16]

The revision of the party's basic principles since the mid-1990s may be seen as a further example of the pragmatic stance of the social democrats, in addition to their earlier decision to become a parliamentary party and their appeal to the middle classes by setting up the Partij van de Arbeid. The radical stance of the 1970s, advocating a planned economy and a maximum ratio of income inequality of 5:1 is now widely considered as obsolete and discussions centre on the revision of the traditional model of the welfare state and the incorporation of ecological issues in the party's political doctrine.[17] However, any criticism of the radicalism of the 1970s must take into account that in both 1973 and in 1977 the PvdA won the elections. In 1973 PvdA leader Den Uyl formed a coalition government, which won ten additional seats (out of 150 in the Second Chamber of Parliament) in the general elections of 1977. The reason the PvdA did not enter the coalition government in 1977 was a disagreement over the specific people taking up positions in the cabinet. Although the policies of the Den Uyl government are now widely criticized, it must be remembered that the electorate did not reject them at the time. Equally, although hardly anyone now believes in the feasibility of a government that can create a just society, the Den Uyl government managed to bring the income inequality down to a ratio between the top 20 per cent and bottom 20 per cent of 5:1.

The location of opposition to the government has recently changed somewhat in the Netherlands. The Green Left is interested in joining a coalition government in the near future and has therefore supported some of the government's policies whereas it would have been hesitant to strive for government participation in the past. A recent example is the intervention in Kosovo. Although pacifism and anti-imperialism were traditionally strong currents in the Green Left, the Green Party supported the intervention in Kosovo. The Socialist Party remains one place where people resisting policies such as the Kosovo intervention can find a home. This party started out as a hard-line Maoist party with a strong anti-feminist position. Now they have seven seats in the Second Chamber of Parliament and their support is growing. Another recent development is the growth of a small Christian party. This party draws some of its growing support from non-religious intellectual women who are concerned with the loss of norms and values in society.

Having sketched a few of the relevant historical and political circumstances for a critical evaluation of the recent changes in Dutch social democracy, the next section looks at the principles adhered to by the Dutch PvdA and focuses on a specific social policy model developed by the last two governments. The shift in the outlook of the social democratic PvdA coincides with a turn-around in Dutch social and economic policy. Whereas the PvdA is not the sole architect of what is commonly referred to in the literature as the Poldermodel, this new type of welfare regime combines some of the insights advocated by the social democrats. As the largest partner in the past two coalition governments, the PvdA played an important role in its development.

The Poldermodel

What is the Poldermodel? Its name refers to another uniquely Dutch endeavour: the creation of land out of water via elaborate engineering projects to build dykes and pump water out of the enclosed 'polder'. The concept of the Poldermodel has been defined in several ways. The narrowest description is as a model of economic and social policy mainly focused on wage restraint in return for job creation. In a slightly wider definition, the constructive negotiations between government, employers' organizations and trade unions over this trade-off are included as an important element. The widest understanding of the Poldermodel focuses mainly on this method of negotiating and applies it to other contexts than the socio-economic one. For example, the concept of a Green Poldermodel has been used to describe (potential) cooperative negotiation between the government, companies impacting on the environment and environmental pressure groups. In this conception of the Poldermodel cooperation in the health and education sectors (with their standing committees of stakeholders) are also examples of a Poldermodel since the method of cooperative negotiation is seen as the central element of the model. The widest definition of the Poldermodel is therefore a model of cooperation where stakeholders aim for agreement in order to prevent polarization and loss of time by entering into conflict.[18]

In this chapter I conceptualize the Poldermodel as the socio-economic model underlying the agreements between the government, the employers and organized labour to give absolute priority to reducing unemployment by accepting wage restraint in return for a reduction in the working week. Since the early 1980s all parties to the annual negotiations between the government, the employers and the unions have agreed on the priority of creating jobs over increased pay. Wage restraint was accepted by the trade unions as a 'responsible wage policy'. In return, they achieved a reduction in the working week through job sharing schemes. The two main characteristics of the Poldermodel are therefore the system of regular cooperation between the three main stakeholders and the consensus on the way forward towards economic growth and reduced unemployment. Any other uses of this system of negotiating could be seen as versions of a Poldermodel approach, but would not fall within the definition of the Poldermodel used here. By the same token, policies focused on the reduction of unemployment through wage-restraint would not add up to a Poldermodel if there were no system of regular corporatist negotiation in place.

Wage restraint should not be interpreted as cutting wages in the Netherlands. The wage demands of the unions up until the late 1990s were at least the level of inflation but they would not cash in on economic success. On the other hand, the government improved purchasing power by tax measures. More recently, with the return to economic growth, wage demands have been a little bit higher than before, but they are still lower than they could be so that there is room left to cut the working week and introduce job-sharing schemes. Most recently, the unions have made a claim for higher wages related to the higher growth figures. However, it is now less urgent to use wage restraints to enable investment in new jobs than it was previously, since economic growth has been at 4 per cent since 1999 and continues to rise.

The working week was cut from 38 hours a week in 1982 to 36 hours in 1993. Now almost 60 per cent of the working population work a 36 hour week in a collective agreement. The employers agreed to this in exchange for longer opening hours. Another part of the policy to reduce the working week is to promote part-time jobs. With many women going (back) to work, childcare has become more of a shared responsibility, and both men and women are looking for part-time jobs.[19]

The results of these policies were researched at the request of the then Minister of Social Affairs, Ad Melkert. He questioned the commonly held belief in Dutch political circles that social security and rough equality undermined the competitiveness of Dutch industries. The Department carried out a large benchmarking study and compared the Netherlands with Belgium, Germany, Denmark, Japan, the United States, the United Kingdom and Sweden. It showed that the Dutch model of social welfare was compatible with good economic growth and a good international position for Dutch business. The study showed that 1) the percentage of inactives (as a percentage of the amount of working people) had decreased fastest in the Netherlands since 1985; 2) expenditure on social welfare in the Netherlands has grown much slower than elsewhere; 3) employment is growing faster in the Netherlands than in the United States, although the Dutch still maintain a model of social protection; and 4) unemployment among lower educated groups is higher in the United Kingdom and United States than in the Netherlands.[20]

The Poldermodel is, therefore, seen as an example of successful social policy. Its results are an improvement in economic performance (for three years all indicators show that the Netherlands performs better than its neighbouring countries); impressive job growth (between 1994 and 1998 over half a million jobs were created); reduced unemployment levels (unemployment in 1998 was at the level of 1981, although many predicted that economic recovery would not bring new jobs); and there is a growing confidence in the future (a lot of people increased their mortgages on their houses over the last year, which resulted in spending and investing the money).[21]

So is there a new social democratic model being discovered in the Netherlands? Is it the social democratic coalition with the Liberals that is behind the success of the Poldermodel? The answer is both yes and no. On the one hand, the historically embedded institutions for cooperation between trade unions and employers' organizations had facilitated an agreement on wage reductions in 1982 – the so-called Wassenaar agreement. However, the neoliberal Christian Democrat coalition government with the Liberal party then unilaterally reduced income even further. A new element in the social democratic social policy is the emphasis on lower taxes and premiums that help to keep the spending power of working people at a decent level.

However, there are some major differences between 'traditional' social democratic social policies and the Poldermodel. These are mainly related to a change in underlying principles and understanding of equality. In the early 1970s large transfers of money and goods beyond the safety net as part of the social democratic welfare regime fitted in with the political philosophy called welfare egalitarianism. The recent emphasis on decent social assistance, access to paid employment for the unemployed and the fight against social benefit fraud fits in with the political philosophy of threshold egalitarianism.[22]

In a recent report by the influential and prestigious government advising body WRR, it is stated that the government ought to aim to 'preserve a decency threshold of social security so that equal opportunities are approximated with achieving outcomes that are said to matter crucially to people's well-being and agency, mainly income and access to the immaterial benefits of paid work.'[23] The underlying considerations are not only the overall goal of social justice, but equally the need for economic growth when the population is ageing and international competition is increasing due to technological changes. The economic growth required to maintain adequate benefit levels therefore requires increasing labour participation.

The economic success of the Poldermodel is based on a combination of the specific social and economic policies of the Purple coalition and the previous neoliberal governments and the institutional corporatism the Netherlands has experienced since the end of the Second World War. Some observers even see the roots of the Poldermodel in the Republic of

the Seven Provinces, when there was a culture of cooperation and con-
sensus-building between policy makers.

The institutions governing social and economic policy in the Netherlands play an important role in the success of the Poldermodel. First of
all, there is a fundamental trust between the major players in the system
and they have built a consensus on the main issues they have to address.
Second, the government appreciates that for successful social and economic policy to be reached, cooperation of the employers and the
unions is crucial. Third, in Dutch industrial relations, two institutions
play an important role: the Social-Economic Council and the Foundation of Labour. In the Social Economic Council, 11 members are
appointed by the government, 11 by employers' organizations and 11
by the trade unions. The Council meets nearly once a month in plenary
session and advises the government on socio-economic topics. The
Labour Foundation consists only of employers and trade unions and is
an advisory body to the government and formulates recommendations
to the collective bargaining process in several industries and companies.
These institutions force the key actors to meet each other frequently in
formal and informal sessions. It is therefore easier to arrive at consensus
and avoid confrontational strategies by either the trade unions or the
employers' organizations.

Cooperation, compromise and consensus building can be seen as
lasting ingredients in the history of Dutch politics. They are regarded
as valuable in contemporary political theory as well as in the Dutch
political culture. De Beus argues, for example, that 'The left should live
up to its egalitarian ideal and it should influence consensus in the real
world as much as it can, yet it should never abolish consensus and
replace it by socialist utopia.'[24] In practical politics the emphasis on
consensus building comes to the fore in the attitude of parties after
electoral victory:

> For example, Dutch social democrats do not impose equality after
> victory in general elections nor do they cancel all measures of right
> wing governments. Instead, they try to articulate an egalitarian mood
> in the ever-changing middle of Dutch society and politics.[25]

Other parties have shown the same restraint when dominating parliament or a coalition government. In some ways this can be seen as a
product of the Calvinist attitude to life, holding that one always needs
to be prepared for future bad luck. So, in case one loses the next elections, one should not force others to reverse their policies because they

may do the same with yours at a later date. Another explanation for the existence of this commitment to consensus is the fact that in the Dutch political system a single party has never had an absolute majority. The largest party is never large enough to dictate its policies to others. The system of coalition governments is another factor that requires careful political compromise. Even the smallest coalition partner can bring a government down if it does not agree with policies implemented by the largest partner. Political parties in the Netherlands understand these dynamics and see it as in their interest to reach agreement rather than let disagreement block policy-making. An early example of this is the so-called 'pacification' in 1917. This was a deal between the liberals and the Christian parties, which brought both sides something they had wanted for a long time. The liberals got consent for the implementation of universal suffrage whereas the Catholics and the Protestants secured the right to equal funding of all schools guaranteed by the 1917 constitution.[26]

An important question for the assessment of the shift in social democratic politics in the Netherlands is whether or not globalization has forced a move to the right. The Minister of Social Affairs Melkert also instigated a research project on globalization and integration in the European context. The research questions were: does the internationalization of the economy automatically mean that the government should and could do less in terms of employment policy and social policy? And does the free flow of goods and capital in Europe necessarily mean letting go of social securities? The answer was that this is not the case at all. Internationalization was seen as good for the economy, but people with low levels of education and low productivity are threatened with social exclusion. So the government is needed more than ever to protect these people, for example, by lowering specific taxes and premiums, which make labour at the lower levels of productivity cheaper. And the government should create extra jobs, especially for those socially excluded at the bottom of society. The researchers also found that in countries where government and social partners react in harmony to economic shocks, the economy does better and so does employment.[27]

However, the story of the Poldermodel is not as harmonious as it seems. Within the PvdA there is modest to harsh criticism of the deconstruction of the welfare state in coalition with the liberals. According to some influential party members the social democrats are getting too close for comfort to the neoliberal economic policies of the liberals. Within the PvdA attitudes towards the market and a capitalist economy have changed. They are no longer seen as a necessary evil, but are actively embraced. The dominant view in the PvdA holds that economic competition and social justice are compatible. Redistribution of income is seen as less important than a strict economic policy that will enhance economic growth. This is then seen as trickling down to everyone in the economy. Problems remaining are, of course, how to avoid creating an underclass to which the wealth of the economy does not trickle down automatically:

> It is generally agreed, however, that Dutch social democracy recon-
> quered its position as 'natural government party' at the expense of
> ... reversal of protracting levelling of income and wealth and a
> return to the level of inequality of the early 1970's. At the same
> time it should be noted that the PvdA is quite militant and consistent
> in its rejection of draconic policies of austerity and exclusion. It
> champions multi-ethnic tolerance, equality of opportunity and Euro-
> pean solidarity.[28]

Within the Partij van de Arbeid there is a new way of thinking about the relation between state and market and the connections between government and business. Former minister Melkert wants to use the market to implement social security policy – i.e. amendment of the traditional corporatist set-up of quangos implementing social security policy. In his eyes whoever can show that social investment is economically beneficial can create alliances, which give the Netherlands a chance to realise its social policies step by step. Melkert believes that cooperation between government and business is not a corruption of the social democratic government, but is a prudent move to create deals, which are beneficial for everyone involved. For example, increased productivity must lead to improved social and economic rights for the workers; or lower social premiums can be exchanged for more jobs. On the other hand, Melkert is also the person who wants to convince the middle classes created by the success of the welfare state of the duties of citizenship. He introduced jobs named after him, which integrate more people into society and increase employment opportunities especially in education, childcare, care for the elderly, hospitals and safety on the streets. Melkert's vision of the society of the near future is one in which people mix periods of paid employment with periods of mainly care for others and combine this with life-long learning. This means there will be a redistribution of care within families, and policies need to be in place to make it possible to interrupt careers without severe consequences in terms of promotion or loss of pension rights.

Social democrats are going through a period of rethinking, brought about by the trauma of neoliberal governments worldwide and by the necessity of adjusting to globalization. It is too easy to call the changes in policy and principle, which are a result of this rethinking, a move to the Right. However, as in every period of change, a lot of debate is about what the underlying principles of the movement are, and new ways of looking at the relationship between state and market are disputed by people who want to hold on to the security of the principles they have always held dear. An important new element is the extent of economic globalization and the power of multinational corporations. Social democracy in the Netherlands will need to look into how they see the role of the state develop in this new era.

If globalization is seen as an economic process that is technologically driven, then the Netherlands may have to respond in the same way as other countries and the options for a national government to regulate the market or compensate for the harshest market outcomes may be limited, whether or not the government social democratic. However, there are at least two counter-arguments to be made here. First, the Netherlands is a transporting economy and therefore open to outside influences. In certain respects economic policy (exchange rates, interest rates, and so on) always had to respond to the larger economies in Europe, especially Germany as the Netherlands' largest trade partner. This did not prevent social democratic governments from implementing redistributive policies. Second, globalization can be seen as politically driven and focused not solely on trade liberalization but also on the regulation of international politics, such as institutions to create more international cooperation, development and respect for human rights.[29] The Netherlands has always seen this as a positive development in international politics and has managed to follow its own path as a welfare state and play a role in international diplomacy. Although a small country, its historic role in the development of international law since the sixteenth century allows the Netherlands to play a larger role in the international community than its size warrants.

Critics of the social democratic shift and the latest response

Although the tripartite corporatism and the historic emphasis on consensus and cooperation have influenced the Poldermodel, there is opposition both within and outside the PvdA to the present social policy.

Critics have focused on two main problems: first, exclusion from the economic benefits of the Poldermodel and lack of concern for real equality; and second, the lack of attention to environmental issues. In addition, the success of the Poldermodel has partly undermined itself. With present levels of economic growth, the unions are less willing to make sacrifices in terms of income.

Members of the scientific bureau of the PvdA, the Wiardi Beckman Stichting (WBS), propose seven amendments to the Poldermodel. They are listed in more detail in the box. Their main concerns are to bring in 1) more international solidarity, 2) a less 'macro' and more 'micro' approach to investment, 3) the incorporation of a labour market policy within an overall anti-poverty and social inclusion strategy, 4) the incorporation of environmental concerns, 5) the inclusion of non-material concerns, 6) more use of high incomes for public goods, and 7) an agenda for democratic renewal into the Poldermodel. In some ways their proposals go beyond amendments and would be better classified as alternatives to the Poldermodel. The idea of a negative income tax, for example, is diametrically opposed to the labour ethic, which lies behind the present 'jobs, jobs, jobs' approach. In the overview of some of the main criticisms, it will be clear that some of the concerns addressed in the seven amendments are quite widely shared, especially the need to get the mix between labour market participation policies and income supporting policies tuned into concerns for a social underclass and the emphasis on environmental concerns are central to the debate on the future of social policy in the Netherlands.

In this chapter I focus on the concern for growing inequality rather than on the environmental concern. This is due to my decision to concentrate on the social policies in the Poldermodel and the lack of space to cover both in enough depth. Very briefly, the current debate on the Poldermodel and the environment centres on the notion of a Green Poldermodel. Prime Minister Wim Kok has proposed such a model, which would include investment in infrastructure from a green perspective. Yet he emphasizes that sustainability is attractive in a period of economic growth, but is unattractive to many voters when it limits economic possibilities.[30] Environmental groups are therefore sceptical of the real meaning of the Green Poldermodel. Since the leader of the PvdA has clearly indicated that it is important to him that the voters are not willing to give up economic wealth for environmental concern, then a Green Poldermodel may not be in a position to get much support from environmental groups. The Poldermodel is deeply rooted in the

1. Rich behind the dykes?
International cooperation is not a luxury but a necessity. Welfare, freedom and democracy are not universally realized and to change this situation should be one of the important goals of social democracy–if not the most important.

2. From macro to micro
Mega-investments in the physical infrastructure are not the best way to strengthen the Dutch economy in the long run. The emphasis should be on a more long-term, less macroeconomic policy aimed at the encouragement of innovative business culture (technologically and organizationally) with respect for the social and cultural environment in which innovation can flourish.

3. Not for work alone
Labour market policy needs a better focus and better balance. It should be embedded in a more general policy of fighting poverty and exclusion, with social renewal and a just income policy as important components. It should encourage individual initiative and freedom of choice of the unemployed, and existing regulations should be scrutinized for limiting participation. A negative income tax could help in this respect.

4. The environment as criterion
Protection of the environment requires a gradual but radical change in our methods of production and consumption. Politics has to make clear the costs and benefits of such a change; confront the settled interests; and be clear about their position that the environment is worth a little bit less growth.

5. Beyond economism
The current debates on the future of our country are focused solely on economic factors. Social, cultural and spatial factors should receive more emphasis and should be judged on their own merits. Not only the material but also the cultural development of people deserves attention and support.

6. What to do with growing resources?
In a civilized society part of income and profit should be spent on collective goods. But the margins for top slicing are too small. A combination of fiscal incentives and social pressure will help to limit excessive incomes and stimulate the use of private capital for public ends.

7. An agenda for democratic renewal
Changing social circumstances (independent citizens, new centres of decision-making, interwoven private and public sphere) demand renewal of democracy. This means better access to political decision-making, a responsive government, and new forms of control and debate. The Poldermodel of consultation and discussion is in need of an overhaul.

Source: Paul Kalma and Frans Becker, *Zeven Amendementen op het veelbezongen Poldermodel* (http://www.pvda.nl/partij/neven/wbs/vpr.html).

new social democratic embrace of the market and a capitalist economy as engines of growth. A reduced growth strategy is not easily seen as an amendment to it.

Critics often agree with some of the reasoning behind abandoning the old welfare state model. Kalma, for example, argues that the welfare state contained too much welfare and too much state. Yet, he argues, the Poldermodel is throwing out the baby with the bathwater. This is not wise for two main reasons. First, the strengthening of the new economy and the weakening of postwar social capitalism pose questions of inequality with renewed urgency. Second, the underlying assumption of progress is still present in New Labour thinking which means that present day politics will have to deal with the dark side of this progress: environmental degradation. So instead of moving away altogether from the social democratic tradition, Kalma argues for a clear commitment to a compromise between capital and labour. This is the traditional position of social democracy since the 1950s and there is no reason to reject it now. However, the contemporary developments in capitalism require new forms of democratic influence and control, and a much higher priority for both social justice and environmental concerns on the social democratic agenda.[31]

The shift away from income redistribution has also been criticized. De Beer specifically focuses on income policies related to the two competing models of social policy adhered to by social democrats in the 1970s and the 1980s–1990s. In the latter period the emphasis of government policy was on creating economic growth and jobs, not on redistribution of income. Social security transfers fell behind the rising incomes of working people and therefore income inequality increased. At last it is recognized that poverty exists in the Netherlands and the level of social transfers is once again linked to salaries and wages. Worries are mounting about some groups in society being left behind whilst others are getting richer.[32]

De Beer is critical of the widespread belief that the main goal of social policy should be participation in the labour market. He argues for revaluing the two traditional instruments of social policy: a progressive income tax and a generous scheme of social transfers.[33] According to De Beer, governments are influential when they actively seek to keep inequality to an acceptable level. He denies the existence of a trade off between social justice and economic efficiency. In his analysis both can only be judged together, since a criterion based on equality only makes no sense (equally poor) nor does a criterion of social policy only based on overall welfare (no limits on minimum or differences).

Finally, de Beer argues that the focus on resources (education, employment) instead of outcomes (income) needs to be rethought. Paradoxically participation in paid employment has increased in the Netherlands between 1984 (48 per cent of 15–64 year olds) and 1998 (62 per cent). Yet at the same time, the part of the total population dependent on social transfers remained the same (25 per cent).[34] Moreover, the number of households dependent on social transfers has increased by a quarter of a million. The explanation de Beer provides for this paradox is that the people who found work were part of a household where someone else was already working in paid employment. New jobs are often taken by women who left work in order to look after children and are now coming back into the labour market and by people who are in school or who have just finished school and students.

Academics, unionists and the circles around the Green Party share the criticism that the approach to social policy of the late 1990s was too focused on participation in paid work, especially the requirement to find paid employment for the 'hard cases' of people with few marketable skills and who may have been out of work for long periods of time. In the long run social integration as well as economic efficiency may be better served by providing general incentives for those people. Examples of such incentives are a partial basic income, participation income and taxbreaks.[35]

Another criticism of the Poldermodel is that it enhances modernization processes that create new forms of division in society. In education there is more attention on individuality, yet the numbers of children attending special schools is increasing. In industry a lot is demanded from employees and productivity has increased, yet there are large numbers of people who are in need of social security since they do not satisfy the criteria of the modern labour market. In healthcare, there is more attention on the individual needs of patients, yet there is more care available for people with the money to pay for it. In housing the proportion of houses for sale is increasing, yet the quality of cheaper rental accommodation is worsening. The current trends are not only accompanied by burdens but those burdens are distributed unequally (van den Brink 1999). Van den Brink also argues that the role of the government is relevant to these processes. The government can still block the modernization of certain sectors, such as the development of 24-hour economy or commercial TV. It can also try to regulate and direct the modernization process, or it can compensate for the negative effects, or it can encourage modernization. With a better understanding of what is happening there is a definite role for social democracy, according to van den Brink.[36]

A central question raised in the introduction to this chapter was whether social democracy in the Netherlands is taking the sociological changes seriously enough to revise and introduce policy. Generally speaking, a lot has changed recently in terms of individualization of taxation and assessment of eligibility for benefits. In housing, too, the government has taken into account that the number of single households is increasing, and this needs to be reflected in strategies for building new properties. The government has also responded to increased demand for accommodation suitable for communal living. New types of families with children living with one of their parents and a new co-parent are taken into account in the general culture of schools writing to invite parents or carers to meetings with teachers.

The next question posed was whether a social democratic strategy of government should include measures to counteract negative consequences of sociological changes. In short, the government should reflect on which effects of people's choices are harmful and which are not. For example, people's move away from traditional authority and organizations like the church is not harmful as long as they find alternative means of associating with others. This option should be open to people with little financial resources, too. A government aim should be to encourage and subsidize social cohesion and participation in order to prevent isolation and social exclusion. It should reflect, too, on the causes of people's choices. Some of the cultural and sociological changes are induced by changes in the economic structure and can be seen as a personal choice only to a certain degree. Migration within and between countries has a severe effect on family life and social integration. The government should be aware of the options open to people and aim to increase the options for people to find meaningful work or other forms of inclusion in their own community.

Since these initiatives by a social democratic government are considered to be desirable, is there evidence that the government can influence these trends effectively? It is possible for the government to shape the process of change, but is the current government doing so effectively? The current trend of the social democratic government is to view most of people's lifestyle choices as a matter of personal preference. In my opinion there is room for more reflection on what the government can do to contribute to people's well-being and social inclusion.

Others argue, too, that the current social policy model is leading to the increasing social exclusion of specific groups of people. De Beus argues that the Poldermodel is excluding those out of work, and that long-term unemployment and youth unemployment, especially among second- and third-generation immigrant families, remain high.[37] Again, there needs to be more strategic thinking about how to avoid social exclusion and enhance the integration of ethnic minorities, young people and people with low skills.

Some fear that real competition is lacking in many sectors of the economy. There is a danger of 'complotting' of market parties against citizens and government. One Member of Parliament recently presented an example of this, which is quoted by a critical journalist in *de Volks-krant*. Before a part of dental treatment was taken out of the national health service, it cost 500 million guilders a year. Now it costs more than 1.2 billion guilders a year.[38]

Summarizing, the critics of the Poldermodel have focused on several main issues. A key criticism made by several authors is that specific groups are excluded from the economic benefits of the Poldermodel. Therefore it is doubted that the Poldermodel can include a concern for the right type of equality. In this context, there are also complaints that there is no longer enough use made of traditional measures, such as a progressive income tax and direct redistribution of income. Here one could argue that there is a shift to more neoliberal policies such as creating equality of opportunity through strategies to encourage training. Clearly, recent changes in social democratic ideology have embraced global capitalism as a motor for social progress. Although there is still explicit adherence to the aim of social justice within a capitalist system, the means by which this can be achieved are more closely linked to neoliberal, trickle-down theories. In addition, the lack of attention for environmental issues is heavily criticized. Social democracy in the Netherlands is still holding on to a model of economic growth and does not prioritize the need for radical restructuring our collective lifestyles in order to preserve non-renewable resources for future generations. Moreover, the recent sociological trend towards post-materialist values has not been incorporated in government policy. Finally, the success of the Poldermodel has partly undermined itself. With present levels of economic growth, the unions are less willing to make sacrifices in terms of income.

The most recent statement of the principles social democrats in the Netherlands stand for has been published in the draft programme of principles.[39] In this document the PvdA responds to some of its critics by putting more emphasis on international solidarity and by warning of the risk of unlimited capitalism. It also calls for the wider inclusion in the Poldermodel arenas of negotiation of groups presently excluded, such as ecological groups. However, the section on environmental problems remains within the PvdA's paradigm of requiring environmental degradation to be paid for by the responsible party. The PvdA is not prepared to sacrifice economic growth for more drastic measures to preserve the environment, even though one of its principles is for each generation to leave the earth in a better state (economically and ecologically) than they found it.

The calls from critics for more traditional forms of redistribution and for the inclusion of ethnic minorities are not explicitly addressed in the new programme. Extreme income disparities are rejected, but no ratios are given for the party to work towards. In terms of the work ethic, the PvdA still holds that paid employment creates the best chances for economic independence. Generally speaking, the document leaves many dilemmas unresolved. One example is that of calling for a multicultural society with acceptable levels of income inequality and the support for the capitalist free market economy. By supporting both, the problem of social exclusion is not addressed appropriately. Another example is the commitment to economic growth and protection of the environment. The programme does not prioritize or defend a balance between those two. The most important criticisms of the Poldermodel are therefore not adequately addressed in the latest document of the PvdA.

European social democracy

In this final section the question is whether the shift in Dutch social democracy in response to globalization and neoliberalism was roughly the same as in Britain and other European countries. In some respects the experience of social democracy in the Netherlands is different. The PvdA shifted away from its traditional view on welfare politics earlier than the UK for example. In the Netherlands the shift took place in response to several factors. In common with other European countries the Netherlands had to adjust to European integration and globalization. And in common with most European countries it also needed to deal with the changes in society, such as modernization and ageing. All western industrialized countries had to find new policies and electoral strategies to handle the increase in numbers of middle class people, the increased individualization of society and the diminishing authority of government and other institutions, such as the churches and unions.[40] Uniquely Dutch were the problems of the 'welfare without work' model of social policy, later referred to as the 'Dutch disease'. Therborn called the Netherlands 'perhaps the most spectacular employment failure in the advanced capitalist world' and with unemployment reaching record levels of almost 14 per cent in 1983 and an almost equal number of workers on disability benefit and in early retirement, this was no unfair judgement.[41] However, also unique to the Dutch is the complete turn around in economic and social indicators in the 15 years since then. Now the Dutch case draws attention for combining unemployment levels of 6.2 per cent with a real GDP growth rate of 2.2 per cent between 1991 and 1996.[42]

Historically, Dutch social democrats had already moved beyond the confrontational attitude towards capital and away from nationalization before the most recent shift. In the 1930s the predecessor of the PvdA, the SDAP, acknowledged capitalism as a force for economic growth and proposed a compromise between labour and capital. An additional difference with the UK, for example, is that the position from which the Dutch social democracy shifted towards more liberal, market-oriented economic policies was from an egalitarian welfare state. During the 1970s the PvdA's ideal ratio between lowest and highest incomes of 5:1 was achieved.[43]

Let us now turn to the question of how Dutch social democrats see developments in Europe. Do they believe in a European social democracy? Interestingly enough, the election of Schröder in Germany and the historical Red–Green coalition, invited some fearful responses from the Netherlands. Whereas Tony Blair reacted enthusiastically, the Dutch prime minister merely sent a telegram of congratulations. However, one commentator holds that the Dutch need not be pessimistic about changes in Germany.[44] He finds it remarkable that something like a European public opinion has developed that has brought social democrats to power in several countries. And the Dutch misgivings about Schröder are based only on the fear that a Red–Green coalition may become reality in the Netherlands, too, according to Roelofs. It is well known that the prime minister does not like that model.

What about the European possibilities for a Poldermodel? In the European context, the Dutch model is seen as a way of fulfilling the criteria for monetary union. The struggle between employers' organizations and trade unions in many countries has delayed meeting the criteria of the Maastricht Treaty. However, Lodewijk de Waal, President of the Dutch Trade Union Federation FNV, holds that it is unlikely that other countries could adopt the Poldermodel successfully. The reason for this pessimistic view is that other European countries lack the institutional corporatist structure the Netherland enjoys. He advises other trade unions to negotiate with employers and government instead of going for a confrontational strategy.[45]

Jos de Beus likewise warns against the direct application of the Dutch model in Europe. The Netherlands was successful precisely because the rest of Europe did not pursue the same policies. Wage reductions mean setting limits to domestic expenditure. The Netherlands could only avoid a recession in the economy, because exports were buoyant. If the rest of Europe limits the spending power of employees, then the whole of Europe will hit a recession.[46]

Two things can be said in response to de Beus. A world-wide recession may be on its way independently and European governments need to react swiftly to that. The social policy the Netherlands has implemented since the last recession may be of help to other countries, too. Second, people's spending power was not reduced under the Poldermodel, because of the lower taxes and premiums for collective insurance. On top of that the model of sharing childcare and sharing paid employment meant that more families had two earners, both working for around four days a week.

Others are more positive about adopting the Dutch example. According to Visser and Hemerijck, lessons can be learned from the 'Dutch Miracle', although they would not want to say that there is a model to be followed. In contrast to the generally negative conclusions on the future of welfare states in Europe, they argue that the experience of the Netherlands shows that through negotiated social policy reform modernization of the welfare state is possible. 'That this has been possible in the Netherlands is significant, because the Dutch welfare state is a specimen of the Bismarckian, continental, corporatist, breadwinner, hence antiquated and compensatory welfare state regimes-the hardest to change of them all.'[47] Crucial ingredients of the successful reform of social policy in the Netherlands were the combination of wage restraint, a focus on labour market participation, as well as a balance between paid and unpaid work, societal consensus and a strong state.

However, critics of the Poldermodel in the Netherlands have something relevant to say in the European context, too. If it is true that Dutch labour market policies have practically created an excluded underclass of unemployed and if this affects the children and grandchildren of immigrants disproportionately, then this could potentially create even more serious problems on a European scale. In addition, the European policies for creating sustainable ways of life are in general far behind the policies in place in the Netherlands or Germany. The critics of the social democratic vision on greening the economy have even more to worry about in the European context. The question is therefore not only whether or not the Dutch model can be repeated on a European scale, but also whether or not it is desirable to do so.

A more socially just Europe is certainly desirable and a more environmentally friendly Europe, too. Even though sceptical about the possibilities of success of a European Poldermodel, Jos de Beus does argue for a more social Europe. He argues for a social pact in Europe to replace any existing regulation in the EU. Such a pact should look like a social constitution for Europe and should replace the existing treaties of Rome and Amsterdam. From 1999 the socialists should actively seek the guarantee of social security of all European citizens in the Economic and Monetary Union. According to de Beus, '[s]ecurity for all citizens increases their willingness to compete in the world market and to accept the risk that is connected to that. Openness of markets increases wealth and creates the surplus needed to create more safety for those citizens at the bottom of society.'[48]

Some argue that there is a convergence between the social democratic parties in Europe already. This is not so much due to their cooperation as to their common response to globalization. The defence of social rights and the quality of public life in a global capitalism is a historical mission, according to Sassoon, that can only be executed well in a European context. The future of social democracy depends on the success or failure of the European Union, according to him.[49]

However, there are still several differences between the respective European social democratic parties. One example is that New Labour emphasizes at least in some of its writings the value of the family and the role of communities, whereas the Dutch PvdA aims to create new types of workplaces and careers that fit in with recent trends towards individualization and liberalization. People will be able to choose a combination of work, education and care in a way that suits their individual needs over a lifetime. The French in their contribution to the Congress of Socialist International in November 1999 made it clear that they hold on to a strong role for the government in regulating the effects of global capitalism and supporting national industries suffering from competition in the global marketplace. In France Keynesianism does not have the bad press it has, for example, in the Netherlands and the UK. Within the Dutch Partij van de Arbeid there is also a growing number of voices that are critical with respect to the much hailed reliance on market forces to deliver care and other social policy objectives. Although there are some critics of privatization in the UK, the overall agenda seems to be towards more involvement of private actors rather than less.

In this context of a wide variety of perspectives within European social democratic parties a truly European social democracy is still largely a fiction. In various countries in Europe social democracy is in transition, but this transition does not (yet) have a common European character. In addition, the attitude towards European integration as a whole, differs widely between the major countries on the continent and the UK. The recent suggestion of creating a European passport invited an overwhelmingly negative response on the part of the British. The idea that the national logo would no longer be on their passport seemed unattractive to most of the British. To imagine a European social democratic unity in the context of British Euroscepticism throughout the political spectrum constitutes science fiction rather than utopianism. Even if politicians may be a little ahead of their troops, if they move too far out of sight, they will not be able to realize their objectives.

Conclusions

The processes of globalization, European integration and modernization form a set of common factors European social democrats have had to respond to. It is no coincidence that the debate on which principles and policies should guide social democracy in the twenty-first century is happening all over Europe and in the US at the same time. In this new era the challenges to social democratic parties are very similar in many respects. The central challenge for Dutch social democracy seems to be to find the right combination of sound economic, effective ecological and just social policies.[50] I would argue that the same is true for other (European) social democratic traditions.

Yet, there are differences between countries in political history and culture that are highly relevant to the feasibility of certain policies in other countries. The Netherlands has an historical political culture of compromise and consensus building. Special institutions exist for cooperation and policy-making in which the government and the social partners (employers and unions) are equally represented. The welfare model the Dutch constructed in the 1960s and 1970s may have led to a deep crisis in the 1980s but it did provide a strong basis to start reforms from. It restricted inequalities of income to a ratio of 5:1 and it put in place social security above minimum levels. It is not advisable to export the Poldermodel beyond the context for which it was gradually developed by different actors in the Netherlands over at least the past 15 years. Moreover, within the Dutch context the debate is still going on. Critics of the Poldermodel have emphasized the social exclusion of mainly unskilled people, the lack of vision on environmental degradation, the need for proper levels of social security for those out of work, the need for redistribution of income and the dangers of relying on market forces in providing social care. Moreover, recently the unions have not been so flexible anymore now that the economy is growing faster.

The positive side of the Poldermodel is, of course, that it has managed to return economic growth with growing employment opportunities. The fact that most jobs are part-time and temporary may be a disadvantage from the position of the traditional breadwinner model, but in terms of supporting a more equal share between members of households of paid employment and care the social democratic policies look promising. Another potentially revolutionary change is the emphasis on life long learning and more flexible secondary education.

However, the proof of the pudding is in the eating. Some of the important challenges for the government are the accommodation of the main critics of the Poldermodel and the practical implementation of its policies. The promise of part-time jobs for everyone and shared responsibilities in taking care of children, elderly and household tasks, has not been fulfilled yet. And the groups of people who are structurally out of paid work need to be included in one of three ways: help with getting the skills needed to participate; adequate social security benefits if the former is not possible; and social inclusion by being recognized through other activities than paid work. The interpretation of equality as equality of opportunity runs the risk of blaming the victim: if people do not have the skills needed for inclusion in the global economy they deserve to be poor since everyone had equal chances. As long as truly equal chances are clearly not realized, this is a dangerous road to follow. The latest documents published by the PvdA do not look hopeful in addressing the points raised by critics.

Finally, I agree with Becker and Cuperus when they hold that '[t]he most pressing issue is now to create credible cohesion between programme and policy.'[51] An important aim for Dutch social democracy should be to combine a debate on just principles, the design of feasible policies to realise those principles and the effective implementation of their programme. The Dutch tradition of open public debate will hopefully be of help to create the most sensible responses of social democracy in the Netherlands to the challenges of globalization, European integration, (post-) modernization and an ageing population. Economic prosperity may assist the government in prioritising policies for socially excluded groups and care of the environment.

Notes

1   I am grateful to Peppe van den Anker, Vera van den Anker, Luke Martell, Neil Stammers, Jos de Beus, Huib Pellikaan and Ian Gough for their help.
2   The meaning of globalization is contested. For critical discussions, see M. Shaw, *Politics and Globalization* (London: Routledge, 1999); and J. Rosenberg, *The Follies of Globalisation Theory* (London: Verso, 2000).
3   This is emphasised for example in the new draft-principles of the PvdA as published on 2 November 2000.
4   The most famous advocate of the triumph of liberalism is Francis Fukuyama, *The End of History and the Last Man* (London: Hamish Hamilton, 1992).
5   Sawitri Saharso, 'Women's Right of Choice?! A Reflection on Women's Rights, Cultural Toleration and Public Morality', *Acta Politica*, 34 (1999), 331–50.
6   For an interesting selection of views on social democracy and Europe, see René Cuperus and Johannes Kandel, *European Social Democracy. Transformation in Progress. Social Democratic Think Tanks Explore the Magical Return of Social Democracy in a Liberal Era* (Amsterdam: Friedrich Ebert Stiftung and Wiardi Beckman Stichting, 1998).
7   For the full text of the document (in Dutch) see the web page of the PvdA at http://www.pvda.nl.
8   The term 'transformation in progress' is used as the central organizing concept in R. Cuperus and J. Kandel, *European Social Democracy. Transformation in Progress. Social Democratic Think Tanks Explore the Magical Return of Social Democracy in a Liberal Era* (Amsterdam: Friedrich Ebert Stiftung and Wiardi Beckman Stichting, 1998).
9   G. Esping-Andersen, 'Social Theory in Democracy and Practice', in G. Esping-Andersen, *Politics against Markets* (Princeton, NJ: Princeton University Press, 1985), 3–38, p. 3.
10   Ibid., 8.
11   K. van Kersbergen, 'The Dutch Labour Party', in R. Ladrech and Ph. Marliere *Social Democratic Parties in the European Union. History, Organization, Policies* (Basingstoke: Macmillan, 1999), 155–65, p. 156.
12   Ibid.
13   For an analysis of Dutch politics and 'Pillarization' see A. Lijphart, *The Politics of Accommodation. Pluralism, and Democracy in the Netherlands* (Berkeley: University of California Press, 1968); and A. Lijphart *Verzuiling, Pacificatie en Kentering in de Nederlandse Politiek*, (Amsterdam: De Bussy, 1982).
14   Kersbergen, 'The Dutch Labour Party'.
15   J. Visser and A. Hemerijck, *'A Dutch Miracle'. Job Growth, Welfare Reform and Corporatism in the Netherlands* (Amsterdam: Amsterdam University Press, 1997).
16   Kersbergen 'The Dutch Labour Party', 164.
17   Ibid., 157.
18   I am grateful to Vera van den Anker for her help in developing the distinction between narrow and wide conceptions of the Poldermodel and to Luke Martell for his demand for clarification on this point.

19   L. de Waal, *Presentation at Siemens*, The Hague, 14 July 1998. Found at http://www.fnv.nl/~toespraak/1998/14–7–98pmodel.html.
20   Ibid.
21   Ibid.
22   J. de Beus, 'The Politics of Consensual Well-being: the Dutch Left Greets the Twenty-first century', in G. Kelly, *The New European Left* (London: Fabian Society, 1999).
23   R. J. van der Veen, 'Participate or Sink: Threshold Equality behind the Dykes', *Acta Politica*, 34 (1999) 351–81, p. 353.
24   de Beus, 'The Politics of Consensual Well-being'.
25   Ibid.
26   D. Mentink and F. Goudappel, 'Religion and the State: A Dutch Case in the Field of Education' Erasmus University Rotterdam/University of Utrecht, found at: *http://www.eur.nl/frg/iacl/papers/mentgoud/html* on 7 July 2000.
27   M. de Rijk, 'Het Land van Paars: het Poldermodel', in *de Groene*, Amsterdam: 5 March 1997.
28   de Beus, 'The Politics of Consensual Well-being: the Dutch Left Greets the Twenty-first Century'.
29   M. Shaw (ed.), *Politics and Globalisation. Knowledge, Ethics and Agency* (London: Routledge, 1999).
30   Y. Albrecht and O. Garschagen, 'Wim Kok: een regisseur op zoek naar zijn script', in *Vrij Nederland* (17 July 1999), 10–13: p.13.
31   P. Kalma, 'Kapitalisme op drift, of: wat de derde weg onbesproken laat', in F. Becker, W. van Hennekeler and B. Tromp, *Hedendaags Kapitalisme. Het Twintigste Jaarboek voor het democratisch socialisme* (Amsterdam: Wiardi Beckman Stichting, 1999), 207–31.
32   P. de Beer, 'Misvattingen en taboes van het inkomensbeleid', in F. Becker, W. van Hennekeler and B. Tromp, *Hedendaags Kapitalisme. Twintigste Jaarboek voor het Democratisch Socialisme* (Amsterdam: Wiardi Beckman Stichting/De Arbeiderspers, 1999), 144–80, p. 149.
33   Ibid., 46.
34   Ibid., 169–70.
35   R. J. van der Veen, 'Participate or Sink: Threshold Equality behind the Dykes', *Acta Politica*, 34 (1999), 351–81.
36   G. van den Brink, 'De modernisering van Nederland en haar dubbelzinnige gevolgen', *Socialisme en Democratie*, 56 (1999), 548–57, p. 557.
37   de Beus, 'The Politics of Consensual Well-being: the Dutch Left Greets the Twenty-first Century'.
38   A. Koper, 'Gevaarlijk Conformisme', *de Volkskrant* (28 March 1998).
39   *http://pvda.nl/hot/02112000beginsel.tpl*
40   van den Brink, 'De modernisering van Nederland en haar dubbelzinnige gevolgen'.
41   Visser and Hemerijck, '*A Dutch Miracle*'.
42   Ibid.
43   P. de Beer, 'Misvattingen en taboes van het inkomensbeleid', in F. Becker, W. van Hennekeler and B. Tromp *Hedendaags Kapitalisme. Twintigste Jaarboek voor het Democratisch Socialisme* (Amsterdam: Wiardi Beckman Stichting/De Arbeiderspers, 1999), 144–80.

44 See, for example, A. Roelofs, 'Succes ermee Schroeder' *de Volkskrant* (2 October 1998).

45 L. de Waal, *Presentation at Siemens*, The Hague, 14 July 1998. Found at http://www.fnv.nl/~toespraak/1998/14–7–98pmodel.html.

46 J. de Beus, 'Modernized Social Democracy and the Fundamental Democratization of Europe', in R. Cuperus and J. Kandel *European Social Democracy. Transformation in Progress. Social Democratic Think Tanks Explore the Magical Return of Social Democracy in a Liberal Era* (Amsterdam: Friedrich Ebert Stiftung and Wiardi Beckman Stichting, 1998), 207–20.

47 Visser and Hemerijck, '*A Dutch Miracle*'. p. 179.

48 de Beus, 'Modernized Social Democracy and the Fundamental Democratization of Europe'.

49 D. Sassoon, 'Introduction: Convergence, Continuity and Change on the European Left', in G. Kelly (ed.), *The New European Left* (London: Fabian Society, 1999), pp. 7–19.

50 F. Becker and R. Cuperus, 'Dutch Social Democracy between Blair and Jospin', in R. Cuperus and J. Kandel, *European Social Democracy. Transformation in Progress. Social Democratic Think Tanks Explore the Magical Return of Social Democracy in a Liberal Era* (Amsterdam: Friedrich Ebert Stiftung and Wiardi Beckman Stichting, 1998), 245–56, p. 254.

51 Ibid.

7

Social Democracy and Structures of Governance in Britain and Germany: How Institutions and Norms Shape Political Innovation[1]

Charles Lees

Introduction

Until the Labour Party and SPD's respective election triumphs in 1997 and 1998, Social Democracy in Britain and Germany had been excluded from national government for a generation. In both countries, social democrats struggled to counter the ideological ascendancy of the Right. Core social democratic values of social partnership, redistributive fiscal measures and some degree of Keynesian macroeconomic management had been eclipsed by a neoliberal discourse of deregulation, privatization and – in Britain – the breaking down of tripartite structures of interest intermediation.

With the two parties now in government, the temptation to draw parallels between them is enormous. Both parties seem to have consciously reoriented their electoral stance in response to the sociopolitical environment of the late 1990s, both have reaped a significant electoral harvest from these changes, both are led by charismatic figures whose political style is more presidential than collectivist, and both were opposed by incumbent parties of the Right that appeared to have run out of steam in terms of ideology and personnel. Moreover, for both parties, the road back to national government was a long one and much ideological baggage had to be jettisoned along the way. However, as this chapter demonstrates, the nation-specific structures and norms of political institutions in both countries continue to impact upon the process of programmatic renewal and shape political innovation. In other words, despite the common rhetoric of the 'Third Way' or 'New Centre' (*Die Neue Mitte*), the scope and scale of modernization within the Labour Party and the SPD remains grounded in the national 'traditions' of British and German Social Democracy.

The unveiling, in July 1999, of the much trumpeted British–German joint policy document on the 'Third Way' or 'New Centre' by Tony Blair and Gerhard Schröder provides a vivid example of how these traditions impact upon political innovation. At the time, the paper's publication was greeted with great interest, not just in Britain and Germany but throughout Europe. In particular, it was hoped that here at last might be concrete evidence of where European social democracy was heading at the end of the twentieth century. Although publication of the Blair–Schröder document had been delayed by the Kosovo crisis, copious leaking on both sides of the North Sea had encouraged speculation that it would pour fuel on the fire in the ongoing struggle between 'traditionalists' and 'modernizers' within both the Labour Party and the SPD. However the reaction was more differentiated than that – and much more interesting.

In the broadest terms, the document was an attempt to reconcile the two parties' social democratic tradition with the basic tenets of the neoliberal orthodoxy of the last decade. This is made explicit in the preamble to the document, which states: 'social democracy has found new acceptance . . . because it stands not only for social justice but also for economic dynamism and the unleashing of creativity and innovation.' The need for 'modernization' was paramount, in order to adapt 'to conditions that have objectively changed', and to do this 'the state should not row, but steer: not so much control as challenge'. The two leaders aspired to a 'new supply-side agenda for the Left' with the aim of 'catching up with the US', by means of a 'robust and competitive market framework' with a 'tax policy to promote sustainable growth' at its core. The details of this policy would include the simplification of company taxation, the cutting of corporation tax, a shift of the tax burden from income to consumption, tax relief and/or lower starting rates of income tax and greater 'flexibility' in the labour market – including the reduction of non-wage labour costs, the promotion of small and medium-sized enterprises and the extension of welfare-to-work policies.

The idea of EU-level cooperation was stressed throughout the document as a means to disseminate this new agenda, albeit using the private sector metaphor of 'political benchmarking'. This process would have three elements. First, there would be a series of ministerial meetings and an ongoing process of staff liaison between Britain and Germany.

Second, Blair and Schröder would 'seek discussion' with political leaders in other EU countries, regardless of political affiliation. Third, they would promote the establishment of a 'network of experts, farsighted thinkers, political fora and discussion meetings' which would 'deepen and continually further develop the concept of the New Centre and the Third Way'.[2]

Within weeks, reaction in some quarters to the Blair–Schröder paper shifted from interest to derision and even outright hostility. However, the reasons for this differed somewhat between the two countries. In Britain criticism focused upon the document's perceived lack of substance and in particular its failure to move beyond policy prescriptions – especially with regard to labour market flexibility – that were already part of the political orthodoxy. On the basis of the document, the 'Third Way' appeared to many to amount to little more than Thatcherism with a human face. In Germany, on the other hand, the *Blair Papier* as it became known was regarded as an attack on the Rhineland model of social market capitalism which had brought social peace and prosperity for more than two generations. Indeed, such was the negative resonance surrounding the paper that the German Chancellor, under pressure from his own party and with the SPD plummeting in the polls, soon began to distance himself from it. By October 1999 SPD news managers were making it clear that Schröder no longer regarded the document as the way forward. On the road to Damascus, he had apparently realized that neoliberal prescriptions were perhaps not as suitable to conditions in the Federal Republic as he had once thought. There were other models of reform to consider, such as in the Netherlands and, more importantly, Germany's closest ally, France. According to the 'spin', Schröder's new course was to be 'more Jospin and less Blair'.[3] Germany's Third Way/New Centre project appeared to have hit the buffers, apparently leaving Blair as the sole – and increasingly isolated – champion of the Third Way agenda.

Aims, structure and theory

It is not the intention of this chapter to assess the true nature of the Third Way or New Centre, although the conclusion of this chapter makes some predictions as to its future development. Rather, the chapter uses the discourse of the Third Way/New Centre 'project' as a dependent variable, the variance of which has some power in explaining the comparative effect of structures of governance on political ideas and political agency. It will throw into relief how institutions and norms shape political innovation within social democratic traditions; not just in Britain and Germany but in all countries were such a tradition exists. Such traditions include modes of intra-party governance, party ideology and policy styles. The chapter argues that these traditions impact upon the modernizing agenda in a different way in the Federal Republic than is the case in Britain. Given the recent avalanche of literature on Blairism – and the relative lack of English-language material on the New Centre – greater empirical emphasis is placed upon the Federal Republic. The relative 'weighting' of the German case serves to illustrate two points. First, comparisons with Germany demonstrate the extent to which the Third Way is grounded in a British (or at least an 'Anglo-Saxon') political praxis and, second, it highlights the potential difficulties in exporting a recognizably Blairite Third Way agenda either to other individual western European states or to the European Union level.

In describing how these traditions have been shaped, the chapter will focus on the facilitating and constraining nature of institutions on political agency at the domestic and European levels. The scope of enquiry will be framed within the following two dimensions:

- party systems, (two-party or multi-party, elected by proportional representation or first-past-the-post, concentrated or deconcentrated), political competition (the presence of Left and/or Green competitor) and election outcomes (whether majority or minority, single-party or coalition governments);
- state structure (whether unitary or federal), administrative structures (whether centralized or devolved) and bureaucratic norms (in particular whether generalist or specialist in nature).

Underlying the arguments is the assumption of institutional autonomy, as well as a fairly loose interpretation of what constitutes an 'institution'. Institutions are considered to be autonomous in the sense that they are more than just the passive settings for political agency. Moreover, types of institutions stretch along a continuum from formal, legally codified practices to more inchoate organizational networks. What they all have in common, however, is that they 'structure relationships in various units of the polity and the economy',[4] to the extent that 'they are political actors in their own right'[5] and therefore serve as potential veto points. Within this context, the exercise of political agency becomes a 'complex decision problem', characterized by 'the lack of complete information, the existence of multiple objectives, and of participants with conflicting interests'[6] which constrain the formation of a dominant coalition in favour of a Third Way agenda. Faced with such a decision problem, decision-makers often adopt a strategy of simplification, whereby alternative or even 'best' courses of action are discounted in favour of one what that is 'good enough' given these constraints. This strategy of 'satisficing'[7] will lead to different outcomes according to the context in which it is undertaken. Thus, even if – and it is a big if – British and German social democrats share similar objectives, the quite different structures of governance in the two countries will tend to generate different innovative strategies to achieve them. We intuitively understand the idea of different social democratic traditions, but these differences did not come about by accident alone. They also came about as a result of institutional design.

Party systems, political competition and government outcomes

The structure and norms of party systems, political competition and government outcomes within a particular polity constitute a powerful institutional filter, through which the ideas associated with political agency must pass. The key variables – albeit related – are three-fold.

First, the particular institutional dynamics of the British and German polities present political agents with their own distinctive strategic dilemmas. In any system, political agents need to form a dominant coalition in order to push through their agenda. This problem is common to both the Labour Party and the SPD, given that the two parties are coalitions themselves. In both parties, diverse interests compete for influence over policy and the appointment of personnel and, in order for the party to function effectively, some degree of equilibrium must be established between party factions. This can take the form of a dominant faction (as in today's Labour Party) or a more balanced relationship between them (as in the SPD). However, multi-party systems increase the complexity of forming a dominant coalition. As the number of parties within the coalition 'game' increases, the number of possible winning coalitions multiplies exponentially.[8] Thus, the problem of forming a winning coalition is more acute in Germany than in the UK because its system of proportional representation tends to increase the number of parties within the legislature that can be regarded as serious competitors for office.

These problems are further aggravated by the second and third elements of party systems and political competition. In terms of the second variable, a deconcentrated party system (involving a hollowing out the 'core' centre-ground) increases the ideological distance between parties, and therefore the transaction costs, as well as the presence of significant 'fringe' parties of the Left and Right. Again, this is relevant for social democratic parties in particular, because the presence of a Left and/or Green competitor further constrains the scope of political agency. Finally, the questions of whether elections result in majority or minority, single-party or coalition governments all present political agents with specific sets of problems that encourage the adoption of the kind of 'satisficing' strategy described earlier.

Britain is a puzzle in this respect. It has more parties in its national parliament than the Federal Republic (ten compared with five), but has traditionally been described as a (concentrated) two-party system (defined as one in which on average more than 90 per cent of the popular vote goes to two big core parties) because in the period from 1945 to 1966 the combined partisan support for the Conservatives and Labour amounted to around 92 per cent of the popular vote[9] and because Britain's plurality or first-past-the-post system of election by constituencies tends to produce disproportional single-party majority government outcomes (which have tended to favour the Conservatives). Subsequent deconcentration of the party system has progressively reduced the share of the core partisan vote, to the extent that in 1997 this core vote amounted only to 74.8 per cent. However, the systemic skewing of the vote towards disproportional outcomes remains a salient factor. Whereas, in 1997, the Conservatives' 31.5 per cent of the vote gave it only 165 seats in the Commons, New Labour's 43.3 per cent gave it 418 seats out of a total of 659. This meant that New Labour not only enjoyed a clear majority of 250 seats over the Conservatives, but it also easily passed the 'minimum-winning' criteria of 50 per cent plus one seat.[10] In a legislature with a minimum winning majority of 380, it enjoyed a surplus majority of 68 over all the other parties combined. Therefore, the discounting of the numerical imperative to negotiate with other parties within the legislature significantly reduces the transaction costs involved in forming a dominant coalition. History and ideological tradition still matter in any party system but, all things being equal, the British electoral system's tendency towards disproportionality makes political innovation easier. In short, Labour's large majority should promote any Third Way agenda.

Apart from providing sheer weight of numbers, there are three other ways in which Britain's plurality system facilitates the promotion of such an agenda. First, it acts as a centripetal force within the party system because it privileges the political centre ground. The disproportionality of electoral outcomes has contributed to a 'political opportunity structure'[11] which makes it very hard for fringe parties of the Left or Right to enter the Commons and, as a result, New Labour's scope for strategic action is not constrained by the presence of a Left and/or Green competitor within the legislature. This privileging of the political centre ground also enhances the electoral influence of moderate 'swing voters' in marginal seats, which makes it rational for political parties to adopt the strategy of pursuing a mythical 'median voter'.[12] This leads to parties gravitating towards the political centre and competing within a very narrow ideological space (although, at the same time, the winner-takes-all effect of the system allows legislation passed by even the smallest majority to be implemented immediately; this can lead to abrupt swings in the direction of UK policy when a new party takes power). New Labour needed to differentiate itself within such a crowded field, and the Third Way – with its claim to 'the radical centre' – was attractive to the party elite for that reason. The Third Way allowed the party to adopt the mantle of cutting-edge ideas, whilst at the same time its apparently non-ideological discourse reassured key centrist voters. As Cowell and Larkin explain elsewhere in this book, the Third Way also allowed the Labour Party to emphasize discontinuity with the ideological battles of 1979–83 and its associated negative connotations.

The second way in which Britain's plurality system facilitates the promotion of a Third Way agenda relates to the fact that, as discussed, the British tendency towards one party majority government reduces the transaction costs involved in the formation of a viable coalition around such agenda. Where New Labour has reached out to elements within the political competition such Charles Kennedy, Ken Clarke, Chris Patten and Michael Heseltine, this has tended to be on normative grounds, such as reinforcing the Third Way's claim to 'big tent' politics or (excepting Kennedy) simply to aggravate internal divisions within the Conservatives. What it is not is a reaction to the need to cobble together a mathematical majority in parliament, as this can be done within the Labour Party itself. Nevertheless, as the record of the 1992–97 Major government demonstrates, a majority in parliament is no guarantee of success for the party elite, especially when that majority is so small that individual backbenchers are able to exert leverage on the leadership because of the need to muster the necessary votes to pass government business. However, for New Labour, if anything the potential for trouble lies in the fact that their parliamentary majority is too great. Over time such a 'surplus majority' means that the payoffs associated with office (promotion, patronage, access for client groups) are spread thinner than would be the case with a minimal/minimum-winning majority.[13] As it becomes clear to individual backbenchers that they have been passed over for office, the use of the 'carrot' of future office becomes less effective when enforcing party discipline and managers become more reliant on the 'stick'. However, in this respect, New Labour appears to have got its retaliation in early! The iron discipline of party whips, as well as the relative passivity of Labour backbenchers who still live in hope of preferment, has become the hallmark of the post-1997 Blair administration.

Related to this last point, the third and final reason why the tendency towards one party majority government facilitates the promotion of a Third Way agenda lies in the monopoly enjoyed by the ruling party over the allocation of ministerial portfolios and other payoffs associated with office. The combination of a lack of coalition partner, strong party discipline and an increasingly 'presidential' norm of prime ministerial power ensures that executive power is firmly entrenched within the Blair circle. Apart from government and ministerial advisory posts, the prime minister approves all senior Whitehall posts, as well as top jobs in the NHS, the BBC, on quangos, and so on. Moreover, as is discussed in the section on state structures, this executive power is further enhanced by a highly centralized civil service and a unitary state structure with a lack of competing centres of power (although this is changing to a certain extent with the introduction of devolution to Scotland, Wales, London and, perhaps in time, the English regions).

The contrast between New Labour's hegemony over the British polity and the SPD's more tenuous position could not be greater. The Federal Republic has traditionally been classified as either a 'two-and-a-half party system'[14] or a three-party system, with the liberal FDP acting as the 'kingmaker' between the two big 'catch-all' parties,[15] the SPD and the Christian Democratic CDU/CSU. This kingmaker function was made possible because of Germany's Additional Member System (AMS) of proportional representation, introduced in 1953. With exception of a brief period of CDU/CSU majority government in the 1950s, over successive legislative periods the AMS system has produced a share of seats in the Bundestag which has made the formation of formal coalitions between the parties a necessity. As a result, AMS produces outcomes that potentially privileges small parties that hold the balance of power.

AMS also produces 'split-ticket' voting, whereby voters divide their allegiance between the first (constituency) and second (party list) votes.

This type of strategic voting first became significant in the 1960s, at around 10 per cent of votes cast,[16] and was especially common amongst Germany's emergent 'new' middle class and technical intelligentsia.[17] In the early years, the bulk of this limited number of split second votes went to the FDP, but in the 1980s, split-ticket voting grew substantially, reaching 14 per cent in 1987 and 16 per cent in 1990.[18] Crucially for the SPD, the main beneficiary of this growth in split-ticket voting were the emergent Greens, who also benefited from the low hurdle to gaining legislative seats, set at 5 per cent of total votes cast. New Left-oriented SPD voters in particular were attracted to the idea of giving their second votes to the Greens, who now compete directly against the SPD along a 'post- materialist' ideological dimension.[19]

Because it is relatively proportionate, Germany's system of AMS is also more prone to reflect the steady deconcentration of the party system itself. Since the 1970s, this deconcentration has become pronounced, first at the margins then, increasingly, at the core of electorate. The first manifestation of deconcentration was the growth in split-ticket voting discussed above, and this had a knock-on effect on the steady decline in the share of the core partisan vote for the two 'catch-all' parties. The SPD has been the biggest loser in this process. Whilst the CDU saw some erosion of support amongst its client groups, the SPD has suffered a severe loss of support amongst its electoral core of Protestants and/or manual workers. Partisan identification for the SPD amongst this group fell 19 per cent during the 1980s,[20] before recovering slightly in 1994 and 1998.[21] Since German unification in 1990, party system deconcentration has also been aggravated by the addition of a 'second' party system in the states of the former East Germany. In these eastern states, the effects of 40 years of communism have generated an 'inverted social profile' of voting behaviour. Although class and confessional (that is, religion-based) classifications are somewhat tentative in eastern Germany, in the early 1990s the SPD trailed the CDU amongst manual workers as well as all confessional groups.[22] This trend was reversed somewhat in the 1998 Bundestag election,[23] but the SPD still has to compete for Left votes with the successor to old East German SED, the Party of Democratic Socialism (PDS), which has established itself as a formidable Left-competitor in the East[24] and is deeply hostile to the revisionist ideas associated with the New Centre.

Given the presence of a Left – as well as a Green – competitor, the SPD's room for manoeuvre is limited compared with that of the Labour Party. Although New Labour and the SPD won similar shares of the total vote in 1997 and 1998, the German Social Democrats are disadvantaged by the (lack of dis)proportional outcomes generated by Germany's AMS system. Overall, the SPD won 40.9 per cent of the party list vote, giving them 298 seats, whilst the CDU/CSU polled 35.1 per cent and received 245 seats. This is in stark contrast to the massive majority enjoyed by the Labour Party over the rump of the Conservatives who survived the 1997 general election. In addition, the minor parties did well under the system, with the Greens polling 6.7 per cent and gaining 47 seats, the FDP 6.2 per cent and 44 seats, and the PDS 5.1 per cent and 35 seats (including four directly elected constituency seats in the East).[25] Thus, although the SPD enjoyed a reasonable majority of 53 seats over the CDU/CSU, in a legislature of 669 seats they fell 37 seats short of the minimum-winning majority of 335 seats. The SPD was presented with the numerical imperative of negotiating with other parties within the legislature, many of whom were not sympathetic to Schröder's New Centre agenda. As a result, the transaction costs involved were raised considerably.

From the point of view of the SPD, the proportionality of electoral outcomes provided a 'political opportunity structure' that privileged its Left and Green competitors within the legislature. This left the SPD torn between two conflicting strategic issues: the need for ideological moderation on the one hand, and the imperatives of coalition formation on the other. Although the party list system does not enhance the influence of moderate swing voters in marginal seats in the way it does in Britain, in aggregate terms it remained rational for the SPD to adopt the strategy of the 'median voter'. Indeed, this was the reason why the SPD made centrist Schröder Chancellor-candidate rather than the more left-wing Oskar Lafontaine. Lafontaine was far more popular with the party's rank-and-file, but all the opinion poll data at the start of 1998 indicated that he would fail once more to unseat Kohl or his putative successor, Wolfgang Schäuble.[26]

However, having maximized the SPD vote on Bundestag election day, the rules of the game changed considerably. If the SPD were to get past the winning post of 50 per cent plus one seat, it had to form a coalition with one of the other parties within the Bundestag. Moreover, for a variety of reasons – including the need to limit the extent of its surplus majority – there was a predisposition towards forming a coalition with the Greens.[27] But in order to do this, the SPD and the Greens had to ensure that the sweep of policy domains where the two parties were broadly in agreement was greater than that which existed between the SPD and any other potential coalition partner. In other words, any 'Red–Green' coalition would have to be the minimal connected winning coalition with the smallest 'ideological range'.[28] In order to do this, the SPD would have selectively to emphasize the post-materialist and/or libertarian dimension to their ideological programme, particularly 'quality of life' issues like the Environment.[29] As it turned out, the SPD's Green 'turn' was executed without undue difficulty. Nevertheless, half-way through its term in office, the Federal coalition still struggles to square the circle between the conflicting ideological strands of the Red–Green model and that of the New Centre.

Such an ideological divide is aggravated because the party system's inherent tendency towards coalition politics aggravates the already existing sectorization within the policy-making apparatus. This is because the principle of ministerial autonomy is formally codified in Article 65 of the Basic Law (known as the *Ressortsprinzip*). The distribution of ministerial seats are central to the processes of coalition formation and maintenance and, given the tendency of parties to staff ministries with their own people, policy-making can become an adjunct to inter-coalition rivalry. 'Junior' partners within coalitions – such as the Greens – tend to be especially jealous of ministerial autonomy, leading to differences in policy style and content across competing ministries. This tendency has continued within the Schröder administration. In particular, the determination of Green Environment Minister Jürgen Trittin to implement the Red–Green agenda set out in the coalition agreement has already led to Trittin's falling out with other members of the cabinet, such as Economics Minister Werner Müller and the Chancellor himself. At the heart of these disagreements has been the inability of ministers to reconcile the pro-business New Centre agenda with the need to impose controls on industry in order to reduce the impact of economic activity on the environment.[30] The problem for Schröder is that Germany's systemic logic means that the SPD cannot simply jettison its coalition partner but, rather, must make sufficient concessions to keep them in the coalition.

Nevertheless, the difficulties Schröder has encountered in developing the New Centre agenda do not stop with the Greens, but go to the heart of the SPD itself. These difficulties are three-fold and again the reasons lie in Germany's federal structure. First, there is a tendency in the Federal Republic for coalition 'models' to be developed at the state level before being implemented at the Federal level. Since the foundation of the Federal Republic, there have been five variants of government in power in Bonn, and all but one of them have been formal coalition arrangements, constituted at the *Land* level before being attempted at the Federal level. William M. Downs suggests that there are vertical linkages between national and sub-national governments and that these state-level arrangements constitutes a bottom-up flow of information to national party elites on the viability of a given political model and the policy agenda associated with it (1998: 243–66). Thus, the development of these agendas at the sub-national level over time enhances their credibility and legitimacy. This disadvantages the Third Way/New Centre agenda, given that the dissemination of such ideas between Britain and Germany, has been primarily an elite-driven process involving top party and government officials, as well as high-profile academics such as Anthony Giddens and Ulrich Beck. By contrast, the Red–Green model has been fine-tuned within the relatively low-risk environment of state government. Thus, the New Centre as an idea must compete with the product of a lesson-drawing process, characterized by the 'emulation of virtue'[31] and the discounting of negative experiences by party elites. The long gestation of the Red–Green model has not only given it a degree of credibility but also means that a whole generation of SPD politicians and activists are familiar with it and have quite often invested a good deal of political capital in its success.[32] Second, the real power enjoyed by state governments in the Federal Republic means that, unlike the Labour Party, the SPD has still enjoyed the trappings of office since losing office at the national level. As a result, the SPD's membership did not become as 'hungry' for power as did their New Labour colleagues during the long period in opposition and are therefore less amenable to what appears to them to be the abandonment of core values. Third, Germany's federal structure is replicated within the SPD, with the party machine at the state level being crucial to an individual's future prospects. Because of this, the SPD has more internal power centres than the Labour Party. These not only serve as additional internal veto points that constrain the strategic actions of the party leadership, but also as the generator of alternative material, informational and ideological resources: many of which are antithetical to the New Centre.

State and administrative structures and norms

The broad structure of British state institutions needs little explanation here and is well documented.[33] Britain is a 'strong' unitary state with a powerful norm of centralized power and, unlike many advanced democracies (including the Federal Republic), it lacks a formal constitution. Traditionally, constraints upon executive power have not been formally codified, but rather have accumulated in an incremental fashion through royal prerogative, statutes, common law, convention and informed opinion. In recent years formally codified external constraints – such as the *Acquis Communautaire* and the European Convention on Human Rights – have imposed further limitations, but the British executive still appears to enjoy a relatively high degree of political agency: at least within the domestic domain.

Administration is carried out by the central government bureaucracy, the British civil service. The civil service is constitutionally part of the executive and its legitimacy rests upon the norms of permanence (they are career civil servants and not meant to be political appointments), neutrality (they are expected to serve the government of the day without partisan bias) and anonymity (civil servants remain 'in the shadows' whilst ministers take external responsibility for policy). The social composition of the higher echelons remains skewed towards white upper-middle-class males at the expense of women and individuals from other social classes or the ethnic minorities[34] and recruitment into the civil service is highly centralized. Modes of recruitment – particularly at the higher levels – tend to favour classicists and, increasingly, lawyers rather than those with more technical qualifications. Given this recruitment bias, it is no surprise that the British civil service maintains a 'generalist' ethos which privileges the norms of systemic stability, evolution rather than revolution, and ideological moderation – although this has changed in recent years, not least because of the reforms of the Thatcher years.

The British civil service is a smooth-running machine which – as governments of all political colours have come to appreciate – can be effectively harnessed as the servant of political agency. Combined with successive parliamentary majorities, it became a formidable tool of executive power used to further an aggressively free-market policy agenda by the Thatcher and Major governments. Nevertheless, in doing so, these Conservative administrations also created the conditions for New Labour. In a recent essay on New Labour's first year in power, David Marquand described this paradox, stating that 'the central theme of the Thatcher revolution lay in a combination of market freedom and state power.... In ten years, the Thatcher governments transformed the political economy and public culture. The new, low tax, business-friendly, union-spurning, Murdoch-courting Labour Party is a tribute to that transformation'.[35]

With the political economy so highly geared towards the neoliberal orthodoxy, it is really no surprise that New Labour looked elsewhere for a 'big idea' and – given that it was so often on the receiving end of

Thatcher's relentless centralism – it is perhaps equally unsurprising that this idea was constitutional reform. Since May 1997, Labour has introduced a substantial raft of legislation that is slowly transforming the constitutional settlement of the United Kingdom. These reforms include devolution for Scotland, Wales and Northern Ireland, elected mayors for the major cities (starting with London), the incorporation of the European Convention on Human Rights into British law, a Freedom of Information Act, reform of the House of Lords and perhaps even a referendum on proportional representation. However, New Labour's declared preference for constitutional decentralization is in direct contrast to its actual approach to the praxis of governance. In the same article, Marquand argues that New Labour's harnessing of state power to pursue these ends is essential if they are to 'stick' in the longer term. He argues that 'the policies... must be pushed through with as much centralist zeal as the Thatcherites displayed 15 years ago'.[36] New Labour is as much a creature of the 'strong' British state as any other government and the combination of constitutional reform driven by a highly centralized and autocratic party machine is at the heart of 'the Blair paradox' the title of Marquand's article.

By contrast, the SPD operates within a structure of governance which is much more consensual and decentralized. Competencies are divided between the Federation, state and local tiers of government, with the states shaping policy at the national level through the second chamber, the Bundesrat. This system of 'multi-level' or 'multi-tiered' governance does not allow for the British style of autocratic leadership. To illustrate this point, consider the Thatcher administration's decision to dissolve the Greater London Council and the Blair government's reform of the House of Lords. In both cases, a German Federal government would have not been able to act in this way, because they would be constrained by Articles 30, 70(1), and 83 of the Basic Law. These articles codify the relationship between the two levels of government and protect the powers of the constituent states from overt interference. This 'sectorization'[37] of the German state apparatus not only imposes clear limits on the ability of German social democrats to change the existing parameters of state power, but also entrenches the status of the various veto points within the system that will resist the imposition of any reformist agenda. The existence of such veto points constrains anything analogous to the 'centralizing zeal' that Marquand advocates for new Labour, and the more consensual tone of 'Schröderism' (typified by the neocorporatist 'Alliance for Jobs') is a reflection of this.

One set of veto points occurs through the horizontal sectorization of policy-making between ministries, which is aggravated by the fact that the German norm of coalition government means that ministries are often 'staffed' by another party, whilst another set occurs through the division of competencies between Federation and state. Moreover, further horizontal and vertical sectorization occurs at the state level itself, although the extent of this varies from state to state. These potential veto points are further privileged by the explicit interdependence of the established parties and the administrative structures. The post-1945 settlement brought political parties into the centre of the governmental/administrative nexus of the new Federal Republic and was formally codified in Article 21 of the Basic Law, which stated that 'the political parties shall participate in the formation of the political will of the people'. This represented a significant realignment within the German polity, with a new norm of state power in which state legitimacy was directly linked to that of the political parties. The extent of interdependence is reflected in the level of partisan penetration of the civil service. For instance, in 1972 the main political parties had staffed over half the senior posts (state secretaries, heads and departmental heads of division) at the state and federal level of the civil service. This was not just a question of restaffing a particular department, but was also manifested in discursive terms, with administrative values permeating internal debate within the established parties[38] and reinforcing the existing consensus between them on the substantive issues of state. The SPD were not immune to this and has acquired a deeply technocratic and non-ideological policy style, with an emphasis upon path-dependent policy prescriptions. At the same time, the persistence of the Hegelian tradition within German bureaucratic norms means that these policy prescriptions continue to contain the idea of the active state at their core. This predisposition towards 'weak' corporatism further differentiates the SPD from New Labour who, although technocratic in tone, are more 'Anglo- Saxon' in outlook and open to neoliberal prescriptions which privilege the private sector.

German state and administrative structures hobble the kind of political innovation associated with the Third Way/New Centre. As Goldberger (1993) points out, Germany's decentralized policy-making apparatus 'makes unified policy-making and co- ordination more difficult than in its more unitary neighbours'[39] and encourages 'a uniform and agreed cooperation of all the participants'.[40] Moreover, this norm of cooperation is further enhanced because civil servants are generally employed by the constituent states – which are often governed by opposition parties – and owe their first allegiance to them. The contrast with the options available to Blair is obvious and demonstrates the limits of Schröder's purchase on the instruments of state.

Conclusion

The chapter demonstrates the central role that nation-specific institutions play in shaping political agendas. They act as a filter or lens through which innovative political strategies must pass. Political entrepreneurs must square interests within their own parties, and in the wider polity, in order to construct a winning coalition in favour of a given strategy. Presented with such a 'complex decision problem', political entrepreneurs resort to a strategy of 'satisficing', in which alternative or even 'best' courses of action are not undertaken. Instead, political entrepreneurs opt for a sub-optimal strategy that is 'good enough' given these constraints.

In the context of Britain and Germany, these institutional filters have skewed the two parties modernizing agendas in distinct ways. In terms of 'input politics'[41] – who makes demands on the state, what they are and the manner in which they are made – the institutional configuration in Britain presents less veto points than that of the Federal Republic. In terms of party systems and election outcomes – despite a degree of electoral deconcentration in recent years – the winner-takes-all effect of first-past-the-post means that Britain remains effectively a three–party system. As a result, governments tend to win workable majorities in parliament and there have been no formal inter-party coalitions in the postwar period. Historically, this has favoured the Conservatives, but now that Labour is in power it is not forced, through legislative necessity, to cooperate with other parties on a formal basis. In contrast, the SPD has always governed through formal coalition arrangements with other parties (the CDU between 1966 and 1969, the FDP between 1969 and 1982, and the Greens since 1998). Moreover, unlike the SPD, the Labour Party does not have to deal with a significant Left or Green electoral competitor.

However, in terms of 'output politics' – particularly policy outputs and outcomes – the picture is more complicated. Despite devolution to Scotland and Wales, Britain still retains a unitary state structure and centralized administration with a strong culture of generalism. Thus, all things being equal, a British government of whatever political colour should enjoy far more command and control over the policy process than is the case of the Federal Republic – with its federal structure, decentralized administration and culture of specialism. But all things are never equal, as a comparison of the records of the Blair and Schröder governments demonstrates. Despite a massive majority in parliament and the centralized powers enjoyed by all British governments, it is not immediately obvious that, in terms of policy making, New Labour has been a more effective government than the Red–Green coalition. In fact, both governments can boast a reasonably impressive record since they came to office. New Labour hit the ground running in May 1997 and can point to operational independence for the Bank of England in setting interest rates, devolution for Scotland and Wales, the introduction of the minimum wage, the New Deal, social chapter, and Good Friday Agreement as obvious policy successes. By contrast, the Schröder administration got off to a very shaky start[42] but has since started to chalk up a number of policy successes – including the partial reform of German citizenship laws, the participation of the Bundeswehr in out-of-area military operations, the phased withdrawal from the use of nuclear power, moves towards the recognition of equal rights for same-sex partners, and reform of the Federal Republic's tax system. In addition, the Franco-German relationship shows signs of resuming its role as the motor of European integration, with Green Foreign Minister Joschka Fischer pushing an ambitious agenda for reform of the European Union (a comparison with New Labour's stalled European agenda is obvious). As a result, rather than looking to New Labour for inspiration, many European Social Democrats are turning once again to the familiar Franco-German axis.

So what does this discrepancy between the pattern of input and output politics tell us? First, it tells us that a focus on nation-specific institutions is no longer sufficient. Elsewhere in this book, Stammers refers to the idea of Social Democracy being underpinned by a 'methodological nationalism' that is no longer appropriate to the conditions of the early twenty-first century – in particular, the hollowing-out of the state and the impact of globalization. This is particularly relevant to European Social Democracy, given the increasing impact of Europeanization on national policy-making.[43] Europeanization also privileges certain political actors at the European level, including those nation-states with institutional structures and norms that 'fit' well with the EU equivalents.[44] In turn this facilitates the framing of European and domestic policy at the national level (this might go some way to explain the weakness of Blair's position on Europe, compared with that of Schröder). Finally, the discrepancy between input and output politics in Britain and Germany also tells us something else – that a concentration upon autonomous institutions at whatever level of governance is only part of the story. Other factors, such as history and ideology, are crucial variables when explaining the divergence between what look, on the surface, to be almost identical agendas. Institutions and norms do shape agendas for political innovation, but such agendas can only be fully explained by reference to the rich context of the political traditions from which they arise.

Notes

1   Many thanks to Luke Martell, Philip Larkin and Stephanie Hoopes for commenting on earlier drafts of this chapter.
2   SPD, *Der Weg nach vorne für Europas Sozialdemonkraten. Ein Vorschlag von Gerhard Schröder und Tony Blair* (1999).
3   *Der Spiegel*, 18 October 1999, 23.
4   P. Hall, *Governing the Economy* (Cambridge: Polity Press, 1996), 19–20.
5   J. G. March and J. P. Olsen, 'The New Institutionalism: Organizational Factors in Political Life', *American Political Science Review*, 78 (1984), 738.
6   K. J. Radford, *Complex Decision Problems: an Integrated Strategy for Resolution* (Reston, Va: Reston Publishing Company, 1977), 11.
7   H. A. Simon, *Administrative Behaviour* (New York: Free Press, 1965).
8   See, for example, Schubik, 1967: 249, cited B. Hinckley, *Coalitions and Politics* (London: Harcourt Brace Jovanovich, 1981), 24.
9   J. Blondel, 'Party Systems and Patterns of Government in Western Democracies', *Canadian Journal of Political Science*. 1 (1968): 180–203. Reprinted in S. B. Wolinetz (ed.), *Party Systems* (Aldershot: Dartmouth, 1998), 111.
10 Cf. W. H. Riker, *The Theory of Political Coalitions* (New Haven, Conn.: Yale University Press, 1962).
11 H. Kitschelt, 'Political Opportunity Structures and Political Protest: Antinuclear Movements in Four Democracies', *British Journal of Political Science*, 16(1) (1986).
12 A. Downs, *An Economic Theory of Democracy* (New York: Harper and Row, 1957).
13 Riker, *The Theory of Political Coalitions*.
14 Blondel, 'Party Systems', p. 112.
15 O. Kirchheimer, 'The Transformation of the western European Party Systems', in J. La Palombara and M. Wiener (eds.), *Political Parties and Political Development* (Princeton, NJ and Guildford: Princeton University Press).
16 R. Dalton, 'Two German Electorates?', in G. Smith, et al. (eds.), *Developments In German Politics* (Basingstoke: Macmillan, 1992), 54.
17 S. Padgett, 'The New German Electorate'. in S. Padgett (ed.), *Parties and Party Systems in the New Germany* (Aldershot: Dartmouth, 1993a), 39.
18 Dalton, 'Two German Electorates?', 54.
19 R. Inglehart, *Culture Shift in Advanced Industrial Society* (Princeton, NJ: Princeton University Press). cited in ibid., 56.
20 Padgett, 'The New German Electorate', 38.
21 Forschungsgruppe Wahlen 1990/1994/1998.

22   Padgett, 'The New German Electorate', 39–41.

23   Forschungsgruppe Wahlen, 1998.

24   C. Lees, 'Paradise Postponed: An Assessment of Ten Years of Governmental Participation by the German Green Party'. IGS95/4. Birmingham: Institute for German Studies discussion paper, University of Birmingham, 1995; C. Lees, 'A Watershed Election: The Berlin State and City Elections of 22 October 1995', *Regional and Federal Studies*, 6, 1 (1995): 63–72; C. Lees, 'The Ambivalent Left: The Greens, the PDS and the SPD's Strategic Dilemma', *Contemporary Political Studies*, 3 (1996b), 1438–51.

25   Statistiches Bundesamt, 1998.

26   *Der Spiegel.* 20 December 1997.

27   C. Lees, 'The Red–Green Coalition', in S. Padgett and T. Saalfield (eds.), *Bundestagswahl: '98: The End of an Era* (London: Frank Cass, 1999), 187.

28   A. de Swaan, *Coalition Theories and Cabinet Formation* (Amsterdam and Oxford: Elsevier, 1973).

29   Lees, 'The Red–Green Coalition', 181.

30   Ibid., 174–6.

31   R. Eyestone, 'Confusion, Diffusion, and Innovation', in *American Political Science Review*, 71 (1977), 441–7.

32   C. Lees, *The Red–Green Coalition in Germany: Politics, Personalities and Power* (Manchester: Manchester University Press, 2000b).

33   Cf. A. V. Dicey, *An Introduction to the Study of the Law of the Constitution*, tenth edition (Basingstoke: Macmillan, 1959; first published 1885); I. Jennings, *The British Constitution* (Cambridge: Cambridge University Press, 1966); R. A. W. Rhodes, *Control and Power in Central-Local Government Relations* (Aldershot: Gower, 1981); R. A. W. Rhodes and D. Marsh, *Policy Networks in British Government* (Oxford: Oxford University Press, 1992).

34   J. Kingdom, *Government and Politics in Britain*, second edition (Cambridge: Politiy Press, 1999), 440–50.

35   D. Marquand, 'The Blair Paradox', *Prospect* (May 1988), 20.

36   Ibid., 20–1.

37   S. Bulmer, 'Domestic Politics and European Community Policy Making', *Journal of Common Market Studies*, XXI, 4 (1983), 349–63.

38   Lees, 'Paradise Postponed', 9.

39   B. Goldberger, 'Why Europe Should Not Fear the Germans', *German Politics*, 2 (1993), 291.

40   S. Bulmer, and W. Paterson, *The Federal Republic of Germany and the European Community* (London. Allen and Unwin, 1987), 187.

41   Cf. P. Dunleavy and B. O'Leary, *Theories of the State* (Basingstoke: Macmillan, 1987).

42   See Lees, 'The Red–Green Coalition', and idem 'The Red–Green Coalition in Germany'.

43   R. Ladrech, 'Europeanization of Domestic Politics and Institutions: The Case of France', *Journal of Common Market Studies*, 32: 1 (1994), 70.

44   C. Lees, 'Reconstituting European Social Democracy: Germany's Pivotal Role', *German Politics* 9: 2 (2000a).

8
The Media and Social Democracy in the United States and Great Britain

Stephanie Hoopes

Introduction

Although the media do not have a direct impact on the political views held by individuals except in certain, and not very common, situations, they do impact on some of the structures of society. The media, especially the changes occurring in the new media, are having a profound impact on some of the key elements of society, which are also central to political theory, including the type of governance, the role of civil society and private enterprise and the levels of equity and justice in society. The changes in media technology have enabled instant access to global information and are often viewed as a key component of globalization because of their contribution to compressing time and space.[1] In this chapter I focus on developments in the United States and Britain and use these cases to compare the effects on social democracy.

In this chapter, after briefly defining the media and establishing the means for comparison between the United States and Britain, I review how the media influence politics in general. Next, I outline three variations of social democracy: traditional, modern and global. Then I consider the impact of the media on several aspects of social democracy, primarily governance, the role of private enterprise, and the means to achieve equality and justice for the disadvantaged in society. I conclude with a comparison of the United States and Britain and discuss the implications for the future of social democracy.

The media have never been a homogeneous entity and in fact are better described as a diverse collection of industries and practices, each with their own methods of communication, specific business interests, constraints and audiences.[2] The media in the United States and in Britain are a massive industry as well as an important purveyor of news, culture, religion, sports and politics. The most important aspect of the media today is the differentiation between traditional media and new media. The traditional media comprise thousands of daily and weekly newspapers, magazines, newsletters, and radio and television stations and networks; the press corps is larger than ever for both newsprint and television.

The New Information and Communication Technologies (NICTs) include a range of developments, including high-speed microprocessing data chips, digital communication, satellite and cable, and the Internet. The speed and capability increases in the computer have resulted in a new information phenomenon. Now information can be carried more quickly, efficiently and cheaply, to the extent that it is possible to gather enormous amounts of information and then group, carry and use it in more and more new ways. The greatest difference between the new and the old media are the costs and therefore the number and types of players. The Internet, with its low start-up costs, for the first time provides a forum for individuals that is not screened by 'liberal' journalists or 'conservative' media moguls. It is a medium that can evade censorship and regulation. It allows for intra-mass communication and ultimately the potential for grass roots movements. Unlike the other media (with the possible exception of talk radio) it is an interactive medium, providing citizens with a forum within which they can react to information. The proliferation of sources also has a downside. One critique, for example, describes the proliferation of information on the Internet as 'exploding quantities of useless and trivial things, cluttering it up'.[3]

In addition to the differences in media usage patterns, the United States is more advanced in terms of Internet, cable and satellite availability than Britain. There are broader structural differences between the two countries too. The United States and Britain are not customarily thought of as social democracies; in fact they are more generally described as neoliberal democratic states. There are aspects of these states where neoliberalism and social democracy merge in their view of the state as positive and a means of enlarging liberty and promoting justice. Both neoliberalism and social democracy accept the logic and structure of the capitalist economy with the subsequent inequalities and deprivations, follow hierarchical statist approaches to both domestic and foreign policy, and rely on an established welfare state. In the wake of the Reagan–Thatcher era of privatization and deregulation, however, it is apparent that liberalism is more dominant than social democracy in these countries.

The more common ideological spectrum in the United States and Britain is considered to be the liberal–conservative continuum. Social democracy is seen as 'the Third Way'. Its tension with neoliberalism and conservatism has helped to define social democracy in practice. Most recently, Bill Clinton's new Democrats in the United States and Tony Blair's New Labour in Britain have given rise to what some call modern social democracy or post-social democracy. In practice, however, Clinton and Blair follow neoliberal principles such as regulation of monopoly power, privatization and paying down deficits, and borrow occasionally from social democratic philosophy. Some argue that they borrow more rhetoric than practices.[4]

The differences between the two countries politically also make them an interesting comparison. The United States has a presidential system with three separate branches of government, a written Constitution and a Bill of Rights. Ideologically, the United States has a strong tradition of neoliberalism and is often described as a pluralist state. Socialist traditions such as the welfare state are stronger in Britain. Britain has a parliamentary system with no separation of powers, no written constitution, and is a member of the European Union. Britain has a larger welfare state than the United States and a nationalized health system. The healthcare system remains private in the United States. Britain's relations with fellow European states (even if tenuous at times), as well as its own history of socialism, give social democracy a strong grounding. These differences can be summed up by saying that the United States is more democratic, more neoliberal and has a smaller state while Britain is more elitist, has a stronger social democratic tradition and a more extensive state. One of the key questions of this chapter will be to determine the extent to which the media have an impact on these differences.

Variations of social democracy

An examination of the media's impact on three variations of social democracy, traditional, modern and global social democracy, sheds light on which variant is most likely to survive the increasing changes brought about by globalization in the United States and Britain. These are discussed at length elsewhere (in particular, see Stammer's chapter and his six criteria). Here I briefly summarize the three variations.

Traditional social democracy believes in democracy and relies on capitalism to generate wealth. It asserts that an elitist hierarchical state can mitigate the inequalities and deprivation generated by the capitalist market through economic and social intervention and regulation. The government dominates the state, orchestrates interest groups and limits civil society. The state compensates for the 'by-products' of capitalism through universalist welfare, which provides an equality of social and economic opportunities for the poor and disadvantaged. Traditional social democracy is associated with the social democratic parties that persevered in Europe against communist and conservative challenges at the national level and as such has a strong nationalist view of domestic and foreign politics. (See Shaw's chapter for further discussion.). In the traditional social democratic view, the state is the only counterbalance to the market. Civil society is small and plays a minimal role in society.

Modern social democracy also accepts liberal democracy. Not only does it accept capitalism as the means to generate wealth, but it also argues that instead of being regulated to prevent inequities and deprivation, it can be harnessed to meet social objectives and promote social justice.[5] As such the welfare state shifts from providing an equality of opportunities for the poor and disadvantaged to one that provides minimum opportunities for those who are currently excluded from them, primarily through education and training. Advocates argue that education and training not only mitigate the inequalities of the market, but also enhance economic dynamism. Modern social democracy thus emphasizes opportunity and provides the means to make it obtainable. The state is still dominant, but the role of non-government actors is increased while the role of civil society is slightly enhanced, but remains small. With an increased understanding and partnership with the market, the state also becomes more outward-oriented and cognisant of the international economy, and therefore a partner in creating international marketplaces through inter-state cooperation.

Global social democracy differs significantly from the others by its transcendence of the state and its advocacy of non- elite governance. It also advocates political democratization at the global level. This shift therefore leaves a much greater role for non-government actors and civil society – though to what degree is disputed between global social democracy scholars.[6] Unlike the previous models, non-governmental groups, social movements and civic organizations play a significant role in societal governance. Global social democracy continues along the path of harnessing the market for positive economic and social advances. It does not, however, rely on the market alone to provide equality and justice, but returns the traditional social democracy view of providing equality of social and economic opportunity for the poor and disadvantaged.

The three types of social democracy are summarized and compared in terms of governance, private enterprise and equality of justice in society (see Table 8.1). In terms of governance, traditional social democrats favour a large state that is hierarchical and, focused on the national level, leaving little room for civil society. Modern social democrats favour a slightly smaller state than the traditional social democrats, but one that can interact with other states in the international arena. There is also more room for civil society. Global social democrats advocate a different kind of government, one that is not elitist and not bound to the nation concept. Not only is there greater room for civil society, but an active non-state sector is deemed important.

The differences between their views of private enterprise are not as great. All three recognize the need for capitalist markets to generate wealth. Traditional social democrats view the state as necessary to compensate for the evils of the market. Modern and global social democrats recognize the possibilities to harness the power of the market and use it to positive social democratic ends. The modern social democrats are most specific about building partnerships with private enterprise. Global social democrats build on the idea of cooperation between the state and private enterprise but also rely on the state and civil society to ensure equality in society.

In terms of equality and justice, traditional social democrats place great emphasis on ensuring opportunities, both social and economic, for all people in society. This is the primary duty of the state and reason for taxing and regulating private enterprise. Modern social democrats are more realistic about what can be achieved and advocate providing minimal standards and targeting individuals. Global social democrats

Table 8.1 Comparison of social democratic types

	Traditional Social Democracy	*Modern Social Democracy*	*Global Social Democracy*
Governance	Big elitist state Nationalistic Small civil society	Medium state, IR cooperation Medium civil society	Non-elite governance, Global cooperation, Large civil society
Private Enterprise	Regulated	Harnessed	Harnessed
Equality and Justice	'Real' social and economic opportunity	Minimum social and economic universal standards	Social and economic universalism

argue that more is needed than a minimal level, and advocate a universal standard for economic and social welfare.

The role of the media

Before assessing the impact of the media on social democracy, it is important to understand how the media influences politics in general. Through its effect on access to and diversity of information, I argue that the media effect on the balance of power between the state, private enterprise and civil society. There are several common misunderstandings about the role of media in society in the United States and Britain. Some argue that the media, controlled by elites, sets the agenda for all political debate (or lack thereof) and subsequent political action.[7] Others argue that the media are run by left-leaning journalists and as such bias our information.[8] Academics have also lambasted the media for reducing politics to spin and personality.[9] The conventional wisdom has perpetuated the view that the media skew elections and policy outcomes to their own ideological ends.[10] In contrast, globalization optimists have heralded the media (at least the new media) as a vehicle for open global democracy.[11] A closer examination of the evidence reveals these views to be unfounded.

The recent literature on the media's impact on politics accepts that its influence is limited, but most profound in setting the agenda.[12] Further work, however, suggests that even agenda-setting is overstating the case. The media will change someone's opinion only if the report contradicts their prior beliefs about the event and they are so uncertain about the event that they pay attention to the news.[13] People are far more likely to view programmes and read newspapers articles that they agree with, and disregard, or turn off, the ones they do not.[14] When individuals are uncertain about an issue, they are far more likely to seek opinions from friends and family, and in forming opinions, education, work environments and personal experience are far more important forces of influence than the media.[15] In addition, an examination of the range of media sources people now use to obtain their information reveals how many choices they have including those with original material.

A useful example to illustrate the role of the media is the 1997 British general election. Commentators focused on the skill and professionalism of Labour's presentation and the shift in the media's support towards the Labour leader, Tony Blair. Studies of the election, however, reveal that the key to Labour's victory was not spin and PR or the endorsements of a majority of newspapers. Rather, factors such as leadership, the economy and the role of the Liberal Democrats had a greater impact on the electoral outcome than newspaper headlines.[16] The main determinant of the election (and of course there were other factors) was the Conservatives' loss of financial credibility after 'Black Wednesday'. On 16 September 1992 the British government led by the Conservatives lost millions of pounds trying to defend sterling in the European Exchange Rate Mechanism. Then they were forced to withdraw, in effect devaluing the pound. Following that precipitous event, the opinion polls were solidly in favour of Labour and barely altered throughout the campaign.[17]

Thus, some might argue that the media had no impact on the election outcome or only helped Labour to maintain its lead. However, a closer examination reveals an important but underlying impact. The capabilities of real-time, instant reporting made public each minute of the falling value of the pound. Not only were the financial markets aware, but voters were privy to the crisis that was unfolding. Such information enabled investors to act in the markets, so exacerbating the situation and limiting the time policy-makers had to respond. Both consequences aggravated the crisis, making it such a profound event that it still had resonance five years later during the 1997 general election.

The impact of the media that I will be exploring in this chapter is much more subtle than that of agenda-setting and election outcomes. I focus on the ways increased access to information, diversity of information and new channels of communication impact on the configuration of society, the balance of power between players and the extent to which individuals and groups participate in the political process in the United States and Britain.

The media and governance

The new media have brought great challenges to the size and role of the state in the United States and Britain. They increase the sources of information, facilitate the means for groups to organize, reduce the time it takes for these groups to receive information and ensure that state officials receive information at the same time as opposition groups. The consequences of these changes include a reduction in the power of the state and an increase in the role and effectiveness of other actors.

The technological developments in the media have contributed to an intensification of politics by reducing the time politicians have to respond to crises and increasing the number of players who have original materials and information almost instantly. The new technologies help provide information for interest groups at virtually the same time that governments receive information about new unfolding events. 'Real-time news' enables people to receive information simultaneously. This has enhanced the role of journalists in the field by eliminating filtering through media production studios or editorial backrooms. The consequences, are twofold. First, politics becomes more open and accountable, as secrecy is more difficult to maintain; and second, there is a new kind of fragility. There is increased invasiveness into the lives of the people involved and a condensed response-time for policy-makers, both of which promote scandal and emotional responses.[18]

Before the advent of 'real-time' reporting the government usually had an information advantage, hours or days to consider new information before responding to other groups and even longer to the public. During the First World War diplomats communicated by letter – so each side had weeks to consider their next move. Now, instead of having time to make a considered response, politicians in most situations are forced to act under pressure in the heat of the moment with a policy that is often geared to public opinion rather than the needs of the situation.[19] If the government chooses not to share information with the public, interest groups often do. Such real-time news played a role in the 1990 Gulf War, the 1991 coup in Moscow and the United States' intervention in Somalia in 1992.

While the government has remained the lead player in policy-making and government budgets continue to increase, there are a few cases that suggest the government's primacy could be threatened in domestic policy and even potentially in its stronghold domain of foreign policy. Interest groups in the United States have long been part of the domestic policy-making process, and although interest groups are not as numerous in Britain, they play an role increasing.

While the participation rate in the United States and Britain in conventional organizations, such as political parties, has declined, alternative forms of participation have increased, ranging from EU interest groups to youth participation movements such as 'Rock the Vote', to environmental protest.[20] In fact, political action in Britain is greater than in any other country, with more people who have either engaged in protest action or are willing to engage. The most common form of protest is signing a petition, followed by attending a lawful demonstration.[21]

The media have been an important tool for interest groups to help raise awareness about their issues and funding for their activities. The new media have facilitated communication between and within interest groups, making them more effective players in the policy-making process. Thousands of interest groups that have been frustrated by their limited access to mainstream media coverage have become a strong force in propelling the Internet. Interest groups have also learned to use, with increasing sophistication, many of the modern media techniques, including direct marketing and focus groups.

There are also problems with the new media. With the increasing number of outlets there is greater competition to reach listeners, to be heard above the increasing 'noise'. Some argue that this information overload only reinforces the role of elites as the average citizen relies on leaders to sort through and analyse the vast amounts of information. Others argue that the increased volume and access allows others access to the raw information not available previously and therefore provides a much stronger basis on which to challenge the establishment.

New media techniques have facilitated interest group communication across borders as well as international business. As issues and problems become global, actors have become so too, including governments. Traditionally, government dominated the foreign policy domain, but this has been challenged by these developments. Cable and satellite bypass state-controlled channels and the e-mail allows almost instant and direct communication. As the protests in Seattle against the World Trade Organization (WTO) in April 2000 demonstrated, the Internet can be a very effective means to mobilize civil society. The coordination of the protests – the array of groups involved, the number of people, and the timing – would probably not have been possible without the Internet. Yet the uniqueness of the Seattle protests also highlights how little the potential of the Internet is being used in this manner.

It is beyond the scope of this chapter to assess fully the role of interest groups in policy-making, but it is obvious that pressure from outside groups has impacted on the conduct of foreign policy, thereby suggesting a need for greater scrutiny and analysis of the issue. The increased barriers suggest some state vulnerability, and thereby a possible avenue for global social democrats to explore.

The 1990–91 Iraq War provides an unusual but telling example of the shift in reporting of news in both countries but the predominance of statist solutions and control in foreign policy remained in place. During the war, for the first time, news programmes opened with colourful graphics and dramatic music, and the war was reported as if it were a football game or an action film.[22] Despite all the entertaining interpretations, the news source was limited to the United States and British governments in the beginning and later included the Iraqi government as well. Because the Gulf War was an essential story to cover, even knowledgeable journalists had to play by the rules of the news source, and journalists reported the image of the Gulf War drawn by military briefers.[23] Although the format of reporting changed and the timing was more immediate than ever before, especially in the beginning, the government controlled the content as much as ever (and far more so than in recent history). Ted Turner of CNN even admitted that their coverage was controlled by outside sources: 'We were manipulated' he said, and added, 'just as much by the United States government, the United States military, as by the Iraqis – the whole media, not just CNN.'[24]

The consequences of the impact of these changes in the media on states and governance for traditional social democrats are significant. Both the decrease in response-time to problems and increased immediate information for non-government actors erode the power of the state and enhance the power of civic groups. Thus, the changes in the media make it harder to maintain the large, elitist state and small civil society advocated by traditional social democrats. In addition, the increased occurrence of international activity by non-government actors does not have a coherent balance in traditional social democracy, which in an age of increasing globalization is a problem.

Modern social democracy is better placed to adapt to the changes in government brought about in part by advances in media technology. Modern social democrats react to the threat to a large elitist state by initiating cooperative measures with interest groups. Modern social democrats have also adapted to an international world, but have focused on the state to act. Interest group cooperation at the international level is less common and may be a future point of contention with non- governmental actors. State action at the international level begins to address cross border problems such as the environment, labour migration and health problems. It also ensures the primacy of the nation-state. Many regional and international organizations, such as the European Union and the International Monetary Fund, are not fully democratic. Therefore, increased state activity at these levels may have increased the state's power in the short term, but at the cost of democratic values.

Global social democrats accept the existence and significance of groups such as ethnic groups, local and international companies, guerrilla and terrorist groups, and social movements.[25] They also promote the proliferation of groups as one of the means to transcend state power and move to better democratic institutions. While the new media certainly aid the plethora of groups emerging, there is nothing intrinsic in their growth that would make them inclined to democracy. Some have noble goals that fit the social democracy agenda, including human rights and social justice. Others, such as child pornographers and football hooligans, however, have selfish or even perverse goals. More work needs to be done on how the growth of interest groups can be harnessed to social democratic ends. It is obvious, though, that the new media technology alone is insufficient to bring about such action.

The media and private enterprise

The old media needed a balance between government and private enterprise. The new media are not as dependent on the government, for licences or information, and therefore are much more difficult to control. Not only are the new media difficult to control, but their technology has swiftly been incorporated by much of the business world, making private enterprise as a whole more difficult to control. These practices include offshore headquarters, the ability to transfer millions of dollars instantly from country to country, and use the virtual marketplace of the web for e-commerce. While the government has also incorporated some of these tactics, such as web pages for political parties and government agencies, these have not made the task of regulating, enforcing regulation and taxing easier. In fact, some argue that business is beginning to encroach on government to the extent that in the United States and Britain incremental privatization is occurring.

The difficulty the governments in the United States and Britain find in regulating the media is representative of the difficulty that the government has in regulating business in general. An example of the reduction of the US government's power in practice is the inability for the Federal Communications Commission (FCC), established in 1934, to regulate interstate and international telegraph, radio and cable communications, to enforce its equality of opposing views doctrine. US law requires that in exchange for licences to operate television and radio stations, the holders must operate 'in the public interest, convenience, and necessity'. The Fairness Doctrine established in 1949, went one step further and required 'objectivity' from broadcasters, who were expected to air controversial public issues and ensure that all points of view were represented.

Although the rules were rarely enforced, they did have an effect but not the intended one. In order not to bias issues, editors chose to avoid them.[26] For fear of a deluge of airtime requests from interest groups or candidates involved in each matter, many broadcasters often avoided controversial issues and instead limited their editorial observations.[27] Thus, the effect was to reduce rather than increase news coverage of political issues and candidates. In 1985 the FCC abolished the doctrine, arguing that with the blossoming of the electronic media in the United States, there was now enough diversity among stations to render unnecessary the requirement for diversity within them.

Even where the government has greater control of the television industry, the pursuit of higher ratings has moved British television programming towards entertainment and away from 'hard news'. For example, in 1991 the BBC established a World Service Television system whose aim was to concentrate not on hard news but, as with the older radio service, greater news analysis.[28]

One of the reasons the new media are difficult to control is size. On the one hand, some companies are now so large they are beyond one state's ability to control them. On the other hand, many new media companies are small start-ups that are often difficult to locate, much less regulate and tax. The drive for profit has encouraged the consolidation of ownership of media and contributed to the trend towards entertainment and away from news reporting. In the United States in 1940, 83 per cent of all daily newspapers were independently owned, by 1990, just 24 per cent remained independent.[29] A similar consolidation has occurred in Britain, where a small number of newspaper conglomerates (e.g. News Corporation) dominate the industry.[30] This is a shift not only within media industries, but also across them. Consolidations have occurred across television, cinema, newspapers, book publishing and the Internet. Disney, for example, owns its production studios, ABC television, book publishing companies as well as radio stations, and American On Line (AOL), the world's leading Internet portal, has just completed one of the world's biggest mergers, acquiring Time Warner, the major book, television and radio conglomerate.

The changes in the media have resulted in many of the media companies themselves becoming global giants. Their markets are larger than one particular country and their profits make them formidable opponents. In fact, as private companies with explicit profit goals, media companies are often at odds with democratic governments. These companies do not hesitate to pursue their primary objectives. A telling example is the personal influence Rupert Murdoch has on his media empire. While Murdoch has long been suspected of exerting personal influence on the editorial content of his newspapers, the most blatant case was with his book publishing company, HarperCollins. In 1998, Murdoch vetoed the publishing of Chris Patten's memoirs of his time as the last British Governor of Hong Kong. Murdoch forced his publisher to lie about the veto and junior executives were instructed to discredit Patten. These moves were made in order to protect Murdoch's billion dollar business interests in China.[31] Macmillan quickly capitalized on the free publicity, and the book was duly published. Although freedom of speech was not impaired, the potential to forgo it for profit is apparent.

There is concern that private enterprise is encroaching into the state through the infiltration of working practices including focus groups, targeted advertising and outsourcing. Some argue that an infiltration of marketplace ethics will follow and use the outsourcing of welfare provision to interest groups as an example.

Politicians have also learned these techniques and incorporate them into their campaign and office. At the same time, they have become media customers. In the United States, they have hired professionals for public and media relations, polling and lobbying and the large amounts of money these groups raise enables them to be competitive and astute customers in the media advertising marketplace. For example, politicians will pay for commercial airtime on a Spanish language station when they want to reach a Hispanic audience. Annual revenue from political advertisements in the United States increased from 2 per cent in 1990 to over 8 per cent in 1999. In fact, the television industry earned $600 million from candidate and issue advertising in 2000, a six-fold increase from a generation ago.[32] Candidates in British elections have also begun to adopt such professional media strategies, with the 1997 general election using sophisticated packaging and presentation. Once elected, officials have continued to use these practices extensively for presenting and promoting politics and governments.[33]

The media have long been concerned with reaching particular 'audiences' that will match their advertisers' consumer profiles – housewives for laundry detergent, for example. Focus groups have facilitated the practice of targeting and enabled its practitioners to become even more sophisticated, tying information, format and advertising to specific audiences. Politicians have used these practices to plan election campaigns as well as formulate legislative strategies.

While social democrats advocate active communities and non-state efforts to combat isolation, poverty and social problems, neoliberals have turned this on its head by advocating non-state action instead of government action. Ideally, individuals stand on their own feet, but when they cannot, neoliberals appeal to compassion and paternalism. Thus, they advocate the rise of volunteerism at the expense of government. In other words, they argue that non-profit groups and businesses can take the place of government, thereby reducing government budgets and taxes. The media have expanded the access of non-state actors to the political process, and so comprise is a two-way street. They have therefore also enabled the government to increase its voice and to do so directly to targeted constituents.

Traditional social democrats favoured big government and big national companies that could be easily identified, held responsible and taxed. The traditional media aided the status quo, particularly the balance between the state and private enterprise, as favoured by traditional social democrats. This view of the market is one where large corporations, though dominant, can be held responsible for their activities and the effects of their actions. The new media, an industry of small start-up companies, have aided the growth of small companies in all industries. These companies are harder to tax, regulate and certainly harder to accept their responsibility of any adverse effects.

New media have helped to change the face of private enterprise so that companies to an increasing degree can minimize government regulation and taxation. In fact, in both the United States and Britain, there has been very little taxation of e-commerce. These changes suggest that unless traditional social democrats adapt, social democratic governments will lose authority and revenue.

Modern social democrats recognize that social democracy is a political theory designed for practice, and therefore has accepted the realities of compromise and electoral survival. The current media systems in the United States and Britain encourage and even demand such flexibility and pragmatism in order for political parties to survive. The current manifestations of this cooperation are the balance between the individual and the community, and partnerships between business, civil society and the state.

In fact, they advocate increased cooperation between state, civil society and business in broad proposals such as the 'Third Way' discussed primarily in Britain and the EU, but also briefly in the United States with stakeholding.[34] Some argue that the new media have made these relationships more feasible in a democracy by facilitating communication between groups, especially government, business and taxpayers, and by making that communication more transparent and thereby more accountable to the public. Actual examples of such partnerships include community development programmes in the United

States and the Private Finance Initiative (PFI) in Britain. Others argue that the new media have made these relationships inevitable. With new media technology, businesses have new means to circumvent the government. Modern social democrats are merely putting a good face on a difficult situation.

Modern social democrats pay a price for their cooperation with business. Business obviously has a bias towards the market, and the market is not democratic. There are few means of recourse should an individual or group feel aggrieved with a private initiative. As a result, ideals such as equality and justice become secondary. With big business actively pursuing ways to consolidate ownership of the Internet and control information flows, it seems unlikely that the voices of the poor and deprived will be the ones that survive. Without government control via regulation or ownership, it may not be possible to maintain the wide array of outlets and information sources. Although the government seems reluctant to tax and regulate the media now, the US government especially was an active participant in the creation of the Internet and helped to design it as an open system. Thus, should the system begin to become limited, there is a history of government involvement that may provide the precedent for future action. By then, however, the state might not have the means to enforce such regulations.

Advocates of global social democracy see the role of media as a powerful driving force to the next stage of social democracy. Anthony Giddens exclaims, 'through the new technologies of computer and satellite, through the new media a new [social democratic] world will be made'.[35] The expectations for the new media are great, and thus far have not been met.

There are two challenges facing global social democrats in terms of relationships with private enterprise. The first challenge is how to maintain diversity of media sources and outlets in the face of the consolidation of media ownership. There is a very big leap, however, from current dissatisfaction and new means of communication to global social democracy. There is nothing intrinsic in local communities or new media that is social democratic. In fact, the evidence suggests that at best a diversity of views has emerged; at worst, the views have been skewed towards business values. So, while diversity is a part of social democracy, it alone is insufficient to create global social democracy. In fact, many attribute violent nationalism, such as that in Serbia, Iran and Afghanistan, to a backlash against globalism, which is conveyed through many forms of the media.

The second and greater challenge is how to ensure prominence to social democratic ideals. Global social democrats recognize that large, possibly even radical, changes are necessary to achieve their goals. The new media have helped to shift the balance of power away from the state and towards private enterprise and civil society. The boost to civil society may be the key to transcend traditional nation-state governance. The boost to private enterprise will probably continue to pose problems for achieving some key social democratic values such as equality and justice (see the next section). The new media may give global social democrats some useful tools, but societal organizations and institutional practices will determine how successfully they can be used to achieve social democratic ends.

The media and equality and justice

The most distinctive part of social democracy may be its concern for the deprived and the means to create equality, including the redistribution of wealth and social justice. While the governments in the United States and Britain have welfare policies to help the poorest and most disadvantaged, social democrats argue that much more needs to be done. There are elaborate progressive tax systems to redistribute wealth, but there are also too many cases of tax evasion by the wealthy while an underclass remains. Both countries have time-honoured judicial systems, however discrimination, prejudice and insufficient resources skew the system against the poor and minorities, and often deny them the due process of law.

In Britain there is more equality in terms of basic needs, especially healthcare. Universal healthcare means all have access to a GP. In practice, the National Health Service cannot provide all the treatments needed. Therefore, it is rationed by health criteria. In the United States, there is no universal healthcare. By default, healthcare is rationed by wealth. Those who can afford it receive the most advanced care in the world; those who cannot are treated in emergency rooms and have no access to preventive care.

The direct impact of changes in the media on equality and justice are mixed. The traditional media have done a surprisingly good job in bringing to the public humanitarian disasters, such as the 1984 Ethiopian famine, and other events such as the protests in Tiananmen Square, the war in Bosnia, and genocide in Rwanda. However, presented as sensational events, each news team sought to show the 'worst' situation, and as a consequence the public has become overwhelmed with 'compassion fatigue'.[36] Thus, half the battle is getting attention for humanitarian crises; the other half is getting viewers mobilized to action. Closer to home, the day-to-day problems of the poor in New York or London are not 'newsworthy'. Most alarmingly, the constant process of starvation and deprivation in less developed countries does not generally get any coverage.

In some ways changes in the media and the new technologies may improve opportunities for equality and justice, but the full effect has yet to be realized. The new media potentially provide new means for the poor and disadvantaged in society to be heard and to participate in the political system. The new media provide new outlets and cheaper procedures such as desktop publishing and the Internet for poor and disadvantaged groups to send out their own information and make calls for help. Examples include the Southern Poverty Law Project in the United States.

The rapid improvements in technology have also contributed to the gap between the rich and the poor. The 'digital divide', the fact that most poor households and many schools do not have computers, is a hard reality. The one area where the new media have the potential to make a profound impact by providing access for the poor and disadvantaged to argue their own case directly has not yet been realized. The digital divide may be one of the greatest obstacles to the disadvantaged achieving equality and justice. Without access to computers, the Internet, cable or satellite, the disadvantaged cannot take advantage of the new time and money saving means of political participation. The United States has taken greater steps to bridge this technology divide by striving to provide computers and Internet access for all public schools. Still more money for communication connections, basic reading and writing skills as well as time and knowledge of the political system, not to mention the technological system, are all necessary before new technology could possibly make a difference to those most disadvantaged.

Not only do the changes in the media impact the level of equality and justice in society directly, through their impact on governance and private enterprise, they also affect how equity and justice can be achieved in society. Because the media in part have contributed to a smaller state with a bigger role for civil society and an even bigger role for private enterprise, the extent to which equity and justice can be achieved has shifted and has probably been reduced. The three variations of social democracy, however, approach the goals of equity and justice differently.

In terms of traditional social democracy, the new media have contributed to a system where the state is less powerful, and civil society and private enterprise are more powerful. The greater power for private enterprise may produce even more 'by-products' of capitalism, which then need to be compensated for by the state. A less powerful state has less authority and resources to sustain a universalist welfare state and provide social and economic opportunities for the poor and disadvantaged. A stronger civil society might be able to compensate for some of the state action, but not on the same scale or probably in the same social democratic tradition. From a traditional social democratic view, the new media do not enhance equality.

Because modern social democrats focus on the ways that private enterprise can be harnessed to achieve social democratic goals, they have a much greater chance than traditional social democrats of achieving greater equality and social justice in society. It depends, of course, on how strong the social democratic element of the government is and the strength of the state vis-à-vis private enterprise. The new media tip the balance towards private enterprise, but there are many other factors beyond the new media, which could also affect the balance. By finding a cooperative arrangement with private enterprise, activities that both mitigate the inequalities of the market, but also enhance economic dynamism, modern social democrats are creating a perpetual circle that will continue to enhance the role of private enterprise. There are many examples of this kind of activity in the United States and Britain. Companies are major contributors to fund-raising campaigns and often organize internal social projects run by their employees, e.g. the company-sponsored Habitat for Humanity houses.

An unintended corollary is that companies are now taking an active role in the setting of beliefs and ethics in society. Company away-days, mission statements and sessions on sensitivity training are methods that companies use to instill ideals in employees.[37] Traditional social democrats who view capitalism as a necessary evil may find this corporate involvement in social issues at best a conflict of interest and at worst an attempt to replace the state. In either case, the goal of social justice is disregarded. Modern social democrats are more likely to view corporate involvement as a necessary form of cooperation and partnership and a pragmatic calculation to achieve the most equality rather than an unachievable universal welfare provision.

Global social democracy continues along the path of harnessing the market for positive economic and social advances. It does not rely on the market alone to provide equality and justice, but turns to the more traditional provider, the state, as well as civil society. Taking the concept of partnership one step further and including civil society, global social democrats believe society will truly be able to provide equality of social and economic opportunity for the poor and disadvantaged. This kind of inclusion and equality also enhances their goal of social justice.

The new media provide an especially useful means of communication linking civil society to the state and private enterprise. While the government, other non-government actors and private enterprise established means of communication, the new media technologies have greatly aided the inclusion of civil society, allowing two-way communication for the first time, for some.

Conclusion

Many argue that politics has become devoid of content and elections are won and lost through spin and slick commercials.[38] There certainly have been changes in the traditional media, especially the loss of the primacy of the network television channels in the United States. At the same time new 'all-news' channels including C-Span, CNN and Sky News, have risen to prominence. With the Internet, more firsthand original documents, sound and images are available to the public than ever before. Most of these are also available quickly if not instantaneously, and for no charge. An historical review of the media shows that there have always been complaints and concerns about sensational reporting. The difference is that today more counterbalances are readily available to such stories than ever before. Despite the differences between the United States and Britain, in terms of history and political structure, as well as media configuration, the same trends are occurring with similar impacts in each country. In conclusion, I compare the impact of the media in the United States and Britain and then consider what this suggests for the future of social democracy.

Comparing the United States and Britain

The slight differences in the media's impact on the strength of the state, degree of democracy, social democratic acceptance between the United States and Britain have produced slightly different outcomes. The power the new media have given to interest groups and private enterprise has forced greater change in Britain where the executive was stronger than in the United States. Real-time news and greater access to information have forced the British government to be more open and more responsive to both the public and the market. While these trends are occurring in the United States, groups and the market have been included to a greater extent much earlier than in Britain.

It should follow that Britain would become more democratic. Some argue that with devolution in Britain that is starting to occur. The new media, with many other forces, may have contributed to such an historic change. Other indicators of democracy, such as voting, open government and executive power, suggest that the government is not as democratic as it claims.[39] There are also concerns about the degree of democracy in terms of decline in voter turnout in the United States and Britain and the media's negative contribution. In the United States voter turnout for presidential elections is below 50 per cent (and even lower for local elections). Turnout is slightly higher in Britain, but it is still declining. Even in the 1997 general election, despite its greatest swing of votes since 1945, there was the lowest voter turnout (71.3 per cent) since 1935.[40] With the greatest percentages of households with televisions, radios and computers in the world, the media certainly have not been a corrective force in voter participation in the United States and Britain. Dissatisfaction with coverage is indicated by the continued decline in the viewing of election coverage, including debates, party political broadcasts and the evening news.

Some argue that the media have reduced politics to such a low substantive level that politics is no longer meaningful enough for people to vote. Others argue that the new media provide the means for individuals to obtain the level and substance they desire. These political facilities on the Internet, however, are not yet well developed. It is therefore still too early to assess the impact of the new media on election coverage and voter turnout.[41]

The level of state control over the media certainly seems to have an impact on the level of public provision of political broadcasting, which may in turn be linked to voter turnout. The evidence suggests that where, in Britain, the government owns the BBC and has strict guidelines for commercial television licences including requirements for all television stations to include free airtime for party political broadcasts, two-thirds of the electorate followed the elections and 70 per cent voted. In the United States where there is no public broadcast for election candidates, less than 50 per cent of the electorate followed the presidential elections through the media, voter turnout was less than 50 per cent.

Though the media have had little impact on the degree of equity and justice in the United States or Britain, the degree of acceptance of social democracy has. The belief in providing equality of opportunity as well as a minimum universal standard has translated in Britain into a stronger welfare state. Both the United States and Britain have undergone different degrees of privatization of social services, which to a small part can be attributed to the media's impact on enhancing the role of business in social life. Both countries have implemented welfare-to-work programmes and increased job and education training. The shift to non-governmental welfare is greater in the United States, with companies providing some welfare services. For example, they provide on-site daycare, flexible hours and telecommuting options for both men and women. Critics argue that they are taking over people's lives, getting them to work more (fewer holiday days) and decreasing their alternative employment opportunities. In addition, these services are available only to employees and not those with the greatest need, particularly the unemployed. The United States has also started, for the first time, allowing religious groups to distribute welfare, for example, government-funded soup kitchens in churches. Besides the issues for separation of church and state, this abdication of responsibility leaves no democratic recourse for those dependent on such services.

The future of social democracy

The new media change many of the traditional parameters in which social democrats worked. The new media have contributed to a reduction in the power of the elite state and have given private enterprise and civil society new means to participate in society. The greatest threat to social democracy is that private enterprise will take over the state. To a large part this depends on whether or not civil society becomes a dominant force. It also depends on the extent to which societies are willing to make big changes. I examine these three concerns in turn.

The rise of private enterprise is especially important in terms of the media. Government may be needed to maintain media diversity. With the proliferation of media outlets, however, the new media may impact on an individual's level of certainty about an event. Individuals who listen to an array of sources may find that conflicting information causes uncertainty. The extent to which these will increase will depend on the diversity of news sources. If all the news comes from the same AP wire or Reuters report, the extent of conflict between media outlets will be limited to that created by the editor's and presenters' interpretation of events. But with interest groups becoming more new media-savvy, there has been a proliferation of websites, radio stations, newsletters and cable channels. Similarly, if there are more diverse outlets and information providers, there is a greater chance that an individual will be exposed to a story, a picture, a set of facts that raises their awareness and then concern for an issue.

Consolidation of media ownership is the greatest threat to the diversity of news sources. Even if the number of outlets remains high, if the same information is simply being presented in different ways, the opportunities for increased democracy and social justice are reduced.

The new media certainly provide useful tools for the growth and enhancement of civil society. And size alone will facilitate some social democratic goals by balancing private enterprise. However, there is nothing intrinsic in new media to move civil society or any part of society towards social democracy. The two greatest threats to the growth of civil society are if there is consolidation of media ownership to the extent that differing views cannot find outlets, or if private enterprise becomes so invasive that people have little time for civil society participation. Conversely, some of the impact of the media and globalization in general has caused people to focus more on their immediate communities.[42] This is certainly borne out by current media and political participation trends. In the United States where traditional news was dominated by the three major networks, viewership has changed so that now more people watch local news (over 67 per cent) than network news (49 per cent).[43] Local television, websites and newsletters are no longer prohibitively expensive to produce and they contribute to a group's sense of community, and enable them to express their dissatisfaction with national level institutions, policies and values. Such forces could potentially contribute to global social democracy.

A closer look at involvement in civil society in the United States is insightful. At the local level some types of participation have increased, charitable giving has increased, membership in community organizations has increased slightly, and nearly half of all Americans say they do some sort of volunteer work, up from a quarter in 1977. In fact, Americans are more likely to be involved in voluntary associations than the citizens of almost any other industrialized nation.[44]

A closer look at local participation tempers these statistics. In terms of charitable giving, as a share of total income, philanthropy has actually shrunk. While membership in community organizations has increased, people attending meetings and holding leadership positions has declined. The Internet and direct mail campaigns have fostered the growth of dues paying members who only participate by mailing in contributions. So while some indicators show an increase in participation, the greatest activity is occurring in groups run by elite organizations in Washington or other capital cities. This, Theda Skocpol argues, 'contributes to the sense of most Americans that everything is going on above their heads', causing them to withdraw from public life.[45] There is no denying the increase in volunteerism, though. Much of the volunteer work is one-to-one tutoring type activity that fits the pattern of increasing local-based action.

Finally, for any of the types of social democracy to emerge fully in the United States and Britain, great structural changes would be needed. Although these are beyond the force of the media, it is important to consider how the new media especially might facilitate change. As the proponents of gradual change, partnership, cooperation and balance, radical action is not a traditional or even modern social democratic method of change. In order to achieve some of their important ideals though, such change is probably necessary. The changes brought on by the new media have already forced great change on traditional social democracy. Unless traditional social democrats can find a means to limit the encroachment of private enterprise and civil society, its means to achieve social democracy will be hampered.

Modern social democrats have embraced some of the changes that have already occurred, particularly advocating state action at the international level. The continuing pressure from domestic and international interest groups as well as international business may force further changes in this traditional nation-state dominance. Modern social democrats do not seem prepared to prevent these threats nor to adapt to them.

Global social democrats recognize the need for extensive change, and create a map for a new kind of governance to achieve basic social democratic ideals. Whether or not their vision can be achieved, however, is not clear. The new media provide some useful tools, particularly the strengthening of civil society and communication in general. The new media have also empowered the private sector, which may hamper efforts to build a new kind of governance. However, the changes needed require more than those brought about by the new media.

Notes

1   M. Waters, *Globalization* (London: Routledge, 1995); J. A. Scholte, *International Relations of Social Change* (Buckingham: Open University Press, 1993); D. Held, 'Democracy, the Nation-State and the Global System', in D. Held (ed.), *Political Theory Today* (Cambridge: Polity Press, 1991), 197–235; and A. Giddens, *Consequences of Modernity* (Cambridge: Polity Press, 1990).

2   A. Briggs and P. Cobley (eds.), *The Media: An Introduction* (Harlow: Longman, 1998).

3   J. Curran and M. Gurevitch (eds.), *Mass Media and Society*, second edition (London: Arnold, 1996), 242.

4   N. Fairclough, *New Language, New Labour* (London: Routledge, 2000).

5   T. Blair, *The Third Way: New Politics for a New Century*, Fabian Society Pamphlet no. 588 (London: Fabian Society, 1998) 4; Giddens, *The Third Way*, 100.

6   For example, Stammers in this book argues for a large role for non-government actors and social movements, while scholars like David Held and Antony Giddens argue for strong role for the state.

7   B. H. Bagdikian, *The Media Monopoly* (Boston: Beacon Press, 1983); and E. Herman and N. Chomsky, *Manufacturing Consent: The Political Economy of the Mass Media* (New York: Pantheon Books, 1988).

8   S. R. Lichter, S. Rothman and L. S. Lichter, *The Media Elite* (Bethesda, Md: Adler & Adler, 1986); D. Bonafede, 'Crossing Over,' *National Journal*, 21 (14 January 1989), 102.

9   N. Jones, *SoundBites and Spin Doctors* (London: Cassell, 1995); N. Jones, *Campaign 1997: How the General Election was Won and Lost* (London: Indigo, 1997); D. Swanson and P. Mancini (eds.), *Politics, Media and Modern Democracy* (New York: Praeger, 1996).

10 J. K. Galbraith, *The Anatomy of Power* (Boston: Houghton Mifflin, 1983).

11 Giddens, *The Third Way*.

12 Iyengar and Kinder, *News That Matters*, 1987; M. McCombs and D. Shaw, 'The Agenda-Setting Function of Mass Media', *Public Opinion Quarterly*, 36 (1972), 176–87; M. McCombs and D. Shaw, 'The Evolution of Agenda-Setting Research: Twenty-Five Years in the Marketplace of Ideas', *Journal of Communication* 43 (1993), 58–67; E. Rogers, J. Dearing and D. Bregman, 'The Anatomy of Agenda-Setting Research', *Journal of Communication*, 43 (1993), 68–84.

13 G. Bovitz, J. Druckman and A. Lupia, 'Stop the Presses: When Can the Media Lead Public Opinion?' paper presented to the 1997 Annual Meeting of the American Political Science Association, 28–31 August 1997.

14 J. Zaller, *The Nature and Origins of Mass Opinion* (Cambridge: Cambridge University Press, 1992).

15 Ibid.; D. Morrison and H. Tumber, *Journalists at War: The Dynamics of News Reporting during the Falklands Conflict* (London: Sage, 1988).

16 I. Crewe, 'Voting and the Electorate', in P. Dunleavy, A. Gamble, I. Holliday and G. Peele (eds.), *Developments in British Politics 4* (Basingstoke: Macmillan, 1993), 92–122.

17 I. Crewe, B. Gosschalk and J. Bartle (eds.), *Why Labour Won the General Election of 1997* (London: Frank Cass, 1998).

18 J. Thompson, *The Media and Modernity: A Social Theory of the Media* (Cambridge: Polity Press, 1995).

19 N. Gowing, *Real-time Television Coverage of Armed Conflicts and Diplomatic Crises* (Harvard University, Cambridge, Mass., 1994).

20 M. Evans, 'Political Participation', in P. Dunleavy, A. Gamble, I. Holliday and G. Peele (eds.), *Developments in British Politics 5* (Basingstoke: Macmillan, 1997).

21 M. Wallace and J. Jenkins, 'The New Class, Post industrialism and Neocorporatism: Three Images of Social Protest in the western Democracies', in J. Jenkins and B. Klandermans (eds.), *The Politics of Social Protest* (London: University College London Press, 1995).

22 J. H. Altschull, *Agents of Power: The Media and Public Policy* (Harlow: Longman, 1995), 11.

23 J. MacArthur, *Second Front: Censorship and Propaganda in the Gulf War* (New York: Hill and Wang, 1992); and M. C. Miller, 'Operation Desert Storm', *New York Times* (24 June 1992).

24 T. Turner, Interview with David Frost on Public Broadcasting System, 27 October 1993.

25 M. Shaw, *Global Society and International Relations* (London: Polity Press, 1994); and Scholte, *International Relations of Social Change*.

26 Altschull, *Agents of Power*.

27 *New York Times* (21 June 1987).

28 S. Prokesch, 'BBC's Global Challenge to CNN', *New York Times* (28 October 1991).

29 H. Stanley, and R. Niemi (eds.), *Vital Statistics on American Politics*, fourth edition (Washington, DC: Congressional Quarterly Press, 1988).

30 D. Marsh, 'The Media', in P. Dunleavy, A. Gamble, I. Holliday and G. Peele (eds.), *Developments in British Politics 4* (Basingstoke: Macmillan, 1993), 332–52.

31 H. Porter, 'Now He's Gone Too Far', *Independent on Sunday* (1 March 1998); P. Routledge, 'MPs Slam Murdoch over Patten Book,' *Independent on Sunday* (1 March 1998).

32 Alliance for Better Campaigns, *Political Standard*, 'TV Stations Get a Revenue Jolt from Record Political Spending' (March 2000).

33 N. Fairclough, *New Language, New Labour* (London: Routledge, 2000).

34 W. Hutton, *The State We're In* (London: Jonathan Cape, 1995).

35 A. Giddens, *Beyond Left and Right: The Future of Radical Politics* (Cambridge: Polity Press, 1994), 27.

36 McNair, 'Technology: New Technologies and the Media'.

37 J. MacLean, 'Towards a Political Economy of Agency in Contemporary International Relations', in M. Shaw, *Politics and Globalization: Knowledge, Ethics and Agency* (London: Routledge, 1999).

38 Hallin, 'Whose Campaign is it, Anyway?' (1991); and N. Minow, Speech at the Gannett Foundation Media Center, New York, 9 May 1991.

39 S. Weir and D. Beetham, *Political Power and Democratic Control in Britain* (London: Routledge, 1999).

40 Crewe, Gosschalk and Bartle, *Why Labour Won the General Election of 1997*, 1998.

41 R. Gibson and S. Ward, 'U.K. Political Parties and the Internet,' *Harvard International Journal of Press/Politics*, Summer 1998, Vol. 3, Issue 3, 14–25; and M. Margolis and D. Resnick, ''Party Competition on the Internet in the United States and Britain,' *Harvard International Journal of Press/Politics*, Summer 1999, Vol.4, Issue 4, p.24; and G. Selnow, *Electronic Whistle-Stops: The Impact of the Internet on American Politics* (London: Praeger, 1998).

42   M. Shaw, *Politics and Globalization: Knowledge, Ethics and Agency* (London: Routledge, 1999).
43   Stanley, and Niemi, *Vital Statistics*, 1995.
44   R. Putnam, *Bowling Alone* (New York: Simon and Schuster, 2000).
45   L. Uchitelle, 'A Political Scientist Renews His Alarm at the Erosion of Community Ties', *New York Times*, 6 May 2000, p.B9.

9

Capitalism, Globalization and Democracy: Does Social Democracy Have a Role?

Luke Martell

This concluding chapter sums up some the main themes of the book. Where, in the light of what the book's contributors have told us, does social democracy stand now? What does it mean today? Are there any meanings or prospects for social democracy, in terms of ideological or policy directions, which bind it together and bridge national gaps? What criticisms have been brought out by the contributors to this book and what alternatives, both for social democracy and to it, are there? Of course, this chapter cannot be fair to everything that all the contributors have said. I concentrate here on critical and prescriptive issues to do with ideological direction and the most appropriate spaces for the development of social democracy in the future.

The context for new forms of social democracy

Debates on the changing role of social democracy reveal a range of factors which explain where we find social democracy today. From 1945 onwards, in many countries social democracy was organized around various ideological and policy features: Keynesian economics, a universal welfare state, working-class solidarity, the trade unions and corporatist arrangements. Of course, such features varied from place to place. In some countries corporatism took off and became embedded more than in others. What form the welfare state has taken has varied, to take another example. And whether such mainstays of social democracy actually always made their way into concrete practice, or were held to throughout all factions of social democratic parties, can be questioned. The main point here is that in the dominant leaderships of many social democratic parties they were important ideological com-mitments. They were also part of a broader ideological consensus accepted by other parties, albeit one in which there were differences between parties on matters of policy.

As Neil Stammers points out, these features are linked to some under-lying characteristics of social democracy, which arguably have been more enduring than the more contingent policy features linked to them.[1] Social democracy accepts, rightly or wrongly, that, for all its faults, liberal democracy works: it is the fundamental basis for demo-cracy, even if it can be improved and reformed for the better. Capitalism is accepted – it can deliver growth and wealth. However, capitalism is not all good, it can lead to inequalities and deprivation which need to be mitigated through government intervention, a characteristic on which social democracy begins to differ, in emphasis at least, from many liberals and conservatives. Francis McGowan takes this point a little further in distinguishing between compensatory policies, which attempt to mitigate or sweep up the social costs of liberal capitalism, and countervailing social democracy, which tries to establish principles which go in a different direction to liberal capitalism. This leads to Stammers' next point, which is that, for social democracy, reform or mitigative policies are initiated and implemented by government from above, elected by the people but then left by the electorate to improve society. Finally, a central feature of several chapters in this book, policy and government has been heavily focused on the national arena, on action via the nation-state.

In case anyone was wondering where the 'S' word had gone, it is worth making an important distinction here, along the continuum that links social democracy and democratic socialism. While democratic socialism may share many characteristics with social democracy – the commitment to pursuing change through existing and extended insti-tutions of democracy, for example – it is concerned with the reform or transformation of capitalism, rather than just mitigation of its worst effects. It aims at change to a society which in the long run may not be so easily or purely identifiable as capitalism but more based on collective control and equality than the dominance of private capital and a social structure determined by market forces. In a sense this amounts to a radical version of McGowan's 'countervailing' social democracy. Com-pensatory social democracy tries to ameliorate the effects of open markets, through redistribution, legal protections, social policy and such like. Countervailing social democracy, however, tries to put forward an alternative model of development altogether, changing the system through, to take an example from McGowan, industrial policy, rather than living with it and mitigating its worst effects. But really trying to provide countervailing rather than just compensatory forces to liberal economics and unregulated capitalism, eventually goes to the leftwards edge of social democracy to some form of socialism. Social democrats such as the French prime minister, Lionel Jospin, feel more comfortable speaking the language of socialism than social democracy, albeit, in Jospin's case, for reasons of national tradition as much as ideology.[2] This is not to say that all democratic socialists are committed to the abolition of every last relic of capitalism, nor that they want overnight revolution. Democratic socialists tend to be committed to democracy and gradualism and do not have an antipathy to all that is private or marketized. But on balance they hope in the end to see a society that is more or as much socialist as capitalist. They are committed to the reform of capitalism rather than merely the mitigation of its worst effects.

From the 1970s onwards the ideological and policy features that had been associated in the postwar period with Stammers' characteristics of social democracy have taken a battering.[3] The size and political loyalty of the traditional manufacturing working class has declined. This does not mean that class as an economic and social division has declined in importance, even if it may have become redefined and restructured. Inequality is still a very important issue. And there have long been significant sections of the middle class who have supported social democracy as well as working-class supporters of the right. But what it means is that, electorally, the core support for social democracy has shrunk with the shift from manufacturing to services and is no longer so loyally social democratic as it used to be. It is more inclined to be instrumental and pragmatic in its choice of voting intention than as partisan and loyal as it was in the past. For some social democratic parties, such as the British Labour Party, admitting its cross-class basis and responding to it took many years of bitter dispute and rethinking. For others, such as the Swedes and Dutch, recognizing that they were as much a middle-as a working-class party has for much longer been quite normal. Either way, to build broader class support has led social democratic parties to rethink their message to suit their electoral constituency.

There have also been policy crises – linked to the issue of changing social base but with other dynamics also involved. In many places it is perceived that state welfare has produced dependency rather than initiative on the part of citizens and the type of government support which would underpin greater opportunities for them. In addition, it is perceived by some social democrats that the willingness of people to support such systems financially through income tax has reached its limits. Furthermore, with growing affluence, welfare or state systems of health, pensions and such like, no longer need to be so universal. Many of us can afford to pay for some of these services ourselves. And such systems have become inefficient, geared to producer rather than consumer interests, undemocratic and unwieldy.

Keynesian macroeconomic policy is also seen to have been undermined, in part by one of the concerns of this book, globalization. The capacity of governments to control the economy within their own borders seems no longer possible (if it ever really was) because capital can move quickly and easily across national boundaries. High public spending and reflationary strategies may, therefore, frighten off capital, more attracted to low spending and stable macroeconomic government policies. Or the wealth it creates could just be spent by consumers on overseas rather than domestic products or lead to price and wage inflation. So social democratic parties nowadays are more concerned with prudence in spending and with attracting investment. Policies for wealth-creation and growth are less about spending and government ownership or direction of industries and more about business-friendliness, maintaining private sector confidence and offering a workforce and incentives which are attractive to potential investors. There is a stronger emphasis on supply-side than demand-side economics, although, of course, this, like other factors being discussed, varies across nations.

Globalization has been a key influence identified in this book, although by no means a main preoccupation of every chapter. Some of the authors who have discussed globalization differ in their analyses, although perhaps not always as much as may at first appear. For both Martin Shaw and Stammers social democracy has been weak at conceptualizing itself beyond the nation-state and is, as such, poorly equipped to respond to fundamentally transformative processes of globalization. Shaw places his hopes in social democracy as part of the 'Western state', an already effectively formed politically globalized formation. Stammers is more sceptical about any accommodation to capitalism or to any politics of the state, albeit (or even especially) constituted at a more supranational level. For McGowan social democracy has already had some engagement with supranational formations and his chapter focused on the European Union. Yet the European Union's liberal economic agenda and the transition from traditional to modernizing social democracy means that for the moment traditional social democratic concerns play a minor and moderate role in the European Union, even when social democrats are significant actors in the institution. Clearly globalization, or at least the perception of it, has been a key influence on social democratic thinking. But other liberalizing influences may have also been influential, the constraints imposed by European Union developments, the Maastricht criteria for instance being particularly important, and in Britain and the United States the legacy of Thatcherism and Reaganism.

Of course, a big question is whether globalization is real at all, or just a discourse which is used to justify policy changes which are really desired for electoral or ideological reasons. Globalization for some critics is merely a tool for justifying ideological change by arguing that a more economically liberal approach is necessary and inevitable. Matt Browne and Yusaf Akbar's chapter analyses globalization as a discourse and its effects as such. But their key point is that even to view the discourse of globalization as ideology does not get it right.[4] This gives its proponents too much of a rational role in the process. The discourse constructs the very agents of globalization as an ideology.

Traditional and modernizing social democracy

Where does this leave social democracy now? There are two ways of looking at this. First, we can take some general categories for understanding where social democracy is today. Three interesting concepts for categorizing postwar and current ideas of social democracy have arisen in this book: traditional social democracy, modernizing social democracy and globalist social democracy. Second, we can try to take the pulse of where social democracy is in different nation-states, classifying it as such along such lines. These two dimensions intersect and I shall discuss them together.

Stephanie Hoopes distinguishes between traditional, modernizing and globalist social democracy. She argues that developments in the new media in the United States and United Kingdom have in some respects undermined aspects of traditional social democracy. The new media provide opportunities for power to shift from state governance to civil society. Private enterprise has benefited and the world of the new media is an unequal one. In these respects social democratic beliefs and approaches are threatened by the new media. On the other hand, democratization to civil society may empower the less well off and so contribute to greater equality and justice and counterbalance the power of private enterprise. Modernizing and globalist social democracy are well in tune with the possibilities offered by global information technology industries. So from another perspective social democracy may be able to gain from developments in the new media.

Modernizing social democracy, which has accommodated itself to quite some extent to neoliberal priorities, is, for most contributors to the book, the current dominant form.[5] Of course, this varies from country to country as a number of the chapters in this volume have shown. To some extent, in some places, social democratic modernization far preceded that recently carried out by the British Labour Party, seen by most as, for good or ill, presently the furthest down the road of liberalization. Germany had its Bad Gödesborg, and Christien van den Anker points to the Dutch SDAP's conversion to the mixed economy and an electoral strategy which incorporated the middle classes as early as the 1930s. She also shows that besides some non-Anglo-American features such as the stress on consensus, the Dutch PvDA (founded in the 1940s) shares a remarkable number of features with New Labour: the rejection of traditional welfarism and Keynesianism, and of planning and egalitarianism; an emphasis on combining economic efficiency with social justice; low taxation policies; competitiveness based on technological innovation; government intervention on social exclusion; a focus on labour and work as the basis for participation; partnership with the private sector; flexibility in worklife; and the importance of education and training. While Sweden has been noted for its high taxation and large universal welfare system, several of these characteristics of modernization noted by van den Anker were also exhibited by Swedish social democracy long before Blair had his day. And many of the criticisms of modernizing social democracy in the Netherlands are also comparable to those made of New Labour in Britain: too much emphasis on work as a solution to social exclusion and too much on opportunities at the exclusion of equality and redistribution, for example.

However, it appears now (and maybe the appearance is deceptive) that the British Labour Party is in the vanguard, if that is right word, of modernizing social democracy. In my view modernizing social democracy, in Britain at least, is not only about finding new means for old social democratic ends – new economic and social policies for pursuing equality and community – in a new globalized context. It has actually redefined old social democratic ends themselves: new times, new means *and* new ends or values.[6] One significant shift is from equality, not only to equal opportunities but to minimum opportunities. Blair does not believe in egalitarian redistribution, and his policies (such as welfare-to-work and the tackling of 'failing' schools and poor literacy) are not geared to *equal* opportunities, but to *minimum* opportunities for those currently excluded from them. Of course, if the socially excluded are granted minimum opportunities this puts them on a more equal footing with others. But beyond that, equality is not promoted and the main dynamic is inclusion and minimum opportunities rather than egalitarian redistribution.[7] After that baseline has been achieved it is not clear that more equal outcomes or even the equalization of opportunities is on the government's agenda.

Furthermore, the oftspoken value of 'community' does not mean class community or the socio-economic community of old social democracy. It refers to moral community with the emphasis on the responsibilities of individual citizens to the state rather than of business to the community, a more old social democratic conception, even if it was not often pursued right down to the hilt in practice.[8] None of this is to say, of course, that modernizing social democracy is just Thatcherism in disguise as critics such as Colin Hay and Stuart Hall have have claimed.[9] There are moderately social democratic sentiments in modernizing social democracy, a point argued in this book by van den Anker as well as Cowell and Larkin – concern for the socially excluded, a role for active government (if not of a directly interventionist sort associated with traditional social democracy) and a commitment to public services like health and education. Like it or not, modernizing social democracy can genuinely claim to be going down a Third Way, breaking with traditional social democracy, but not quite the same as the new right.[10]

In other countries, such as Germany, the journey to modernized social democracy is a more difficult process, the government being subjected to a number of forces, neatly outlined by Charles Lees in this book, which have allowed Blair-like policies to be carried out in some areas but greater social democratic traditionalism retained elsewhere. The need to combine moderate electoral appeal with more radical appeal to coalition partners, the social market culture, and the devolved nature of the German political system and institutions are likely to lead to different outcomes from Third Way policy agendas there compared to other countries where institutional and cultural pressures are very different – in Britain a more centralized state, a political system which gives the modernizers greater control, and a *laissez-faire* market culture, for example. Similarly van den Anker shows the Netherlands has embedded in its culture consensual norms which counteract or balance some of the more economically liberal developments in social democracy there and elsewhere. And the Dutch PvdA places more emphasis on individualization and liberalization and less on moral communitarianism than Blair.[11] In France, of course, the rhetoric is quite hostile to modernizing social democracy for reasons of national tradition (French exceptionalism and the statist and public sector tradition, for instance, which transcend partisan boundaries) and politics (such as the need to hold together a coalition of the Left), although in policy practice the French socialists have not in all respects differed radically from modernizing social democratic policies elsewhere.

Cowell and Larkin show well how differences between social democratic parties in Europe, real as they are, can be exaggerated and how similarities in policy agendas are sometimes as equally noticeable, even if the outcomes of those agendas may vary nationally because of the sort of institutional and cultural differences outlined by Lees and van den Anker. Across Europe social democratic parties are discussing or implementing more flexible labour markets, privatization, welfare reform, cuts in business regulations and taxes, low inflation and macroeconomic stability and supply-side policies alongside continuing social democratic concerns for social inclusion and minimum social standards. But the contexts in which such issues are being addressed vary and so the outcomes of comparable policy agendas may differ from nation to nation: dependent on factors such as the degree of centralized control or devolution in political systems; the extent to which modernizers monopolize power or have to share it with the Left or other parties; and historical traditions of statism, consensus or economic liberalism, to take just some examples. So even if different social democratic parties are all experimenting with Third Ways between neoliberalism and old-style social democracy, these are third ways in the plural, there being different Third Ways rather than just one, varying by national background amongst other factors.[12]

Globalization and national social democracy

There is a third category of social democracy discussed by Stammers and Shaw: globalist social democracy. However, it is not the only possible social democratic response to globalization and before discussing it a few more words are needed on both the meaning of globalization and on differing social democratic responses to it. Globalization as an idea has been applied to many different contexts: economic, social, political, cultural and military, for example. Some advocates of globalization theses argue that factors such as the growth of information technology and telecommunications as well as of the global economy have eroded national cultural and communicative boundaries, such that there is easier, faster and increased contact across national boundaries and across cultural groups. For some this may be leading to greater cultural homogeneity; for others to increasing appeals to the security of local or national identities; or maybe a bit of both. Militarily, some commentators argue that wars between nations have declined. Many wars are now between ethnic or cultural groups within or across nations, with the participation of military forces often based on intra-national ethnicities or national or religious groups or transnational political alliances, for example.[13]

However the key concerns of this book and chapter are with economic and political globalization. For many social democrats the key issue in globalization theses that underpins modernization is the increasing mobility of capital. National governments, it is argued, can no longer control their own economies or regulate capital. States have limited autonomy because they cannot do anything that will stop capital leaving the country. Government policy – for example, on public spending, taxation and regulation of business – has to be tailored to the need to attract and retain investment. This is particularly problematic for social democrats because it is said to force them to accommodate to business interests and neoliberal policies. Along with this comes a concern with the growth of transnational political organizations, such as the United Nations and European Union, not to mention global financial regimes such as the IMF, G7, World Bank and the World Trade Organization, to take just a few examples, or international law, to extend even further. Because of such institutions many decisions which affect nation-states are said now to be taken above the level at which those states mainly operate. Many of these may be on matters previously the preserve of nation-states, for example, legal prescriptions on human rights, or social or environmental policy. Many may have arisen because of the growing consciousness of problems which transcend national boundaries and so require international collaboration to be resolved, for example, ecological problems or crime. For advocates of globalization theses the growth of economic and political globalization poses a challenge to social democrats to rethink, to some extent at least, the way they have traditionally done things at a national level. They have to engage with processes and institutions which extend beyond the borders of the nation-state and confound the abilities of nation-states alone to deal with them.[14]

Of course, there are many sceptics. In this book Browne and Akbar analyse globalization as a discourse that forms agents' views, interests and reality. There are many who see globalization as a tool used by politicians to justify electorally or ideologically driven preferences, rather than as a real constraint. Social democracy is seen as constrained by the perception rather than the reality of globalization.[15] The extent of globalization also varies according to the level at which you deal with it. Because, for example, there may be global capital mobility does not mean that companies do not have national allegiances or that production and trade are as globalized as capital is, nor that it necessarily follows that there is cultural globalization. Alternatively, globalization may be more a feature of developments in media or consumption than of developments in other spheres. Others argue that the extent to which nation-states are vulnerable to globalization may vary from nation to nation dependent on balances of global power. Vandenbroucke, for example, suggests that the idea of globalization explains better what has happened in culture, media and responses to ecological problems than in the economy, and in so far as it does describe the latter it more closely does so for the US experience than Europe which has seen regionalization rather than than globalization.[16] And for some commentators while there may be instances of globalization this may be nothing new: analyses of a new global era may exaggerate the power of nation-states in the past and play down the extent to which globalization has long been around. Furthermore, there are questions raised over the extent to which nation-states remain autonomous actors. On one level they actually play a key part in global structures themselves, constituting and influencing them in the pursuit of national interest as much as being constituted and constrained by them. On another they still retain significant powers within their own boundaries, for instance, over education, welfare and defence. This claim has been supported by much evidence of policy variations across national boundaries, often diverging from the neoliberalism that economic globalization is seen to require. This evidence may dispel false images of globalization, or at least that if there is globalization it acts with the effect of a structurally determining force. Globalization may be mediated nationally and leave open to nation-states considerable choice. This claim underpins one of the social democratic responses to globalization that I shall discuss below.[17]

I wish to outline three main possible social democratic responses to globalization: neoliberal acquiescence which accepts the case that economic globalization severely restricts the power of national governments and has to be accommodated to; continued nation-state interventionism which may accept that we live in some sort of globalized economy but argues for less passivity, that there is still space for national governments to pursue social democratic ends within it; and political globalism which accepts the case for economic globalization but not passively nor just at the level of the nation-state and says that social democrats can achieve their ends if they participate in and develop global democratic forms to take some control over the global economy.

So, three current main meanings of social democracy have been identified:

1. traditional social democracy;
2. modernizing social democracy;
3. globalist social democracy.

And I intend now to discuss three main social democratic responses to globalization:

1. neoliberal acquiescence;
2. active nation-state interventionism;
3. political globalism.

Neoliberal acquiescence is, to some extent, the road that modernizing social democracy is going down, or already has in the case of New Labour. In this approach macroeconomic policy is designed to attract investment and deter capital from leaving the country. As such it is based on national competitiveness and relative acquiescence to the desires of private capital. So policies may include low business taxes, labour market flexibility, macroeconomic stability, an emphasis on fiscal prudence and restrictions on public spending and business regulations. This is not to say necessarily that such policies are forced on social democrats externally, as some of them may claim; they may well be a chosen response to globalization. And they could be based on the perception as much as reality of globalization. Furthermore, they need not involve completely giving into neoliberalism. As I have discussed above, modernizing social democracy in practice includes policies on social inclusion and minimum opportunities, and a commitment to spending on education and health, demonstrating that national governments can continue with moderately social democratic policies within the context of perceived economic globalization. Furthermore, while

New Labour, for example, may to some extent take globalization passively in one sphere, they are determined to be more active in another. While relatively passive in the face of economic globalization they have been at the forefront of attempts to create cross-national military alliances which can intervene in instances of perceived significant humanitarian crises.

This leads us to the second form of social democrat response to economic globalization: using autonomy and choice at the national level despite globalization. A number of possible policy spaces for national social democracy have been put by authors such as Garrett, Vandenbroucke, Wickham-Jones and Hay.[18] From this perspective globalization may exist, but does not determine national government policy. The acquiescent approach gives too much determining and constraining power to globalization and underplays the extent to which restraints on social democracy have been as much domestic and internal as external and it ignores possibilities for political choice. Hay, for example, argues that globalization has been less of a contraint on the pursuit of social democratic policies in the United Kingdom than political will or the internalization of the *idea* of globalization. He argues that the British Labour Party could choose to follow a different path – one that was less neoliberal and instead attempted to foster an indigenous investment ethic through a more *dirigiste*, developmental supply-side approach, more favourable to industrial than financial capital. For Vandenbroucke it is internal domestic constraints which have affected possibilities for social democratic policies more than external constraints. He is dubious of the claims of those such as Giddens that Keynesianism is dead.[19] For example, he claims that countries such as the Netherlands which are very exposed to the global economy have maintained redistributive policies. More neoliberal paths taken elsewhere have suffered from internal constraints not shared by the Netherlands – such as the lack of a culture of consensus or strong unions integrated into politics. Factors that affect the capacity for redistributive policies seem more to do with domestic social democratic and consensual institutions and cultures, or the lack of them, than external global economic compulsion. In fact, Garrett argues that economic globalization positively favours social democracy because it leads to feelings of insecurity and vulnerability amongst voters who may then become sympathetic to interventionism and redistribution. Businesses, meanwhile, may be persuaded that social democratic economic policy could actually be in their interests.

A number of possibilities are put forward by authors such as these for ways in which governments can pursue social democratic ends whilst not leading to exit by employers. First, national governments have a great deal of national autonomy outside the realm of the economy narrowly defined. Whatever the fact of economic globalization they can pursue reforms to welfare, education, health, defence, and law and order, to take just some examples, which may be different to right-wing preferences without necessarily frightening off capital. Second, Garrett, Vandenbroucke and Wickham-Jones argue that a social democratic government in a country where trade unions cover a range of the workforce, are united, strong and can command the obedience of their memberships, can make deals with capital, promising moderation in wage demands in return for agreement to redistributive, Keynesian or other social democratic ends. Countries such as the Netherlands may be in a better position to succeed with this approach than others such as the United Kingdom where broad union membership and centralized conformity does not exist and conflict or the exclusion of unions is historically more characteristic of industrial relations than consensus.

Authors like Wickham-Jones are more optimistic about the chances of transplanting such structures into places like the United Kingdom than others like Garrett. Wickham-Jones favours a shift in the British Labour Party back to its approach of the 1980s when attempts were made to align it more with mainstream European social democracy. However, where more corporatist structures cannot be developed, there is a third active national possibility identified by Wickham-Jones which is that social democratic governments can promise moderate wage demands on the basis of maintaining a weak role for trade unions and a tough public sector pay policy, again in exchange for agreement to social democratic ends. This is not very social democratic on the trade union side of things, but still perhaps capable of delivering social democratic ends in exchange for the maintenance of such a balance of power.

Fourth, there may be other more moderate things that social democratic governments can offer capital which would make it worthwhile employers sticking around and agreeing to concessions to social democracy: collective goods in the form of, say, supply-side interventions in infrastructure, research and development or training and education – things the market alone will not supply adequately – or policies which deliver economic, political and social stability. Clearly, some social democratic governments have tried a moderate form of this supply-side and stability incentives approach and have managed to pursue modest social goals, although it is not clear whether this was the result of any active exchange with capital. It is also unclear whether such strategies themselves, which put a heavy emphasis on human capital, can alone provide the sort of economic prosperity and stability employers require for them to tolerate social democratic advances in other areas. Economic success is based on wider factors than these – some of which may well be out of the hands of national governments. Furthermore it may be that supply-side strategies are insufficient in themselves to deliver social democratic goals. For that more directly redistributional and Keynesian approaches are needed.[20]

There are similar problems with all of these proposals for active national government within the context of economic globalization. The viability of each in different national contexts could be debated. Some seem appropriate for some countries but less relevant for others. There is also the question of the extent to which deals with employers are being, or can actually be, pursued. For some what is offered by the social democratic governments may seem unlikely alone to deliver the desired economic goals, or may be too modest in its demands to secure any really significant social democratic goals in return.

Globalizing social democracy

However, another perspective is that, without denigrating what national governments can do within their own boundaries, the approach just outlined stays too much at a national level. Whether national concessions can be won for social democracy or not, such an approach alone leaves out the necessity for engagement with international organisations and possibilities that could be pursued at a supranational level by social democratic governments. In addition it pitches one national social democratic government against another, each pursuing their own national interest and competitiveness rather than common cross-national social interests. This leads to the third category of social democracy, one which is discussed in this book by Shaw, Stammers and Hoopes – globalist social democracy. This is an idea of social democracy as a movement organizing politically at global levels in response to the globalization of the economy, politics and the military. This is globalization of a proactive sort, with social democrats trying to carve some sort of human-chosen root for world order, rather than one determined by market forces or the priorities of global capital or merely national interests. For van den Anker also, social democracy needs to take globalization not just as an economic given to be accommodated to, but also as a political possibility, where global regimes can regulate globalized capitalism, explore new modes of redistribution and protect those excluded from the labour market internationally.

David Held is a prominent advocate of globalist democracy and his proposals have an implicitly social democratic slant.[21] Like his fellow globalist Martin Shaw, his arguments are both empirical and normative, referring to real developing processes of political globalization and arguing for their extension. Held does not argue that the nation-state has lost its role and his prescriptions are compatible with the active nation-state social democracy outlined above. In fact, he argues that states have initiated many of the global changes, are active participants in them and may even be more powerful today than their predecessors. But he does argue that politics has been globalized and that nation-state powers are being reconfigured. The development of human rights regimes undermines state sovereignty; security and defence are international industries sometimes organized into international military alliances; environmental problems are global and increasingly require international collaboration to solve them; and the deregulation of capital markets has increased the power of capital in relation to states and labour. Nation-states have to share power with a myriad of other agencies at all levels and nations cannot, therefore, be said to be self-determining collectivities. The fate of nations is determined partly by forces beyond the national level, both political and otherwise, and so nation-states have to extend to wider levels to build political forms appropriate to democratic accountability to relevant communities and to control over their fates. Communities' fates are increasingly bound together so that if they want to make decisions concerning themselves and be accountable to those affected they have to extend democracy and representation to broader transnational levels. Held argues that new global forms of democracy, therefore, require citizens to be 'cosmopolitan', to mediate between different national traditions, communities and cultures. Institutions developing in such a global cosmopolitan direction already exist: they include the UN which delivers important international public goods (in air transport and telecommunications standards, disease control, refugee aid, peacekeeping and environmental protection, for instance) and the European Union which pools national sovereignty in some areas of common concern (including social rights and the regulation of markets). Furthermore, international law – on war crimes, environmental issues and human rights – limits the power of nation-states.

Held argues that this globalization of democracy can be deepened by some immediate steps such as increasing regulation of markets (on child labour, union rights and social rights), new forms of economic coordination to overcome the fragmentation between bodies such as the IMF, World Bank, OECD and G7, stave off financial emergencies, and steer international capital markets and investment and spending priorities. He advocates measures to regulate the volatility of capital markets and speculation – via taxes on turnover in foreign exchange markets, capital controls and regulations to ensure the transparency of bank accounting. Held proposes a new 'Bretton Woods' introducing greater accountability and regulation into institutions for the coordination of investment, production and trade, and greater responsiveness to less developed countries needs. All this requires the reform and extension of transnational forms of democracy, such as found in the European Union, the United Nations, international financial organizations and human rights regimes. And already there are social democratic forces pushing in such directions – for example, within the European Union to greater integration, inclusion and democratization and amongst some national governments, New Labour in Britain for example, more globally for the transparency and democratization of international institutions and their strengthening and extension.[22]

Martin Shaw in this book also argues that political globalization of the sort envisaged in globalist social democracy already exists to some extent, in the form of an integrated and interdependent (albeit internally complex and differentiated) military-political 'Western state'. The Western state is something that emerged during the Cold War and became victorious and dominant at its outcome. It is based in democracy established in North America, western Europe, Japan and the British Commonwealth, with its social democratic elements strongest in western Europe and Australasia. These states came to make up, for Shaw, what was basically an American-led consensus during the Cold War. It now combines enormous dominant economic and military power. Militarily it is committed to western-defined universal human rights to which common adherence beyond the West is expected, and on which force is seen as a legitimate means for enforcement, the intervention in Kosovo being a high profile instance which exemplifies this approach.[23] Economically and politically it is based on free markets and liberal democracy. Yet its concerns, Shaw argues, need to be focused on the non-western world, a point that van den Anker also stresses, because it is here that the need for democratization and protection against infringements of human rights (whether political or economic, caused by dictators or poverty) are greatest. Globally inclusive democratization, for Shaw, is the precondition for the pursuit of economic and social rights world-wide and requires international institutions governed by the Western state norms just outlined as much as internal democratization within poorer nation-states.

Social democrats within the Western state, after much struggle and division on the issue, as McGowan also shows, have become integrationist within the European Union (although, as both McGowan and Shaw agree, the liberal market element of integration has come out stronger than its moderate and less numerous social democratic aspects). For Shaw, political globalization is already a fact, and social democratic involvement in a US-led Western state and in the integrationist European Union is part of that story. Social democracy within that state has evolved, less divided on a fundamental level than in the past over European integration and alliance with the United States, relieved of the fraught question of relations with communism, and with European peace movements having shown social democrats the possibilities for forging pan-European coordination. So social democracy has become more unified, more integrated into Europe, more settled with US relations and, in many places, open to relations with liberal, Left and Green movements and parties beyond social democracy. There is, in short, in Shaw's view, a new more unified and open configuration for social democracy within the Western state.[24]

Democratization plays a big part in providing the underpinnings for pursuing traditionally social democratic norms. In fact, as I have just suggested, casting democratization on to a global scale can force social democrats to a more global consciousness of economic and social welfare, less domestically or even regionally focused and more responsive to acute inequalities and needs outside the first world. Yet, while democratization brings to the fore social democratic concerns, its global dimension will require inputs from outside the historically domestic focus of social democracy. This may well come from international institutions, Green politics and peace and feminist movements which have a greater consciousness of globalism and of global organization around what are often quite typical social democratic concerns. Such movements may well have to be involved in the reconstitution of what are still essentially domestically interested social democratic parties. Even those which are most integrationist in the European Union are seeking primarily national or regional self-interest rather than a genuinely open globalism. Shaw argues that social democracy needs to be just one amongst many social movements, its own distinctive contribution being not to input social democratic concerns into politics so much, as these can be found in other movements, but to play a key role in using its political leverage to develop the international institutions through which those concerns can be enacted.

How does the Western state compare to other models so far outlined in this chapter? In Shaw's model there is some leaning towards modernizing social democracy. Free markets are part of the Western state, although on one hand this is less a case of acquiescence to economic liberalism than its positive promotion, while on the other Shaw's appeals to democratization and attention to global inequality imply some serious restrictions on free markets. The emphasis on free markets implies less of a role for traditional social democracy, but traditional concerns come out in his consciousness of global inequalities and of the need for democratization. There is not that much of a place for active nation-state democracy, but this is not necessarily precluded by Shaw's model as long as it does not undermine globalist social democracy. There could be space within globalist social democracy to pursue what is possible within nation-state forums. The danger is that this could drive national governments to a preoccupation with domestic structures and competitive national interests to the extent that globalist consciousness and structures could be undermined.

Problems for globalist social democracy

The gloomy picture painted by McGowan – gloomy if you are a traditional social democrat, and I do not mean this as a criticism of McGowan's valuable dose of hard-headed realism – implies that global social democracy is a long way off if the difficulties of establishing regional social democracy are any guide. Where supranational proactive social democratic organization is possible – via the European Union – the liberal orientation of this institution and national differences between parties, make any EU-wide reconfiguration of traditional social democracy unlikely for the time being. This is the case even in the most propitious of scenarios for social democrats, where most of the members of the European Union are governed by social democratic governments and where social democrats are well organized in the European Parliament. Despite all this, the European Union has become a liberal project, with social democratic inputs of the compensatory or countervailing sorts mentioned above more of a minor part, few and far between and with a moderate impact. The European Union is more concerned with negative integration, about removing barriers to free trade, than with positive integration, agreeing common policies to coordinate government and business behaviour and pursue mitigation of the effects of the market or even redistribution. Negative integration hinders social democracy at a national level and constrains its reconfiguration at a regional level. EMU convergence criteria have gone against the achievement of social democratic ends through macroeconomic measures such as borrowing and running deficits. And while the European Union may currently offer more immediately realistic possibilities for coordination than what for some are as yet relatively less developed global regimes, it is also regionally focused, concerned with the interests of Europe in rivalry with other regional blocs in the world, rather than concerned with global solidarity and overcoming inequality on a more universal human scale.

Van den Anker also points out the need for various traditions of European social democracy which are pulling in different directions to combine and coordinate more. And she, McGowan, Lees and Cowell and Larkin have pointed out some of the differences that divide social democratic parties: traditions of consensus and collaboration and corporatism versus more Anglo-American individualism; Euro-reluctance as against enthusiasm for European integration; countries where the state and public sector involvement are more valued as against those where privatization and deregulation have so far been embraced more enthusiastically; those who have been through a neoliberal experiment and those that have not; those with centralized systems with one party government as opposed to those with complex decentralized systems and coalition governments, often of very many parties; to take just a few examples of some differences. As I have discussed, all these lead to different national rhetorics and different receptions and fortunes for what may often be quite comparable Third Way agendas. Sometimes left and right parties within the same nation may appear to have more in common with each other than with their sister parties abroad. These are the sorts of problems for coordination that a supranational social democracy has to counter. Furthermore McGowan argues that many of the problems of using the European Union in a positive social democratic way lie not just with the liberalism of the European Union and such national differences, but also with the national social democratic parties themselves who have as a matter of choice decided to shift away from their more traditional agendas and constituencies to more economically liberal approaches and middle-class bases. He argues they have never really been all that internationalist in reality anyway, as Shaw and Stammers both also point out, and that their attitude to the European Union is often constrained by the need to tailor it to domestic political consumption. How negative or positive they can be about the

European Union is often constrained by what they feel they need to say to domestic audiences – the electorate, business interests and coalition partners, for example.

As a pragmatic idealist I am inclined to share McGowan's pessimism but also Shaw's ambition.[25] Social democracy across Europe has been marked by a shift to modernized forms and liberal economic priorities. This is partly to do with liberal constraints imposed via the European Union in forms such as the Maastricht criteria and the Single Market rules. In part it is because of the economic liberal inheritance of places such as the United Kingdom. It is also to do with the desire of governments to attract capital and so adapt themselves to business priorities. However this desire results from their fear of losing investment to other nation-states in a globalized marketplace. If, on the other hand, nations which together have a monopoly on the workforces and consumer markets that capital needs can collaborate to enforce common standards and regulations on businesses and common social and redistributive programmes then capital will be left with nowhere to go and will need to reconcile itself to such norms. To put it another way, a proactive, combined, political globalization allows for a more social and egalitarian agenda of a traditional social democratic sort which the passive focus of modernising social democracy on economic globalization does not. Of course, as McGowan points out, social democratic governments now are often too tied to the desire to retain national powers and advantages to go too far down this road, although this is obviously far more the case for the liberal Blair (on issues such as tax harmonization) than, for example, for the political-integrationist Joschka Fischer in the German coalition government. Yet this is a necessary road for social democracy if it is to continue to impose a role for social democratic priorities in world politics, although as a supplement to, rather than replacement of, the powers of nation-states within their own boundaries which continue to be very important. McGowan may be right to express gloom about the prospects for such a direction of change, but Shaw is certainly right to say that this is where social democracy has to go or it will lose a handhold on significant opportunities for pursuing social democratic ends.

But while McGowan appeals to my pragmatism and Shaw's prescriptiveness to my idealism I am less convinced by the conclusions of radical communitarian criticisms such as Stammers'. These reject social democracy's accommodation to capitalism and see global political organization which encompasses social democratic governments as potentially authoritarian and flawed for failing to break with government and the

nation in 'inter-national'.[26] For Stammers, the six identifying characteristics of social democracy he identifies need to be transcended if social
democracy is to be a part of democratic global governance – it would
have to go beyond liberal democracy, beyond an acceptance of capitalism, beyond mere mitigation of inequalities, beyond top-down and
statist leadership and beyond a privileging of national levels. In short
social democrats need to discard social democracy to make anything of
global democracy.

Certainly democracy is incomplete within the limits of these six
characteristics, at a purely liberal democratic, national and elite/statist
level and undermined by private ownership and the inequalities
of capitalism. But an important question is how you deal with this
strategically in current and future political conjunctures. Stammers
argues that any trajectory has to start from where we are – a set-up of
nation-states and an inter-state system with asymmetries of power – but
his call for transcending the six characteristics of social democracy
entails giving up such bases for change. The radical communitarian
call for transcending these characteristics undermines opportunities
for political leverage and for what social democracy can do from within its own limits. Global economic democratization through global
social democratic initiatives is one way of regulating and constraining
capital and subjecting it to more democratic control. The conditions that radical communitarians argue need to be transcended for
global democracy to work actually offer the openings for intervening
to democratize globally. Forces for mitigating capitalism offer possibilities which an anti-capitalist rejection of such forces do not, and are
a basis through which stronger reforms of capitalism can be pursued
both now and in the long term. Social democratic parties are democratically legitimated and recognized institutions in national societies,
with financial resources and potential power once in government.
They are involved in regional, supranational and international forums
and are participants in processes of global political and economic
change.

Capitalism also has certain benefits in its economic incentive and
allocative systems. This is not to say that non-capitalist forms of incentives or allocation are not also important; nor that those benefits don't
also produce social bads – inequalities and losers; nor that because of
those benefits the bads of capitalism should not be curbed; or that there
are not dimensions which can be restructured and reformed without
losing these benefits. But it does mean that the advantages of capitalism
need to be retained within the context of a regulated and constrained

market, rather than ultimately abolishing capitalism along with its advantages, unrealistic as that is anyway for the foreseeable future.

Radical communitarians also argue that existing state forms, whether at a national level or reconstituted internationally, have to be transcended for democratic global governance to be a possibility. Stammers, for instance, raises two problems with the social democratic approach: 1) that it equates globalism with the international too much, continuing to reduce the global to relations between nation-states rather than recognizing that globalism goes beyond and above nation-states; and 2) that it hands too much power to a global state, in place of which he would prefer to see global governance without global government, that is democracy through movements and civil society forums other than states. Both of these points are problematic.

First, to disengage from state power and international collaboration on a global level leaves aside forums which offer possibilities for global change. States offer legitimate and accepted means of representation of one sort, amongst others, and are blocks on which democratic representation can be built globally, in the short and long terms, to offer powers countervailing to those of global capital. Democratic forums have to be made out of recognized and legitimate identities and political forms such as nation-state governments, associations and social movements. Globalism is something different from international state collaboration, but cannot be constituted without it. Governance that is composed of a lot more than government is necessary, but governance without government is an impossibility in anything like the current world system. Second, making global institutions linked to an international composition is, in fact, one way of keeping them accountable to a constituent membership and so restricting the possibility of the authoritarianism radical critics fear. A really global institution which transcends an international composition would be more detached and open to abuses of power. State power at national and international levels is potentially authoritarian – any formation of power is. But the best response to this is to build in liberal, democratic and popular constraints: global government in combination with state and civil society politics, not replacing state forms.

Of course, these are not the only criticisms that might be levelled at globalist social democracy. There are other complex and strong points that globalist social democrats have to respond to.[27] One is that it tries to establish democracy at levels for which there is no established political community. In other words, it lacks a social or cultural basis to give it legitimacy and support. The social bases for global democracy are ones of conflicting and diverging identities and interests who do not share any common global identity or sense of political citizenship. For communitarian critics, politics should be aligned with political forms where there are real cultural and political identities, maybe nation-states or other more devolved forms of territorial or functional representation. Second, and relatedly, it is assumed in globalist democracy that the meeting of conflicting interests will bring about harmony and consensus when in fact it may actually exacerbate conflict and disagreement. Politics cannot solve disharmony which rests at more economic and cultural levels. This has been demonstrated by the record of global forums in failing to reconcile conflicting interests or solve common global problems, such as war, ecology or development. A third criticism is that global democracy is merely a means for imposing western norms and ideas on the rest of the world. Shaw's outline of the 'Western state' makes this clear. Global democracy's proponents may think twice about their proposals were global democracy likely to lead to a different set of values achieving hegemony through global institutions. And what if such values were to be anti-democratic or illiberal? Does the possibility of global politics being dominated by such values suddenly make it seem less desirable? And if western values were not to retain hegemony or to be shifted in a leftwards direction what realistic possibility is there that global democracy would be accepted by powerful western interests such as the 'western state' or multinational corporations?

These are complex problems and some of the responses global social democrats can make can only be touched on here. Global social democracy is an empirical as much as normative project. This is clear from many of its advocacies which analyse as much what *is* going on in the global transformation of politics and other spheres – for example, the growth of supranational political forums, social movements and human rights legislation – as what it is thought ideally *should* be going on. Furthermore many problems are widely seen as requiring the extension of existing international institutions and agreements – on environmental problems, crime, peace and security, development and debt, for example. And global democracy is also envisaged as transformatory, building on existing changes in the economic, political and cultural world but also advancing or reconstituting them. So, from this point of view, it may seem slightly less utopian than at first sight for political forums at a global level to find common bases and problems upon which productive democratic negotiations can take place. Transformatory possibilities are grounded in real institutions and dynamics which already exist. Furthermore, if you look at the historical shifting foci of political institutions over time you find that the social basis of citizenship is a complex and dynamic process and that both historically and now legitimate political institutions often have a social basis which is as diverse and complex as it is united. Many nation-states, for example, could barely be said to be based on anything much less complex than diverse ethnic, national and cultural mixes yet still remain legitimate and accepted.

As far as Western dominance goes, global democrats advocate forms which institutionally qualify as much as advance this. Power relations at present are based on factors, economic and military for example, other than political enfranchisement. Any move to entrench power relations more in political equality – including economic democracy and the democratization of international military alliances – would, done in the true spirit of global democracy, actually reduce western dominance. So the extension of liberal democracy itself limits the ability of the west to *impose* western values through global democracy. But in answer to the charge that global democrats wish to pursue, *democratically*, western values the answer has to be 'guilty as charged'. At the level of values global democrats argue, with qualifications, for western values – such as liberalism and democracy – and that these are becoming generalized across the world and should be further extended. For global democrats the real problems with western values of liberalism and democracy include the need to extend them further (to a wider range of spheres and a broader range of actors) to realize their own logic more adequately. The problem is the failure of the West to apply them consistently and the need for them to be further enforced, recognized, institutionalized and extended into deeper forms of democracy – rather than the undesirability of them as the basis for global political forums. The alternative is a failure to establish such norms at global levels so allowing democratic accountability to remain limited, and giving illiberal and undemocratic practices and beliefs within and beyond the West one less obstacle in their way.

A future for globalist social democracy?

So what sort of model of social democracy does this leave us with and how does it compare with the other models discussed in this book? The sort of social democracy which is left by the comments I have made is one that is in alliance with social movements and forces in civil society, rather than either ignoring them or leaving aside its own position in politics to civil society activism alone. These offer ideological inputs and participatory channels in addition to social democracy's and can increase pluralism, inclusion and popular accountability. In this way it departs from both traditional social democracy and anti-politics approaches and is in accordance with some of the prescriptions of Shaw on the role of social movements. And it draws on radical communitarianism, even if it is not reducible to it. In reaching out to movements in civil society it also addresses some of the socio-cultural issues that Christien van den Anker is one of the few to address in this book – the loss of legitimacy of politics and democracy in European and other societies, especially the lack of participation or representation of working-class and disenfranchised people, and the growth of cultures and ideas around individualization, identity, democracy, personal lifestyle and family form, post-material and environmental issues and multiculturalism. Such issues have often been initially established on the political agenda as much by civil society initiatives and social movements as by social democratic or other parties.

In one other respect it allies with the general approach that Shaw has argued for because it puts at its centre the need to integrate with social democratic and other left actors at supranational levels, whether regional, as discussed by McGowan, or global as Shaw himself suggests, in pursuit of social, regulative and democratic goals. In this sense it goes beyond the neoliberal acquiescence response to globalization. So it is a *globalist* social democracy, although in saying that I do not preclude the enduring importance of state action within national boundaries or in international cooperation. There is a place for the active nation-state social democracy that has been discussed, even if globalist social democracy goes well beyond this. Nation-states are still very important and, as I have argued, it is impossible to conceive of global politics outside international cooperation. However this social democracy differs from traditional social democracy, not only because of its appeal to social movements but also because of the aim to integrate and combine at supranational levels. Some might argue that social democracy and socialism are by tradition internationalist movements. But as Shaw, Stammers and McGowan all note, this has often been overridden in practice by a focus on national politics and national solutions. Traditional social democrats have in fact often been averse to involvement in supranational institutions certainly of an integrationist or global sort because, as McGowan points out, of their identification of this with the furthering of capitalism, or with the undermining of national government powers. Yet social democracy today needs to engage with supranational political forums in order to reconfigure them in social democratic directions, and to participate in capitalism in order to regulate and democratize it in pursuit of more social and less liberal-economic goals.

The globalist social democracy outlined engages with Shaw's analysis of the history of social democracy as tied in with the evolution of wider *democratic* movements and ideas.[28] As he argues, democratization is not just about relations within states but about relations between them. Democracy does not just mean establishing standards within nations, but doing that by establishing standards across national boundaries. So social democracy needs to establish social democratic norms by reconstituting itself as a supranational force for democratization. A global regulative social democracy is about democratization, by which I mean the attempt to counter the unaccountability of private capital which operates relatively unfettered on a global scale, sailing across any possibility of attempts by states to regulate within national boundaries. A global social democracy is in part an attempt to democratize the world order which is currently dominated by global capital, with, at present, democratic actors having little in the way of public or political powers to provide a counterweight or corrective through their own global organization (or lack of it). As Shaw points out, democratization in aid of social goals is what the social democratic project was always supposed to be about – *social* and *democratic*.

McGowan will be sceptical of these sorts of possibilities, at least as far as the constraints of the liberal economic European Union is concerned and in the light of national differences which divide social democracies. And maybe he is right to be. Certainly different nations are more or less likely to be leading or reluctant actors in such a globalized social democracy and, beyond the military sphere and on economic and social policy, the United Kingdom is likely to be more of a reluctant participant or even an obstacle – both because Blair is keen to preserve national instruments of economic policy and pursue competitive national interest and also because he inclines to the liberal, business-friendly rather than regulative approach. Modernizing social democracy – or Blair's New Labour in this case – is open to the collective endeavours of states to create international military alliances. But as far as political globalization to ensure effective controls and authority structures in the economy and social policy goes it is a positive obstacle to greater globalism. As Stammers puts it, modernizing social democracy focuses on the effects of economic globalization inside the nation-state while globalizing social democracy looks at broader political restructuring outside the nation-state which might be necessary to cope with globalization. Within social democracy the more interventionist-minded and those more open to integration – the French and Germans obviously lead this pack – are more sympathetic to this sort of thing. Either way a key point here is that the recent growth of support for globalist social democracy needs not only to expand on arguments for it and analysis of the forms it could take but also on the political bases, spaces and resources for such an approach.

This globalist social democracy also involves a shift away from modernizing social democracy, even if Shaw is right (and some would contest his claim) that modernizing social democracy is the form that is grasping the nettle of global democracy.[29] This is because it returns to the ends if not means of traditional social democracy. It goes back from the social liberal concerns of modernizers – with equal worth, minimum opportunities and community obligations on the citizen – to stronger social restrictions on liberal capitalism, egalitarian redistribution (not to flat equal outcomes, but to *more* equal and just distributions more responsive to need) and the obligations to the community of business. While different from anti-capitalism and anti-statism and from the national focus of traditional social democracy and its unresponsiveness to social movements it also departs from modernizing social democracy's liberal accommodations. But even globalist social democracy is a broad church. It could, at a push, include the British Chancellor Brown's plans to reform the IMF and ally globally to counter world debt or Blair's and others' belief in humanitarian military intervention on a transnational scale. However the values of the globalist social democracy discussed here, while not antipathetic to this, are traditional enough in the social democratic sense to be calling for more regulations of capitalism and common transnational social programmes than Blair and Brown aspire to. And it is more inclusive of NGOs, social movements and civil society politics than global politicians such as Blair would imagine. At the same time, as far as it is global and open to civil society, it is also not a globalism or alliance with social movements which goes beyond the role for nations, states and for the international because these are all recognized building blocks and components for any global order. This is where social democracy is currently located and this is where movements for global democratization have to start.

Acknowledgement

Many thanks for their advice and comments to, Christien van den Anker, Matt Browne, Stephen Driver, Eunice Goes, Stephanie Hoopes, Phil Larkin, Charles Lees, Francis McGowan, Martin Shaw, Neil Stammers and Caroline Welsh.

Notes

1 All references to authors are to the chapters of this book unless otherwise indicated. For an outline of other, slightly more specific definitions of social democracy, see S. Thomson, *The Social Democratic Dilemma: Ideology, Governance and Globalization* (Basingstoke: Macmillan, 2000), introduction.

2 See L. Jospin, *Modern Socialism* (London: Fabian Society, 1999).

3 Some of the shifts and the reasons for them discussed here are also summarised in C. Pierson, *Socialism after Communism* (Cambridge: Polity Press, 1995).

4 See, for instance, M. Watson, 'Globalization and the Development of the British Political Economy', in D. Marsh et al. (eds.), *Postwar British Politics in Perspective* (Cambridge: Polity Press, 1999).

5 Cowell and Larkin in this book may choose to dispute such a hard and fast line being drawn between traditional and modernizing social democracy. See also D. Rubinstein, 'A New Look at New Labour', *Politics*, 20:3 (2000), 161–7; and P. Larkin, 'New Labour and Old Revisionism' *Renewal*, 8:1 (2000), 42–9.

6 This is contrary to Tony Blair's sometime claims that modernized social democracy is about applying new means in a new context to achieve old social democratic values, a claim he sometimes contradicts when explicitly rejecting equality as a goal. See also S. Driver and L. Martell, *New Labour: Politics after Thatcherism* (Cambridge: Polity Press, 1998).

7 See also R. Levitas, *The Inclusive Society? Social Exclusion and New Labour* (Basingstoke: Macmillan, 1999).

8 A more extended development of this argument is in S. Driver and L. Martell, 'New Labour's Communitarianisms', *Critical Social Policy*, 17:3 (1997), 27–46.

9 S. Hall, 'The Great Moving Nowhere Show', *Marxism Today* (November/ December 1998); and C. Hay, *The Political Economy of New Labour: Labouring under False Pretences?* (Manchester: Manchester University Press, 1999).

10 This claim is made in T. Blair, *The Third Way* (London: Fabian Society, 1998), T. Blair and G. Schröder, *Europe – The Third Way – die Neue Mitte* (London: Labour Party, 1999), A. Giddens, *The Third Way: The Renewal of Social Democracy* (Cambridge: Polity Press, 1998), A. Giddens, *The Third Way and its Critics* (Cambridge: Polity Press, 2000), A. Giddens, *The Third Way Reader* (Cambridge: Polity Press, 2001).

11 Something that also differs the Third Way of Anthony Giddens, in emphasis at least, from that of Blair. See Giddens, *The Third Way*; and S. Driver and L. Martell, 'Left, Right and the Third Way', *Policy and Politics*, 28:2 (2000), 147–61.

12 A good discussion of the modernization of social democracy in different European countries can be found in G. Kelly (ed.), *The New European Left* (London: Fabian Society, 1999). Some of the comparative points in this paragraph are developed further in S. Driver and L. Martell, 'Blair's Third Way: the British Debate', in O. Schmidtke (ed.), *The Third Way and the Quest for Social Justice: The Normative Claims and Policy Initiatives of the New Social-democratic Left at the end of the 20th Century* (London: Routledge, forthcoming).

13 See, for example, M. Kaldor, *New and Old Wars* (Cambridge: Polity Press, 1999).

14 For a good discussion of the globalization literature, including a substantial contribution to it in its own right, see D. Held et al., *Global Transformations: Politics, Economics and Culture* (Cambridge: Polity Press, 1999).

15 For example, see C. Hay, 'Globalization, Social Democracy and the Persistence of Partisan Politics: A Commentary on Garrett', *Review of International Political Economy*, 7:1 (Spring 2000), 138–52.

16 F. Vandenbroucke, *Globalisation, Inequality and Social Democracy* (London: IPPR, 1998).

17 For criticisms of globalization theories, see, for example, P. Hirst and G. Thompson, *Globalization In Question,* (Cambridge: Polity Press, 1996); and J. Dearlove, 'Globalization and the Study of British Politics', *Politics*, 20:2 (2000), 111–18.

18 G. Garrett, *Partisan Politics in the Global Economy* (Cambridge: Cambridge University Press, 1998); M. Wickham-Jones, 'New Labour in the Global Economy: Partisan Politics and the Social Democratic Model', *British Journal of Politics and International Relations*, 2:1 (2000), 1–25; Hay, 'Globalization, Social Democracy and the Persistence of Partisan Politics'; Vandenbroucke, *Globalization, Inequality and Social Democracy.*

19 For example, in A. Giddens, *Beyond Left and Right* (Cambridge: Polity Press, 1994).

20 A point of view argued by Vandenbroucke, *Globalization, Inequality and Social Democracy* and in support of which he cites the American economists Paul Krugman and Robert Reich.

21 See D. Held, 'Regulating Globalization? The Reinvention of Politics', *International Sociology*, 15:2 (2000), 394–408; D. Archibugi et al. (eds.), *Reimagining Political Community: Studies in Cosmopolitan Democracy,* (Cambridge: Polity Press, 1998); D. Archibugi and D. Held, *Cosmopolitan Democracy: An Agenda for a New World Order* (Cambridge: Polity Press, 1995); D. Held, *Democracy and the Global Order: From the Modern State to Cosmopolitan Governance* (Cambridge: Polity Press, 1995); A. McGrew (eds.), *The Transformation of Democracy: Globalization and Territorial Democracy* (Cambridge: Polity Press, 1997). Anthony Giddens is another advocate of global democracy who addresses this issue more directly within the context of the future of social democracy but does not always integrate globalization into the whole of his analysis. See Giddens *The Third Way,* and *The Third Way and its Critics.*

22 Tony Blair and Gordon Brown have made many speeches on the need to reform, extend or strengthen international financial and military organisations – see the 10 Downing Street and Treasury pages at *www.opengov.uk*. For Held and others the approach of the New Labour government is far too timid or misplaced in its aims: see, for example, D. Held, 'The Timid Tendency', *Marxism Today* (November/December 1998); and M. Watson, 'Sand in the Wheels, Or Oiling the Wheels, of International Finance? New Labour's Appeal to a "New Bretton Woods"', paper to the Political Studies Association, April 2000.

23 Although this is not to say that intervention to enforce such standards is done consistently, or that other interests are not also involved in external interventions. Furthermore, it should be noted that some in the West wish to move away from notions of international responsibilities that require external interventions, either in preference for a focus on domestic self-interest

(usually a point of view which comes from the Right) or because such interventions are seen as furthering western interests (which usually comes from the Left). Others (I include myself here) may have problems with the inconsistency and hypocrisy with which principles of universal human rights are sometimes applied, but argue that this implies that they should be applied more universally and consistently rather than not at all.

24 Other chapters in this book do not share this picture, seeing social democratic parties in Europe divided in terms of ideology and policy – this sometimes resulting in part from national traditions and pressures – and some as far more open to movements outside social democracy than others, often on the basis of factors such as whether the electoral system requires them to seek coalitions or not.

25 Without necessarily agreeing with all aspects of what Shaw endorses.

26 See also John Burnheim who puts forward positive proposals for alternative forms of global democracy from a radical communitarian perspective not dissimilar to Stammers': J. Burnheim, *Is Democracy Possible?* (Cambridge: Cambridge University Press, 1985); and J. Burnheim, 'Democracy, Nation-states and the World System', in D. Held and C. Pollitt (eds.), *New Forms of Democracy* (London: Sage, 1986).

27 I only have space to touch on these issues here. For a slightly more developed outline see A. McGrew, 'Democracy beyond Borders? Globalization and the Reconstruction of Democratic Theory and Practice', in A. McGrew (ed.), *The Transformation of Democracy? Globalization and Territorial Democracy* (Cambridge: Polity Press, 1997).

28 For the democracy emphasis, see, amongst others, Held, *Democracy and the Global Order*; and McGrew, *The Transformation of Democracy*.

29 See, for example, Watson, 'Sand in the Wheels, or Oiling the Wheels, of International Finance'.

Index